MISUNDERSTOOD
The Brian Molko Story

Chloe Govan

Bright Pen

A Bright Pen Book

British Library Cataloguing Publication Data.
A catalogue record for this book is available from the British Library

ISBN 978-07552-1271-2

Bright Pen
19 The Cinques
Gamlingay, Sandy
Bedfordshire SG19 3NU
England

This book is dedicated to:

1) My father, William Govan.
2) My very own Special K, Khalid – however restless my feet or even my temperament, my heart belongs with you.
3) Last but not least, Placebo for their contribution to music, an international language that can break all barriers. Thanks for the memories.

Love, Chloe

About the Author

Chloe Govan is an author, journalist and entrepreneur. She has seen Placebo more than 50 times in 21 countries, including Brazil, Iceland, Malaysia, Japan, Turkey, Lebanon and Singapore to name but a few. Over the past 12 years, she has seen both the birth and the death of Nancy Boy, and everything in between. To join her forthcoming mailing list, email chloegovan@aol.co.uk

Acknowledgements.

Thanks to the following magazines and newspapers:
Alternative Press, Bassist, CMJ, Cream, FHM, G-Spot, Guitarist, Kerrang, Les Inrockuptibles, Melody Maker, NME, OK Australia, Orkus, Record Collector, Piranha, Pulse, Q, Rock and Folk, Rock One, Rock Sound, Rock Star, Rolling Stone, Samsonic, Scene, Select, Sonic Seducer, The Daily Star, The Sun, The Sunday Telegraph, Visions, Viva, WOM.
Particular thanks go to Simon Breed plus Gerald Lidstone and Robert Gordon of Goldsmiths College, London for their participation.

Contents

Prologue.

Expected to be a God-fearing, Conservative voting banker with a virtuous wife and 2.4 children, Brian Molko dashed, confounded and then exceeded everyone's expectations.

The son of an influential businessman and his deeply religious partner, it was never going to be easy. First craving a career in the circus as a sad clown and then as an androgynous sex symbol on the silver screen, Brian finally discovered music as his purpose.

His unswerving commitment to eccentric individuality earned him a record deal at just 22. Yet for Brian, there was a darker side to fame – and one that would rapidly become apparent. He was to battle mental illness, death threats and drug addiction, all less than a year later.

A combination of punk-rock tunes, tender love ballads, leopard skin tights and kohl eyeliner, the Molko brand was born. In a world of mass produced and manufactured pop stars without so much as a personality to their names, the singer stuck out like a sore thumb.

Unlike obvious female impersonators such as Boy George and David Bowie, Brian provoked the genuine question 'Is it a boy or a girl?', speculation that most people put behind them at birth.

He certainly wasn't for everyone. Seen as a 'fallen angel' by some and merely a 'drug hoover' by others, Brian was both loved and hated in equal measure. To critics, his vocals might have been no more than a 'raucous whine', yet it was that raucous whine that sold over ten million albums worldwide.

While NME journalists branded him 'delusional to the point of mental illness', his CDs were flying off the shelves. The same year he was described as having 'thicker skin than your average psychopath', and was generally belittled, scorned and despised in the popular music press, Black Market Music went 3x Platinum in France. Meanwhile, the 2006 album Meds earned the number one spot in seven different countries.

However, these figures were not to earn him instant credibility. Suffering the same fate as Amy Winehouse, Brian's excesses were far more of a talking point than his music ever was. Salacious gossip paired with tales of drug addiction and debauchery quickly adorned the media.

Whether it was hurtful headlines or harmless cartoons, Brian struggled to overcome 'so many people having a strong opinion of me without ever having met me.' It was the price of fame.

The following account peeks beneath the tearstained eyeliner for a look at the real Brian Molko. As one third of Placebo, he has been to hell and back and survived to tell the story. Along the way, he has achieved one of his long-term ambitions – never to be forgotten. Misunderstood plays its own part in sustaining that.

Chapter 1.

'At first I was alone, but that was only the beginning' – Brian Molko.

'Obviously it makes perfect sense,' chides the NME sarcastically, 'for Placebo to expose themselves to hypothermia four metres under the water miming along to a track they can't hear.'

This, of course, is the backdrop for Placebo's famed music video, 36 Degrees. Chris Cunningham, infamous director with a taste for sadism, seems to derive a curious pleasure from witnessing bands suffering for their artistic endeavours – and Placebo is no exception. Proudly categorising himself as the man responsible for 'almost destroying Madonna's career', he was only too happy to be part of Placebo's latest new project.

36 Degrees, featuring the refrain 'Someone tried to do me ache', is the ultimate tale of fraught and disconnected relationships. 36 degrees being 1.5°C below standard body temperature, it represents cold-bloodedness and what better way to convey this visually than an underwater scene which is just as painful as it looks?

Singer and lead guitarist Brian Molko braved sub-zero temperatures and a fear of hypothermia to appear amid scenes of drowning guitars. For his fans, he had become a master of suffering in the name of art. Cunningham later proudly announced that he'd been able to make the singer cry, and had refused to let the group take the breaks they so desperately needed. 'Brian was begging to get out,' he confided. 'His nuts shrank to the size of raisins.'

However without pain there can be no pleasure, and the band had more than paid their dues. Just moments later, during his post-filming interview, Brian was understandably not in the best of moods. Heating up by way of his temper, he groaned 'There was never a chance of us being Britpop – for a start we're not British.' It was to be just the first of many misunderstandings about the group.

The truth is that Placebo represents ambiguity. Try as they might to portray themselves as they are, their identity is cloaked in uncertainty. From tales of crack cocaine to battles with mental illness, the group has hardly held back, yet in spite of their candour, their demeanour remains one of mystery. Dangerous yet intriguing, it's a Pandora's Box of thrills that at first is best viewed from the exterior. Should you accept the invitation into Placebo's hypnotic world, be aware that you won't emerge unchanged. But what brought them to the painful yet privileged position of sharing their trauma in the name of music?

The answer lies at the beginning of Placebo's long and eventful journey towards fame. The location was de Shaerbeek Hospital in Brussels, Belgium. It was here on December 10th 1972 that one of the most influential, original and uncompromising successes ever to grace rock music was born. With Brian around, the world would see a blurring of traditional gender boundaries and a dramatic shake-up of music, theatre and politics – in fact, things would never be the same again.

Brian was born to an American Jewish father and a Scottish Catholic mother, and had a mixed cultural heritage including French and Italian descent. Devout Catholic Mary Molko met the love of her life on a New York business trip and after a whirlwind romance, agreed to marry him. Brian was the second of two sons, with an elder brother Stuart conceived ten years previously. He grew up around the spoken word in a kaleidoscope of languages – French, Luxembourgish and, due to his father's business, a little Arabic. His destiny for fame was portrayed even in his surname – Molko is the direct translation of 'royal one' in Hebrew although Brian, ever the subversive, has teasingly quipped that it is Hebrew for Queen.

The family relocated to Lebanon soon after his birth but their stay was to be a short one. In the wake of the civil war, they moved to Liberia where they were plagued by a relentless and unforgiving climate and 'head fuck flies' that could lay eggs under human skin.

Brian was confined to a stiflingly hot nursery most days, watching helplessly as maids and servants attended to the housekeeping. He recalled 'I remember being in my cot, and there was a large and lovely black woman sweeping up around me.' However it is no coincidence that his earliest memories were those of entrapment, and he recalled with poignant melancholia that his cot 'already seemed like a jail cell.'

Those memories were to set the pattern for his childhood – the misunderstood kid who constantly moved and – at the mercy of his father's working life – never truly belonged anywhere. His childhood years were also characterised by a longing for attention, one so strong that it would ultimately catapult him to fame. He once recalled his delight at throwing toys from his pram in a bid to break the tedium and the silence, and forcing his long suffering nanny to pick them up again.

Financially solvent yet emotionally bankrupt, even at Brian's tender age his life was fraught with sadness. Unfortunately the constant and hectic travelling would provide a framework for his future.

Moving several times more, which he jokingly attributed to 'my father falling out with Sheikhs here and there', the final destination was Luxembourg. A hauntingly quiet city, it was the base where Brian spent the majority of his painfully isolated adolescence.

The family settled in Remich, a small town on the road to Zonnweiler. On arrival he was enrolled in the European School of Luxembourg, an experience that was memorable for all the wrong reasons.

The first school ever to exist in Europe, it was renowned for producing actors, actresses and 'born performers.' Enjoying drama but hating sports and academic pursuits, he excelled at school nonetheless. After all what better place for a budding dramatist than an institute with a reputation to rival Sylvia Young's famous stage school? This was the location where Brian started his love affair with the stage. However, his happiness was to be short-lived, as the mischievous young man goaded his peers to breaking point.

'I actually had to leave because I was being bullied too much,' smirked Brian. 'I had a tendency to goad people until they basically lost it, people twice the size of me. They'd then be faced with this saggy, diminutive little tranny in front of them; I think they were embarrassed to hit me.' Instead he was dangled perilously from a 10ft wall in the playground, clinging on by his shoes. 'If they'd dropped me, I would have broken my neck, definitely. I faced mortality at a very young age.'

He enrolled instead in the American International School of Luxembourg, a private institution for the most influential members of society. The school claims to have over 40 nationalities in its midst, in contrast to Brian's original claims that it was 'insular and full of whiny Americans.' From bankers to politicians, the school has a reputation for receiving children from the most influential families in the country. On paper, Brian fitted in perfectly at the prestigious school, yet in reality he faced a miserable existence.

Firstly, he hated Luxembourg with a passion, seeing the quiet countryside as deceptively idyllic. In fact, he would later compare it to the setting of the David Lynch series Twin Peaks. 'The funny thing about Twin Peaks is that it all looks really nice on the outside but underneath is a whole load of nasty shit going on,' he warned at a live show in the country years later. 'I've always felt that way about Luxembourg.'

As time passed, he saw AISL as the home of 'spoilt American brats who complain if they don't get the right flavour of chocolate chip cookies.' Believing himself to be modest for his background, Brian detested displays of spoilt behaviour.

He failed to fit in with his classmates, not least due to his parents' influence. 'I was always the black sheep of the family, raised by a born-again Christian mother and a social misfit businessman so I was always the little weird kid.'

He also hated sports at school, much to his classmates' bemusement. Although yearbook pictures depicted him as a beaming participant of school sports classes, he did stand out as the opposite of his more mainstream classmates. A mischievous, unusual looking young boy with an undeniable glint in his eye, there was no mistaking Brian among the rows of otherwise identical schoolboys. Confessing to distaste for almost all sporting pursuits, he recalled insecurity at being the last to be chosen for sports teams. 'I'd be standing there as this little insecure kid, thinking "Oh no, no-one likes me."'

With few friends in whom to confide, Brian quickly tired of Luxembourg. There was little to do there and musical companions such as the Smiths and the Cure were often his only saviours on a rainy afternoon. He did attend the occasional daytrip as a child however. At the age of 11, he crossed the border into French territory for a concert in the town of Arlon featuring the Belgian group Telephone. Accompanied by his protective 21-year old brother, Brian clinched a place in the front row. 'Being so small, I climbed over the barriers,' he chuckled. Today a DVD exists that pictures him as an audience member – a cherubically handsome young boy with chubby cheeks dressed in a light blue denim jacket. He was one of the youngest fans to be pictured, but made up for his lack of years with enthusiasm and charisma. Brian excitedly recalled 'It was filmed by Luxembourgish TV and then six months later, I saw myself on screen. I thought "Oh wow… what a cute face!"'

It was to be the start of a passionate love affair with fame – and, his detractors would insist, his own image. The youngster used fantasies of fortune to while away the lonely days. Mesmerised by the stage, and longing to see his own image there, the young Brian conducted imaginary interviews with himself, usually on the toilet. 'My parents must have thought I was weird, talking to myself as I was shitting.'

Despite the glamour puss's disinterest in the mundane, Brian was intellectually gifted, enrolling in numerous Advanced Placement (AP) classes, optional rigorous courses to gain college credits. These can be used to gain entry to universities nationwide, and are particularly useful if seeking a place at a university overseas. According to the website College Board, 'AP can change your life. Through college-level AP courses, you enter a universe of knowledge that might otherwise remain unexplored in high school… you have the opportunity to earn credit or advanced standing at most of the nation's colleges and universities.'

However his real interest was rapidly emerging – a taste for all things musical. Alternative music was not widely available in Luxembourg, and chart music was scarce too so he resorted to Snub TV for his few fixes of musical discovery. 'We were lucky,' Brian laughed later. 'We were never exposed to Phil Collins or Rush.'

Despite this musical desert, he did manage to view David Bowie's video Ashes to Ashes at the tender age of ten. He was immediately drawn to the dramatic image and especially to Bowie's abundant use of makeup. Most of all perhaps, he was inspired by the lack of reservation and the open celebration that Bowie employed in matters of being different. Whilst Brian was transfixed by his new idol, he very much upset his mother. 'Is that a man or a woman? You can't tell these days. It's disgusting!' she had shrieked in falsetto tones. Little did she know that in the future, her son was to inspire exactly the same reaction.

From the age of single figures, he had regularly been mistaken for a female. Long hair combined with an already feminine facial appearance sealed his fate, and he frequently inspired confusion as his mother took him on holidays in her hometown of Dundee. 'I used to have really long hair, much longer than it is now, and I remember walking around Dundee with my mum and her bumping into people that she knew from years ago and they'd say: "So who's your little girl then?"' Instead of reacting with embarrassment, he relished the ease with which he could slip into a female role, and by the age of 11 had already begun to take female parts in plays.

Living with a religious mother and an ultra-conservative banker father in one of Europe's smallest countries was probably not the best place to explore the deviations which held such fascination for the boy. 'My parents expected me to be a Republican-voting, God-fearing conformist,' he recalled with a touch of sadness.

Despite loving his mother dearly, age meant that he was already beginning to clash with her. It went without saying that she did not approve of his rapidly emerging tendency to defy normal gender roles. Eager to please, he did take on a brief flirtation with religion, strongly encouraged by Mrs. Molko, with whom he attended church every weekend.

Recognising his leadership qualities, the pastor invited Brian for private Bible study meetings where he would be primed for a career in the ministry.

Mischievously, he responded by subverting religious teachings, arguing his point remarkably persuasively. This caused a great deal of embarrassment for Brian's parents, particularly when they heard he had brought Dead Kennedys albums into his Sunday school classes. He would routinely horrify the pastor by analysing their subversive, anti-governmental lyrics in infinite detail.

'When I was 13 years old, I was really into the Dead Kennedys,' Brian confirmed. 'Living in Luxembourg, there was nothing to channel my teenage energies into – I wasn't big on vandalism and too chicken to be a petty thief, so as an unhappy teenager, they were a band that I managed to channel all of my isolation and aggression into. I was obsessed by them. I went from being groomed for the ministry to throwing myself into the anti-establishment politics of [singer] Jello Biafra.'

At Sunday school, he introduced his peers to Biafara's anti-corporate socialist values. The singer condoned eliminating taxes for the working class whilst increasing them for the wealthy by way of compensation. Like Brian, he also condoned the legalisation of drugs. With titles such as Kinky Sex Makes the World Go Around, and Too Drunk to Fuck, the group was hugely incongruent with church etiquette.

The lyric 'Is my cock big enough? Is my brain small enough?' gave a nod to lad culture with a huge dose of irony. It demonstrated the scathing ambivalence he felt about the culture and Brian could relate. Meanwhile 'I Fought the Law' with the line 'The law don't mean shit if you've got the right friends, that's how this country's run,' echoed Brian's dissatisfaction with the concept of hierarchy, one where influential people won regardless of justice. Brian was one of the privileged few referred to in the song, but it didn't change his views. In fact Biafara's manifesto couldn't have been more different from that of Brian's own parents.

Combining punk-rock music with a message as powerful as its beat, this fiercely political frontman was termed a 'visionary, incendiary performer' by famed punk-rock author Stephen Blush. 'I had all his spoken word albums,' enthused Brian, 'and they all had a really big effect on me, one that went way beyond music. He really tapped into that alienation and aggression that you feel as a teenager. I could channel all of that through him.'

Brian also expressed his rage through Black Flag, another alternative band. 'They took the piss out of American frat boy culture. It told me everything that was wrong with lad culture.' By appearing as a female, Brian was to bear the brunt of the dangers of lad culture first hand, which increased his loathing for it. 'Don't call me pet!' he would snarl at groups of drunken and predatory men.

As he learnt more about the world, Brian was becoming increasingly disillusioned, but no more so than with organised religion. He despised its strict gender roles and attitude towards homosexuality. Yet, at his mother's request, he would spend many summers reluctantly attending Sunday school camps to meditate and reflect on the questions of life. The luxurious Swiss mountain resorts where these took place formed one part of Brian's life, but for the remainder of his summers, he was engaged in a different pursuit – theatre camp in Oxfordshire. There was a tremendous gulf between these two opposing worlds and in Brian's eyes, the glamorous life of the stage was winning.

Despite being quite a controversial member of the Catholic community, he nevertheless began to turn away from all that it represented. He appreciated the rich metaphorical imagery within the Bible and yet for him religion left many questions unanswered. 'I gave my life to Christ at 11 and took it back at 14,' Brian reflected. 'I told my mom "I don't want to go to church anymore. I'm discovering who I am."'

To complicate matters further, there was the issue of Brian's sexuality. 'My sexuality is very fluid but it's very real,' he claimed. 'I have had confusing and contradicting emotions since I have awakened sexually, and it's something that I have come to terms with and that I have managed to live with in a very positive way.'

Plus as a fiercely independent soul, Brian also resented the implication that he should unquestioningly accept a rulebook that was not of his own creation. He was unable to embrace the predefined rules set by the Church, preferring to embark on an individual journey to find his own morality. For him a world of sex, drugs and rock and roll was eminently preferable.

Sure enough, shortly afterwards Brian began to have sex. He lost his virginity at the age of 14 to a beautiful and glamorous Parisian woman, Carole, and concealed this from his absent parents by attributing it to a nose-bleed. Two years his senior, she prompted Brian's fascination with all things French. He none too romantically described the moment as 'You get it over with, and then you become strongly acquainted with your right hand.' However he did concede that the romance had been special. 'She was my first girlfriend,' he remarked blushingly. Explaining away the red blood stains that adorned his covers, Brian successfully concealed the secret from an overzealous mother. 'It happened in my room. I convinced my mother that I'd had a nosebleed on the duvet but she said, "You must have been lying in a strange position."'

The demons that confronted him on his involvement with the Church did not cease, and this was the year that his attendance stopped. Meanwhile, the issue of sexuality came into play. His first flirtation with the concept of sex with other men occurred at the age of 16. Whilst recovering from chicken pox, he played a game in the woods with a handsome male friend. Noting his friend's bare-chested physique, Brian felt an inexplicable rush of attraction, which was to pave the way for his later experimentation. 'I got chicken pox when I was about 16, and in order to relieve the stress of it, a friend of mine came over, and we were just running through the woods pretending to be Indians or something,' Brian recalled. 'We might have had something to smoke that day. And he had his top off, and I remember going, "Well, that's quite nice, isn't it?" That set the whole thought process going.'

This was yet another turning point for Brian's turbulent relationship with religion. His feelings clashed with the values of Catholicism, which regard homosexuality as a strict sin. Brian withdrew. 'I remember my mother saying "When Jesus knocks at your door, it's your choice to open the door or leave it closed. Jesus will knock for a while but then your heart will become hardened and he will leave."'

Evidently Brian's heart was hardening already as he turned his back on religion for good. Despite receiving a letter from the pastor declaring 'You may have strayed from the path and you are a lost sheep in the flock, but you will return,' he never did. 'He hasn't seen you lately then?' chortled a bemused journalist when Brian recounted the story years later.

Despite keeping his feelings a secret from his overbearing family, his mother continued to disapprove of his interests. Brian also clashed with his father – despite employing full staff in the family home, Mr. Molko expected his son to be responsible for menial jobs such as mowing the lawn and 'picking up the dog shit.' Brian did so whilst apparently entertaining the belief that his dog was gay.

Birthdays were also a sad time for Brian. 'They're a reminder of how everything was a complete fuck up in my family, and no one was ever really around,' he mourned later. However, one stood out in particular for being a happy occasion. For his sixteenth, Brian was bought a Telecaster guitar as a gift, something that would mark his entry into the musical world. As a stoned teenager, he was also introduced to Sonic Youth, a band that would change his life forever.

Music gave Brian the confidence to break the mould. There was an expectation in the family that Brian would excel academically and that, like his father and elder brother, would maintain an unsatisfying but financially rewarding career. Brian could not appreciate this notion, feeling the nagging desire to 'forge his own identity.' As someone who has experienced opposing views from birth, Brian was in the perhaps enviable position of knowing his own mind through necessity.

Raised in a culturally diverse environment and unwittingly pulled in opposite directions by his parents, one of whom wanted him to be a minister and the other a banker, Brian was unable to fall unquestioningly into the socially typical roles of his culture. Simply, there was no one culture, but a variety of different ones.

Despite the relentless pressure from his parents, Brian did enjoy a relatively close relationship with his brother Stuart. Despite a ten-year age gap and different ambitions for life, the two were supportive of each other and even became firm friends. 'He's my best friend," Brian gushed. 'That ten-year gap, once I got to a certain age, meant that there wasn't going to be any competition between us, which was great, and once I got to a certain age we could start partying together.' Stuart also took on the role of bank manager for Brian once success showed its head in a financial sense.

However, the two were polar opposites. While his brother had achieved a sensible job in the financial sector and was always dressed conservatively, Brian's reputation was one of breathtaking flamboyancy. At school he was known and criticised for his trademark baggy clothes in an array of fluorescent colours. He later admitted to the fashion crimes that had made him a laughing stock, claiming 'It was horrible.' However in a peculiar twist of fate, a 15-year old Brian was selected by his classmates for the title of Best Dressed Male in his year group. Whether it was a cruel joke and a moment of irony, or genuine admiration, it achieved yearbook history. Brian later mused 'This was a paradox that made me understand the duality of emotions I can provoke in people.'

He wasn't mistaken. From his earliest years, not unlike the present day, he inspired an intensity of sheer emotion in all who encountered him. He was loved and hated with equal passion but notably never induced indifference. So here was a man who was mistaken for a girl from the age of innocence, was subject to ridicule for his unusual appearance in school, and who was an outsider in almost all environments.

Worse still, aside from the student bars of Luxembourg, where, according to Brian, students spent their time consuming 'dodgy E', Brian's opportunities for socialising were strictly limited. So for someone who did not like work and who, despite being intellectually gifted, lacked the inclination to become an academic, what would become of Brian?

Having made the grade at school, it was now time for university, which he saw as a welcome escape. Tired of being a voyeur of many cultures and belonging to none of them, his adventurous spirit took over. Fleeing the intensely cloistering environment in which he lived was to be a priority, and he swapped Luxembourg in favour of its polar opposite with the same initial – London. 'I didn't want to go to America,' Brian asserted. 'The kids I went to school with were like the ugly American abroad, totally arrogant. That gave me a tainted view of what Americans are like, because I was mixing with the upper-middle class spoilt rich kids.'

A large cosmopolitan city where diversity is accepted, anonymity comes easily, and quirkiness is often celebrated, the location seemed like the perfect solution to cure Brian's heartache. Despite having its fair share of prejudice in some ways, it was also home to vibrant nightlife where even the most lost soul could find his niche.

Fuelled by a desire for escape, plans were quickly made for Brian to attend the biggest creative arts college in the UK. His passion for theatre saw him enrol on a Bachelor of Arts in Drama, where he awaited a new and brightly lit future.

Whatever fantasies Brian had indulged in about the bright lights of London, he was to be sorely disappointed. Far from the sophisticated scene he was familiar with from short trips abroad with family, his choice of university had brought him to Deptford. A small and uninspiring district on the suburbs of south-east London, it was better known for its gang violence than its buoyant nightlife. Gritty and bleak, it nevertheless embodied some of the dangerous atmosphere a young Brian was looking for to ease the tedium.

The New York Times christened the region 'the Wild West of London' and 'top of the charts for shabby chic', instantly establishing it as a place for the bohemian and outrageous. However, according to locals, the newspaper's affection was misplaced. Amid cries that American tourists should holiday there, a local barmaid laughed 'I hope Americans like hoodies, muggers and junkies – there are enough of them around here.' Local mechanic David Ferndale told the Mail 'Have a look at the local paper – there are stabbings and shootings here all the time. You might as well be done with it and book two weeks all inclusive in Kabul.'

Unflatteringly enlikened to Afghanistan's biggest warzone, its sole redeeming feature for Brian was to be the local Deptford Arms pub. It played host to a number of little known local indie bands, and later Brian himself. Rejecting groups like Nirvana for being too commercial, he sought more obscure bands on independent labels to satisfy his listening pleasure. For that reason, the live nights at the diminutive local suited Brian's tastes perfectly.

The only other attraction in a relatively spartan neighbourhood was of course Goldsmiths College. Amid the den of inequity, it represented one of the many colleges that formed part of the University of London. Despite its art focus, the university enjoys a good reputation academically, ranking 45 out of 114 institutes in the Times' Good University Guide 2010. With its reputation as a creative arts place, the university is notably absent of the would-be scientists and earnest careerists in suits that normally inhabit places of study. The laid back environment was a perfect match for Brian's temperament.

Despite entering an environment which embraced creativity and individuality, Brian still stood apart from the rest. At just 17, he was younger than his contemporaries in both age and appearance, and equally set apart in his manner.

Instantly recognisable, he represented a shy, introverted boy who, according to his tutors, was initially bashful about revealing the hidden spark within. Surrounded by intensely competitive students, Brian kept a distance and inhabited his own world, behind which lay a powerful intellect and a passion for his work. As a tutor commented 'You only truly saw how powerful his work could be at the end.'

Brian's favourite lecturer was Gerald Lidstone, now a senior member of the drama department. 'I do remember him quite distinctly in his first year,' said Gerald. 'He was quite individual and looked much younger than the other students, probably because he was smaller. He also had a very different background because he hadn't studied in England before and was only 17 when I started teaching him.'

He is said to have shared a small group of close friends, just as he had done in his Luxembourg days, and remained on the periphery of the class rather than commanding his tutors' attention in a typical drama student style.

Yet he must have been extremely special to have inspired the breadth and intensity of memories which his tutors recall. For someone who graduated more than 15 years previously, the recollections have amazing clarity. Gerald, Brian's personal tutor over the three years, got to know him amongst a small group of just five other pupils. In this intimate context, he had the opportunity to see beyond Brian's bashful exterior into the dangerous actor he aspired to become.

Despite an intensely subversive nature, Brian was astonishingly quiet, and Gerald believed that hinted at the troubled upbringing with which stories of his formative years are now synonymous. 'He was a typical shy exhibitionist,' Gerald mused. 'He was not a show-off in an obvious way. He would hide behind his mask rather than push himself to the front.'

As a brash student in Luxembourg, Brian had also made a conscious effort to soften his approach by thinking before he spoke. Such measures were likely to prevent him from meeting an unfortunate end in the Thames, rather like previous encounters where he was dangled from a wall at his Luxembourg school. The newly diplomatic Brian was head and shoulders in front of his less sophisticated classmates. Gerald recalled his steps into maturity, commenting 'Everyone was trying to show off a bit, but he was too clever for that. He thought "Well, that's everyone's game, so I'll bide my time, wait a bit and then make my statement when I feel ready."'

'He was friends with some of the more avant-garde members of the year group,' Gerald recalled. 'They were quite unconventional and very creative, which was unusual in those days – very much the art-school type.'

Gerald was equally unusual, with a subversive nature and self-confessed love of anarchy, which was atypical in his role of tutor. His tutorials comprised a note of contempt for authority and tradition, and in that the pair shared what Gerald describes as an 'unspoken bond.'

'He got on very well with me because I'm a bit anarchic myself,' chuckled Gerald. 'Especially in those days and he enjoyed that. Our classes were quite anti-authority and I think it surprised him as well as appealed to him that any of the teachers would be on that wavelength.'

Musing on Brian's shared love of deviation that so closely resembled his, he continued 'He'd always be challenging. He'd always question rather than accept peoples' judgments and he'd always want to know why. He had a sort of naivety in those days – he wanted to know why things were like that, and why he should do it like that.'

Brian's contemptuous attitude to authority extended to his work as well, where he would shun assignments that failed to interest him. 'He wasn't the kind of student who would do the whole aspect of the course, so I think with the purely academic work, if he didn't see that it was interesting for him to do it, he wouldn't. He was very passionate about certain aspects of the course, the creative work, anything original that he was allowed to do. I think everything that was self-generated he loved, and anything where he had to follow form he wasn't so interested in – he would do it, but again he would question it.'

Brian's love affair with makeup and inspiring gender confusion began in full-force in his first year. Far away from his parents' cloistering influence, he began to experiment with makeup, wearing pale foundation and on occasion a spot of black eyeliner. Gerald recalled 'I remember he wore makeup but it wasn't outrageous – it was just a definite choice and more to do with self-presentation at the time than trying to be the best performer. I think that came later.'

Years on, in conversation with noted fashion designer Xavier Delcour – ironically given his reputation for an appalling fashion sense – Brian confirmed this observation. 'I had heroes but I was more attracted by music than image. My interest in image began the moment I had to present myself to the public.' Indeed, unlike contemporaries such as Kiss, Brian's visual portrayals seemed natural, a mere reflection of who he was rather than a publicity stunt or a false face to hide behind. In the eyes of his fans, he had a strong image in collaboration with the music, not one which was adopted to hide the mediocrity of the sonic output – he had never required image for that.

From the nine-year old child who'd worshipped Michael Jackson's 1981 hit Beat It for its rocky Van Halen guitars to the shy teenager with a penchant for Bowie records, Brian did try to emulate his musical heroes, but never copied a look just for dramatic effect. When it was time to appear in public, he avoided allowing image to overshadow performance, although it might contribute an important message to it, and he enjoyed tricking his audience, seducing them in the revelry of pseudo-identities.

One notable example of this was his third year performance piece which formed the dissertation requirement of the course. Critical to graduation, it was important to deliver something special and by all accounts, Brian did not disappoint. A pseudo-autobiographical piece about the perils of gender issues, the project, entitled Scar Tissue, raised eyebrows all around the school.

'He created a very effective video because he was someone who at that stage we didn't expect to do those things,' tutor Robert Gordon recalled. 'He was quite private as a student, and he wasn't one of those that constantly craved your attention. However I got to know him better because of the tutorial, and I knew there was something different about him. In class he didn't push himself to the front, so you only truly saw how dangerous his work could be at the end.'

'Brian wasn't deliberately outrageous or provocative in those days,' agreed Gerald, 'but later on he did do a performance piece that was pretty provocative and quite brave actually. It was this self-created piece about gender and he was nude in this piece. Again all the students always threatened they were going to take their clothes off for the final project, but none of them did – apart from Brian. It was about gender and something to do with a man in a woman's body.'

These recollections were correct and his piece, Scar Tissue had an intriguing plot. On her 13th birthday, a young girl named Brandy experiences Testicular Defeminisation Syndrome and overnight her identity as a woman irrevocably changes. She realises the painful identity crisis of being a female trapped in a man's body. Her transformation leads her to the role of an adolescent male known as Brian. This hinted at Brian's own experience growing up from an effeminate boy to a grown man and facing some gender conflicts.

Gerald explained 'Out of all the pieces we saw that year, it was the most radical and probably the most self-defining. It was also very teasing. Was this really him or was this just a persona that he had created?' He added flatteringly that it reached an element of danger – one that other students, perhaps more conventional in nature, had hinted at, aspired to but never quite achieved. Causing a ripple of envy amongst his more exhibitionistic but less daring classmates, he appeared completely naked, covered only by a screen.

For someone who had been so self-conscious as a child that he had refused to wear revealing clothes such as a swimming costume, this was a feat indeed. It was to be just the beginning as he later recalled 'I wanted to be taller than I am. I wanted to be sexier than I am, and I wanted to have less zits than I have. On stage I am all of these things.'

The angst, intensity and new found confidence he portrayed in his multiple gender story surely paid off as he earned top marks for the piece. In fact it was only his written work that became a downfall, earning him a 2:2 en balance. The grade was a compromise between his high-ranking practical performances and his lower-graded academic work. The singer has openly described himself as being 'ridiculously bad at written work' in a disarmingly self-deprecating moment – but just how accurate is this analysis?

'Written work?' chuckled Gerald. 'He didn't like it. He was looking at what we had to offer that he wanted to learn, not what we thought he should know.' Another tutor recalled giving Brian a 'ridiculously low' mark on one essay, commenting 'If he wasn't interested, he didn't bother.'

Indeed, Brian had little concern for keeping up appearances. 'I basically flunked all my academic stuff, and scored top marks on all my practical work,' Brian confessed to Vox years later.

His fearless and unconventional approach to learning indicated a need for control and a desire to manipulate the learning experience to suit his own needs. Instead of fitting his words to another person's context, he preferred to create his own boundaries.

'I always felt there was an honesty about Brian,' Gerald reflected. 'He didn't seem to feel any need to hide what was naïve. If he didn't understand something, like a Shakespeare play, when the others would think they ought to know, he would just say "Well, what does that mean?" He'd say it directly, when the other students were embarrassed to, so he had no shame about feeling he ought to be sophisticated. And obviously now he seems very sophisticated, because he's so clever at what he does, but I think he was very open to learning.'

Aside from performance, the curriculum was varied and challenging. Students studied psychodrama, 'a form of human development which explores through dramatic action problems, issues, concerns, dreams and highest aspirations.' It was certainly true that Brian could exorcise his demons through drama, using it as a therapeutic context – the performance piece was an example of that. They were also versed in philosophy, studying Sartre, Camus and the greats of ancient Greek theatre. Brian had a fondness for them and incorporated them into his work. Psychoanalytic theory and gender in the theatre were other specialisations that appealed to Brian. He was also a fan of Shakespeare, his favourites being Twelfth Night and As You Like It.

Gerald had a vivid memory of Brian seeing the famed Robbie Le Page production of A Midsummer Night's Dream. 'That was the one in the mud baths', Gerald smiled, 'and he loved that because it was so quirky and outrageous.' It had been a group theatre trip, and it was the inspiration of one of many performance pieces that Brian co-directed during his time at Goldsmiths.

Brian's rapidly increasing love of music also found its way into his performance. He incorporated music into what he describes as a 'punk-rock version of Shakespeare', with a soundtrack featuring the adored Sonic Youth, and the Butthole Surfers. This version, like many of Brian's plays thematically, focused on gender. The plot saw war ensue between the sexes, with the male and female fairies fighting and Brian playing a female fairy himself.

The memory of the play was said to be an inspiration for many of the songs on Placebo's debut album. Brian recalled a six hour editing marathon with a friend where, fuelled by amphetamines, they created a fast-paced version of a Midnight Summer's Dream. 'The authorities hated it, but it was the most popular play that year,' Brian quipped mischievously. 'The character of Titania was so lifeless that we replaced her with a blow-up doll, and during the last scene she'd deflated and the King of Thieves would end up in tears, hugging a deflated doll.' He added 'And we never ever fucked that doll. A friend stole it, but he was sad. We spent a great deal of time touching it, thinking how weird it would be to actually fuck it.

And maybe it's like the closest thing to fucking a groupie, because you have no connection with either.'

Senior staff member Robert was one of the first to recognise his growing interest in music when he incorporated a song into Scar Tissue. 'He wasn't a good singer back then- not that you'd notice. He wasn't special. However not many students would choose to sing at that part of the course, so it was noticeable.'

Nonetheless, Brian continued to immerse himself in rhythm. 'I wanted to be an actor more than anything else. The thing is you spend a lot of time working on other people's ideas in films – you spend about three to four months working on a film before you actually see the fruits of your labour. Music is much more instant,' he recalled.

He delighted the public with his distinctive image, so much so that Robert had a vision of Brian as a visual artist. 'I felt he might want to become a visual artist. I see the Bowie connection there, because Bowie worked so much with artists such as Lizzie Kemp and I think he had a great affinity with that, anything where he would use his imagination.'

He continued 'He came across as an artist on video, which shows you someone with a very strong visual sense as well as a desire to perform. I think in all his performances the idea of presence, of being there as a real person within the role play was something that intrigued him. It was something about role play with the tease of being yourself as well.'

If his tutors could write a script specifically designed for Brian based on their perceptions of his life and character, what would it be? 'I think a fallen angel,' Gerald suggested. 'He did have a dark side. But he also had a very playful, teasing side. I think he's somebody who's intelligent yet self assured. I feel that he's got a maturity, a very good sense of himself amongst other people, and that maybe that comes from having to look after himself as a child. Someone who's careful – he's very open, yet very guarded. And when I first said a fallen angel, I meant someone who knows how to look after himself. I think he's vulnerable. He has vulnerability and a great sort of openness – a sort of innocence about himself – an unashamed openness to his own femininity.'

This type of character was first demonstrated in his childhood years when friends of his mother mistook him for a girl. Meanwhile Robert could see Brian in a Charlie Chaplin film role, concurring 'He could project vulnerability and hurt without too much effort.' Indeed, Brian mirrored Chaplin's curious mixture of depression, fieriness and hidden optimism. The words 'Smile though your heart is aching, smile even though it's breaking' were Chaplin words yet could easily describe Brian.

Clearly his tutors had immensely high opinions of him, but his personal life was rapidly coming undone. Characterised by loneliness and sexual frustration, his last year at college was to be a miserable one. After a year of celibacy, something which he wryly remarked gave him 'no inner peace,' he hoped for better luck the following year.

At around that time, Brian fell in love with a man, an all-consuming mutual infatuation that developed between him and a fellow drama student three years his senior. Brian chuckled 'I think he probably relished the idea of breaking me in more than he was actually in love with me!' A far cry from his oppressive Luxembourg upbringing, the anonymity that London provided was allowing Brian to emerge from his shell. He began to experiment and his regular visits to drag queen clubs allowed him to contemplate the sexual possibilities available to him.

Yet his time in Deptford was infused with drama as well as decadence – from clinging to a tree trying to reconnect to the world after a bad acid trip to immense pressures from his family. His troubled thoughts were understood by Gerald. 'I think you could see evidence of his troubled upbringing. It wasn't that he was difficult or demanding attention – he seemed like a bit of a fallen angel, with a rather cherubic face, and you did know that he was a loner and had been as a child. But he didn't seem to make a big fuss about it. He just seemed to deal with it. It came out in his work and mental abilities and thoughts, but he didn't act it out in the college situation. You could definitely feel that sometimes he wanted reassurance, and sometimes he wanted to stand back and not commit himself. I think he'd been through a lot of mental trauma, so he was defensive.'

Gerald offered a telling anecdote about his family relationship, which persisted in its angst beyond the barrier of an ocean. 'Brian would sometimes say rather humorously "Oh, my father's coming to London" in such a way as if his father was checking up on him that he was doing his education properly, but there was a slight tease about that, and I never quite knew why it might be a bad thing.'

Memories of Brian were always defined by intrigue, ambiguity and mystery, something that would change little even years on.

Finally as his course concluded, without so much as a second glance, Brian left behind the college that had been his home for the last three years, and began his plunge into freedom.

What lasting impression would the aspiring actor leave his lecturers with? 'I saw him on Jonathan Ross years later,' Gerald remembered. 'He was really cool, and very much the same Brian I remember – just a little more confident and a little clearer about who he was.'

Chapter 2.

'We're like transvestites on crystal meth!' – Brian Molko

'I don't know if I believe in fate, or if I really believe that chance rules our lives,' Brian mused. 'It would be a real shame if predestination existed. That would mean that free will would have nothing to do with your life.' It's a bold statement for Mr Molko, but ironically it was fate that put him where he is today.

By June 1993, Brian was euphoric. He had finally graduated and fulfilled parental expectations of him – and now he had the freedom to pursue his own destiny. In many ways he was relieved to have left as, whilst he had a passion for drama, his living conditions had been far from ideal. 'I used to go to sleep every night with the sound of my neighbour to my right fucking his girlfriend, and then every morning the guy to the left would listen to Lionel Richie really early and go to breakfast.' Yet if dorm life had been bad, the worst was yet to come.

He had also fallen prey to the agonies of depression and sexual frustration, his involvement in the drug scene playing no small part. Formerly quiet and introverted, he had fought the ties of repression in his university days to compensate. He had been introduced to ketamine, a powerful horse tranquiliser used recreationally, which had been an intensely unpleasant experience.

'I don't recommend it,' an older and wiser Brian commented later. 'It's fucking horrible. You walk around tripping up because you no longer have any concept of gravity.' However, flaunting his new-found rebellion, he had continued to flirt with danger and began to sample the highly toxic hallucinogenic LSD. His compulsive experimentation had led to one occasion where he feared for his life. The experience had been so bad Brian had decided to give up hallucinogenic drugs for good. 'I literally felt like every muscle in my body was about to sort of tear itself apart, and I thought I was going to die. I found myself in Greenwich Park in London, and I'm embarrassed to admit it, hugging a tree. Trying to calm myself down and tell myself "It's only a drug. This will stop. You may be a casualty after this but you will still be alive."'

Aside from the bad trips and shockingly inadequate marks in academic work, university life had never run smoothly. The main difficulty for Brian however was his growing dependency on marijuana. He had reportedly said that he felt 'unable to function' without at least five joints per day. Living away from home for the first time and experiencing far more than Luxembourg's limited nightlife, he was certainly making up for lost time.

He had gone from sexual frustration to constant bed hopping, a schizophrenic phase which he would later bitterly regret. 'Due to low self-esteem, a lack of pure love when I was a kid and because I was a serious attention-seeker, I did once try to find meaning through being a bit of a slut,' Brian mused.

'In fact, as I was finishing college, I'd enforced celibacy on myself for 11 months because I'd reached the point where I was suffering from post-coital depression. I'd sleep with people and on the point of coming, I'd be filled with complete revulsion for them. I stopped having sex because I was sick of throwing people out of my flat at 4am and just going "Fuck off, I don't want to see you anymore."'

Instead of sexual entertainment, Brian settled for much more wholesome fun – a life of music, transsexual bars and drunken swimming contests in the Thames.

'I used to go swimming in the Thames when I was really, really pissed,' Brian revealed, 'which was a really fucking stupid thing to do – I swallowed some Thames water once too. I'm lucky I didn't die.'

Another issue was Brian's run-ins with the police. 'I was once in Greenwich Park and sparked up a spliff just as a cop car pulled up in front of me. They broke it into bits and let me go.' On another occasion, he was stopped and searched, yet despite possessing a gram of speed in his pocket, the police were unable to find it. Since that day, Brian has been adamant that a guardian angel watches over him in times of crisis.

If he had been confused and in turmoil throughout his time at university, that was nothing compared to the reality of graduation. He moved from his college dormitory into a housing-benefit funded flat on Deptford's Drakefell Road where he was desperately pulling together a budget to make a series of short films. Unapologetically perverse, these included a man who could breathe underwater and a woman who bled every time the phone rang.

Brian's ideas were as eccentric and non-commercial as ever, and he was having trouble obtaining financial support for his niche-market movies.

Jobless, friendless and isolated, he relied on his fortnightly income support cheque simply to get by. Naturally for a type as sensitive as Brian, this was far from ideal as he struggled to balance the incongruence of his dreams for success with this dark new reality.

'I lived in glamorous Deptford,' Brian had shuddered later. 'I was on income support and housing benefit which I considered to be my artistic grant from the Government.' Unfortunately he spent this grant on marijuana instead. 'I lived under the dark cloud of dole, daily violence on Deptford High Street, cheap beer and scraping up enough money to get a tenth of hash.' He sank even deeper into despair, culminating in a panic attack on the high street. To Brian, this was a tell-tale warning sign that his lifestyle was not for him.

It was the immediacy and instant feedback of being in a band that Brian truly wanted. It would satisfy his musical cravings and allow him instant praise, eliminating the insecurity he suffered from so greatly. This deeply impatient new man knew the rock music industry was for him, evidenced by his love of guitar and atonal rock artists. Stating that it was, after all, the place where the freaks go, Brian embarked on a new journey – a frenetic search for his place in 'the rock and roll circus.'

Under these miserable circumstances, success was to show its head sooner than he could ever have imagined. Brian arranged to meet a female friend to catch an art exhibition in the cosmopolitan district of Chelsea. The crisp white rows of Georgian houses and the upper-crust environment were not new to Brian, but they were certainly different from his recent experiences of London.

Strolling into South Kensington tube station, he caught the eye of none other than his Luxembourg classmate and polar opposite, Stefan Olsdal. Brian breathed an ill-disguised sigh of frustration. It had been several years since the two had met, and over the seven years that Brian had been at school, they had 'barely exchanged one sentence.' Brian had been what he terms a 'big girl's blouse', on the 'loser team', and an introverted soul who preferred the theatre and marijuana to sport. Stefan on the other hand had been the archetype of masculinity, a tall jock and basketball team player.

Originally they had met at a school production of 1950s play 'The Boyfriend', in which a millionaire schoolgirl, wary of gold-diggers, dupes her first crush into believing she is a penniless secretary. The romantic comedy saw Brian operate the lights whilst the more popular Stefan acted as a young musician on the stage. They were also to meet at a club for those interested in starting a band, but unfortunately the pair did little more than eat pizza. Those two meetings were to be the only times they spoke.

'He was the youngest to make varsity basketball so he was in the jock group and I was more interested in the drama club and making smuggling trips to Holland, so I was in the loser group. We didn't mix,' assured Brian sardonically.

Their paths had rarely crossed, yet by divine intervention, seeing that tall figure with a guitar strapped to his back, Brian had let out an unguarded shriek of 'Stefan?' The two eyed each other awkwardly and began to make polite conversation. 'I was trying to avoid you and talk to the girl you were with,' Stefan had admitted later.

Studying at the Musician's Institute in Wapping, not so far from Brian's own east London university, Stefan had already been in the city for quite some time. Noticing his guitar, an unlikely item to be associated with Stefan, Brian's curiosity was immediately piqued. In a twist of fate neither would forget, he invited him to an acoustic show he was performing in at Deptford pub Round the Bend.

Stefan attended somewhat reluctantly as he had been more interested in getting Brian's friend's phone number than his, but was, to his surprise, completely blown away. At school their paths and indeed social circles couldn't have been more different and few could have predicted the unlikely meeting of minds that was to follow.

The moment the show was over, Stefan approached Brian offering to be his bass player, and over an evening of drinks, they discovered they shared much more in common than either had initially supposed. United by the East London line, it was to be the first of many meetings to follow.

Stefan's parents were wealthy, owning commercial aircraft and enjoying numerous high-flying business interests. However the young Stefan, like Brian, was desperate with boredom and had channelled his frustrations into music. A metal and heavy rock fan, his hero in childhood had been Steve Harris of Iron Maiden. This unlikely idol had first inspired him to pick up the bass. It wasn't a secret the young Stefan had shared with his basketball team. As time had gone on, he'd patriotically supported childhood heroes Abba instead and his tastes gradually became more sophisticated. Adamant at all costs that he would become a musician, he moved to London where fate had led him to Brian's show.

'After the gig Stef came up to me and said "I really like what you're doing – let's make some music together and see what happens," recalled Brian, 'and two people that thought they'd have absolutely nothing in common found we had a really common bond between us. Five minutes into our drink, Stefan turned round to me and said "I think I'm gay." I said, "That's cool, because I'm bisexual." Then – BANG – we hit it off like that. Finally, we'd find something tangible that we both had in common.'

Indeed, throughout his teenage years, Stefan had been disguising a secret life beyond the school gates, one he felt his fellow pupils could never hope to understand. The gentle Swede confessed 'I really didn't feel comfortable in the locker room with all that "Woooargh! Let's go kick their asses!" I was playing music all the time.' Despite appearing to be the popular guy whilst Brian was seen as 'the gay one' by visiting parents, it had turned out that unbeknown to either their roles had hugely overlapped.

Steve, the third piece of the puzzle, met Brian in the less than glamorous location of a Lewisham branch of Burgerking. Chatting over soggy fries and cholesterol-loaded burgers dripping with grease, it didn't seem a likely place to make a connection but when Brian entered with a mutual friend at the time, connect they did, and it was there on Lewisham High Street that destiny began to take its course.

Steve's background couldn't be more different from that of Brian and Stefan's eminently more privileged lives. A Mancunian born in Cheshire, he was at the mercy of his father, an ICI chief engineer, and his musical preferences. 'I was brought up with Elton John and Wings, because that was all my dad would let me listen to, I think. Then I discovered my own brain.'

The rebellious Hewitt began to borrow his brother's record collection and developed a passion for AC/DC. 'My dad wouldn't let me buy a drum kit when I was 11, but I was like "Fuck you, I'm gonna do it anyway!"' Steve grinned.

His debut into music was distinctly unglamorous, performing Fleetwood Mac's 'Albatross' at a school assembly. Steve disliked school intensely and dreamed instead of success with his group Mystic Deckchairs, although his strict father had other ideas. Much to his horror, just a week after leaving school, he found that his father had organised an apprenticeship for him as a joiner. Understandably Hewitt Senior was keen for his son to start work, but Steve was determined to find success on his own terms. Seven months later he walked out.

As time went on, he found a new vocation. In between working as a mechanic on Formula 1 racing cars – something Steve both enjoyed and had an aptitude for – he managed to find a limited amount of success with music. He was the percussionist on the album 'Ichabod and I' by the Boo Radleys and on 'Rhythm is a Mystery,' a 1989 K-Klass offering.

However, his most notable success before he met Brian was as the third part of Breed, a dark and broody rock group who found fame as the support act on Nick Cave tours. Steve joined the group as a naïve 17-year old and was instantly adored by lead singer Simon. 'He pretended to like all the albums we'd got when really he didn't know what he was going on about, but he had so much enthusiasm for my music it didn't matter,' said Simon. Auditioning for a drummer, he soon saw Steve's aptitude. 'There weren't any contenders- we tried several people but no-one clicked like Steve. I thought, he's got attitude, raw talent, was cocky as hell and looked like a young Nick Cave. He was in! His first words as we watched some inept shambling act were "Let's twat 'em and jam!"'

These first words proved to be beguiling and the three set off for Germany, where the young Steve would attempt his first international tour. The first show the group played together was in Hamburg at the Kaiserkeller, an infamous music venue commonly associated with being the Beatles' Hamburg home.

Despite disguising cringes of embarrassment at Steve's eclectic fashion sense, penchant for clogs, and backcombed hair which earned him the nickname of 'tarantula', Simon and bandmate Andrew quickly formed a bond with him. At the bar that night, they were astonished to learn that Steve was underage and in fact 'not even legal to buy a drink. He'd lied to us about his age basically so that we wouldn't think touring or bars would be a problem.' Chuckling affectionately, Simon continued 'Steve has always lied when it's been in his best interests – still does.'

However there were tangible benefits to having a young drummer in tow. His mother regularly supported them, offering a place to stay and dishing up home-cooked casseroles. These moments were to be brief respites from the tough life on the road. Steve's mother would tease him relentlessly by collecting pictures of La Toya Jackson, Michael's sister, and claiming that there was a resemblance. Mischief like this provided laughter and comfort at what was a difficult time for Breed. They also developed their own spirituality in the form of an Anti-God called the Masta Konfuser. 'He was a deity responsible for chaos and idiocy at every turn,' Simon remembered. 'Our motto was "Feels good, looks stupid."'

Simon delightedly recalled one of their most memorable tours: 'Steve did a runner from a Parisian restaurant only to be chased by a knife-wielding waiter to the van – and then we found out that our digs were next door to the same restaurant.'

If that wasn't disturbing enough, the group then had a huge argument live on TV at a hippie commune in Copenhagen. 'The interviewer was so stoned that it just degenerated, and we took over the camera. I interviewed Steve live on TV. "What matters about Breed, Steve?" "I dunno man, you never tell us. What is it fucking all about?" Cue a tearful fight – live on TV.' Their tours were certainly eventful, but above all successful.

The group travelled the UK and Europe achieving cult recognition and made their first big break touring with Nick Cave. Just when it seemed that their hardships were over however, disaster struck. 'I came back from the Nick Cave tour to find that my girlfriend was pregnant,' Steve recalled. The touring lifestyle and as yet scant financial rewards were too hectic to bring up a child, but there was more bad news. 'Our record company had gone bankrupt, then Breed split up and I thought I would never become a professional musician.'

It was at that moment that Brian met Steve. Coincidentally Brian had been a huge fan of Breed, remarking that their style had given him the inspiration he needed to adopt an art-rock style. He believed that the group had transformed his performances and consequently his friends had thought that Brian had a crush on Steve. Their chance meeting led to frequent partying together, and after much discussion, Brian and Stefan realised they'd found their drummer.

Steve had shared Brian's experiences of abject poverty, once living in a disused warehouse and surviving on a diet of mouldy cheese. Both had admittedly had their fair share of disastrous jobs, with Steve's mechanic tasks almost invariably ending in misadventure, while Brian had once taken a summer job shredding documents. He would frequently take illicit breaks to masturbate in the toilets and amused himself by seeing which objects he could successfully put through the shredder without breaking it – from paper clips to glass. The machine promptly ended its life when he attempted to shred plastic, and that spelt the end of his shredding career. As a magazine journalist commented, he would have looked considerably more foolish had he been wearing eyeliner at the time.

From the moment Steve joined Breed, lying about his age to gain the coveted position of drummer, he had been quite an adventurer. Now as Brian, Stefan and himself found themselves rehearsing constantly, desperate to make the big time, life was tough. Unable to afford a taxi, Steve recalled the ardour of transporting an amp and drum kit all the way from Camberwell, south London to Brian's dismal Deptford flat with his slight companion. Bemused spectators could hardly have anticipated that this dishevelled two piece could ever have made it as a famous group, but they were to be spectacularly proved wrong. Little could onlookers or indeed the band themselves have known that their future success would be a far cry from their humble beginnings.

Stefan fondly recalled their first jams with Steve. 'We started with broken keyboards and old guitars, writing arty punk-rock songs at the front room of Brian's council flat,' he said. 'We practised between cheap pints of lager at the pub round the corner.'

Steve had equally fond memories of his introduction to the hybrid monster that was the original Placebo. 'Me and Brian went to parties together. Our earliest incarnation was probably in the hallway, me on bongoes, him on guitar drunk on fucking Thunderbird or something.' Brian shamelessly countered 'It was White Lightening – the Happy Shopper version that came in two litre bottles.'

Despite the insalubrious environment and financial problems, the group was undeterred and quickly began writing some demos. Brian remained angry at his closeted upbringing and began to write about 'shedding the sceptre of Jesus,' fuelled by disappointment towards the church and his fraught childhood. Cheerier topics included 'accidentally castrating' his lover's prize poodle and embarking on an illicit affair with his daughter. 'Well, I can't help who I fall in love with, OK?' whined Brian in a pseudo-lovelorn voice. Another demo, 2468, was a withering and sarcastic tune with the popular cheerleaders' refrain '2 4 6 8, who do we appreciate?' These demos were never formally released. However four of the more commercially friendly songs were released on CD – Nancy Boy, Bruise Pristine, 36 Degrees and Bionic.

A name had also been decided upon. Initially naming themselves Ashtray Heart as an ode to Brian's favourite performer Captain Beefheart and his song of the same name, they soon discovered other possibilities. At that time there was a craze in the rock world for naming bands after drugs. Inspired by Codeine, Morphine et al, Brian hit upon Placebo. A drug of no pharmaceutical value which works purely due to the belief effect, it was a cunning name that would mirror Placebo's love affair with trickery and ambiguity.

However, Brian later acknowledged 'Our PR people told us to say it was chosen for the deceptive appeal of the name. In fact, we just thought "What would sound best if 30,000 people were screaming it in unison?"'

Latin for 'I shall please', exactly what the group set out to do, they confirmed themselves as Placebo. The awkward naming sessions aside, they could now focus on the new material.

However, Steve was in the group purely for fun at that time. Another group, Jaguar, with whom he had jammed, had found a record deal with

Warner Bros. Delighted, Steve accepted their invitation to become a percussionist for them full time and fled to a recording studio in Wales to seal the deal.

In Steve's absence the search for a new drummer began in earnest. Stefan's Swedish friend and musical associate Robert Schultzberg was also studying in London and with all three sharing a passion for rock music, the next step was clear. He joined in October 1994.

Brian and Stefan had just made their first public debut to a live audience, when the two joined 98 other guitarists for a composition of '100 Guitars' by Rhys Chatman. The show took place at Queen Elizabeth Hall in London. Brian had also been involved in film work for the Edinburgh Film festival that year but both side projects were short-lived and it wasn't long before Placebo became the main objective.

On January 23rd 1995 the group played their first show with Robert as drummer, at the Rock Garden in West London. Here, their unusual sound and appearance coupled with Brian's distinctive voice earned them the attention of A & R men up and down the country. Arriving on the scene amid a musical climate of Blur, Oasis and a long list of Britpop wannabes, Brian's voice refreshingly satisfied a thirst in the desert that was alternative music.

The band's first single was the independently released Bruise Pristine, a raw early version of the much-loved favourite, and it was released on Fierce Panda on October 30th 1995. 'Dangerous, mysterious and utterly addictive,' the NME mused appreciatively. On hearing his first radio play, Brian felt a rush of elation, combined with embarrassment at what he termed his 'Mickey Mouse vocals.' Early detractors blasted his 'helium-soaked' tones and the song was played at half-speed on the radio to counter the squeakiness. However, largely undeterred, Brian responded to Geddy Lee comparisons with threats to give the reviewers a 'broken leg.'

Ever kind to their friends, and as yet untouched by rock-star elevation of egos, the group had persuaded executive producer Brad Wood to let their fellow musician friends Soup star in the double-A side single for Bruise Pristine. Irritatingly persuasive, the Placebo effect seemed to have formerly sensible businessmen on their knees, complying with all manner of requests just to continue being bewitched by this deceptive yet curiously alluring drug. They could not resist, knowing instinctively that Placebo were about to become something huge. And so the pattern began.

The single's release was followed by an exclusive show at Café Freedom in the heart of London's prestigious West End. Presented by Riverman management, it would pave the way for important networking opportunities.

The location was right and the band finally had an opportunity to make it big. Tickets were just £2 on the door, an irresistibly cheap proposition and a chance for Placebo to unleash their punk-rock theme on the public. The bill also comprised of label mates Soup, the group whom they had coerced Fierce Panda into signing.

Soon afterwards, Placebo travelled to Manchester to play Unsigned in the City, a yearly bands festival targeted at big names in the music industry searching for new talent. Appearing alongside the now defunct Kula Shaker and Performance, Brian was the star of the show. 'Dip me in honey and throw me to the lesbians!' he squeaked in the distinctive trademark voice that had been wowing those in the know for months, before launching into the brand new Bruise Pristine. His feminine appearance, accentuated by his pale pink t-shirt bearing the slogan 'Don't label me' was a message to all that attended that evening. Whilst most had no intention of categorising him – even in the unlikely event that they'd be able to – there was an increasing desire to label him in a different way by signing him up and giving him the much coveted record deal.

An industry mogul reported 'When I thought the singer was a girl, I wasn't overcome. But when I heard it was a boy, it immediately changed my attitude towards them.' He was cited strange and unsettling, which was presumably nothing less than what the band set out to achieve. Another executive interested in signing them up quizzed 'Do you think he takes helium before going onstage? Maybe I should.'

There was no winner that night. It was reported, much to Brian's televised distaste, that all three groups showed a different side of the music industry and therefore all three were equally worthy of the prize. None were too pleased at this perceived cop-out – Brian in particular, who scowled furiously at the camera. However, this did not deter the group in their search for fame, and they were soon inundated by interested reps.

Back in London a few months later, Brian was living the dream – assaulted at every turn by overly enthusiastic representatives from the music industry. In fact coming off stage in Kings Cross one night, Brian threw his first rock-star tantrum, when a beer was knocked out of his hand by a record company executive. Brian sweetly refused his offer of a replacement until he was safely deposited around the corner and out of earshot. Then he turned to his press officer, kicked broken glass against the wall in a blaze of glory and in a loud voice yelled 'Shmuck!' Brian had achieved diva status ahead of his time.

Meanwhile the bidding war started. People were desperate to sign this group with its unusual front-man. Placebo was invited to perform a live set for management company Riverman. That day was a moment of suspense for the group – they had satisfied so far but in front of a potential management team, could they deliver?

They needn't have worried – Alex Weston claimed she was enraptured the moment Brian sang Lady of the Flowers. Setting the standard in a live context was her criteria for worthiness and, having proven their finesse not just as a studio band but as a competent live act as well, it led to Riverman becoming just one of the managements that were anxious to sign them. They had never taken on a band before, but seduced by Placebo's presentation, they knew that they would have to make an exception. The offer was reported to be £1 million, a claim which the group has firmly denied ever since.

Brian was equally enthusiastic in reciprocating their praises. 'Signing to Hut Records was an emotional thing.' He believed that Hut and Riverman offered some of the creative freedom they needed to express their stormy personalities with clarity. 'They had stars in their eyes rather than dollar signs. They were the people that we really felt cared about music. We met a lot of people for whom it was all about money, drugs, women... the lifestyle. For Hut it was about letting us be who we were, and that's exactly who we needed to be.'

By special arrangement with Hut Recordings, the group devised their own label, Elevator Music and Brian and Stefan became company directors. Despite now owning its own record label, the band was yet to release so much as an album. That, of course, was about to change.

Come Home was released as a single on February 6th 1996. The B-side featured Drowning by Numbers, a punk-rock track about someone unable and unwilling to change their sexuality, and Oxygen Thief, a harrowing and dark instrumental.

'There's a really strong water metaphor going through the whole single,' Brian revealed. 'Oxygen Thief became the sound that you might hear if you were drowning. People who have almost drowned and come back and spoken about it have said that as you begin to let go and your lungs start to fill with water, you have this sort of psychedelic trip and it's really quite peaceful. It became a soundtrack to that for us.'

There was no disguising the band's love of hallucinogenic states, derived from water or otherwise, and this theme was proved by illustrating the single cover with a child's inflatable wrist band. This completed the drowning metaphor. There was a naughtier side to Oxygen Thief too, inspired by a friend from Goldsmiths College. 'It came from a guy I know who was complaining that mainstream pop artists thieve his oxygen.'

The visual accompaniment to Come Home apparently embarrassed Brian so much that in later years he banned it altogether, cringing in shame when it was accidentally screened at a fan club show in 2000.

The video was created on a low budget but Brian's silver metallic lipstick, a sight that might look unusual on a woman let alone a man, and bright red 'God is Love' T-shirt, attracted some attention. The singer playfully head butted his platinum blonde bassist throughout the song.

By this time, the group's original demos had come to the attention of none other than the gender-ambiguous Mr David Bowie. He liked them on the strength of a poor-quality recording of Nancy Boy, 'a great name for a bunch of chaps to give a song.' To the group's delight, he had wasted no time in inviting them to fill the support slot of his prestigious Outside World tour, beginning on February 7th 1996. Sharing the stage with high-profile rockers such as NIN, it was clearly a momentous opportunity. 'Morrissey had unexpectedly walked out of the support slot – he went home to his mum,' Brian had laughed gleefully, 'and we went from playing Camden's Dublin Castle one night to an 8,000 seater stadium the next.'

So why would Bowie instantly fall in love with the trio? 'I don't know – we remind him of his younger self, perhaps,' Brian blushed modestly.

Bowie, a prestigious musician who had publicly flaunted his bisexuality and use of makeup, needed little introduction. Brian recalled only too well the face on his TV screen that had satisfied his adolescent yearning for deviation and excitement. However, whilst Bowie's gender confusion had been largely dismissed as little more than a publicity stunt– a rumour he did little to quell when he retracted his interest in the male species years later – were Placebo different? There was little doubt among their most ardent fans that far from being out to court press headlines, this group adored, lived and breathed the rock and roll circus.

Joining Bowie in Geneva, Milan, Lyon and finally Bologna, the hometown of Brian's grandmother, on February 9th 1996, he had some major adjustments to make. 'We went from 300 capacity venues to 8,000 and 12,000 capacity stadiums almost overnight, which was freaky.' However, Placebo was adored by Bowie's audiences. 'Remember where you heard it first,' was David's trademark statement, sensing that this was a group with the potential to make it big. He wasn't mistaken.

In fact, although they made a phenomenal mark on the music industry when they toured with Bowie, paradoxically it was their solo shows in the UK that intrigued the most. 'The ruby-lipped, trashed-out Brian Molko IS Courtney Love,' observed the NME of their Norwich Arts Centre show on

June 3rd 1996, adding with a trace of hero worship 'It's physically impossible not to love Placebo.' Though the crowd might be drunken students equally fervent in their drug-induced haze no matter what the soundtrack, there were some who had truly noticed the talent.

The two pictures published in the NME that week were testimony to the paradox that was Placebo. One sees Brian in an unusually macho pose, strumming the guitar in orgiastic rapture and with Sonic Youth inspired fervour, whilst another shows him gazing angelically onto that night's crowd, his femininity fully restored. It is this short-sharp-shock of dichotomous sexuality that was the most appealing for audiences.

If the image was striking, the music was even more so. Describing the unsettling silent movie that then accompanied a Placebo live show, a reviewer reflected 'A woman fervently digs her own grave, slits her throat, punches her arm with hypodermic needles, claws, scratches, beats herself, and lets out hollow screams.'

The fact that the music should fit in perfectly with these extreme emotional states is certainly no coincidence. Raw, alive and honest to the point of disgusting its listener, Placebo set out to inspire mystery and confusion. Admitting to relishing groups who could make their audience vomit with the sheer intensity of their musical vibrations, Brian clearly knew how to make an impact. Discussing sonic overload with unsettling enthusiasm, he claimed 'Some frequencies can make you physically ill or make your bowels loose. The Swans used to do it. By the end of gigs people would vomit because the frequencies were so nasty.' Not content with blowing listeners' heads off sonically, or doing 'covert research into crowd control,' Brian had mischievous ambitions for his audiences. 'If some guy comes to one of our gigs, and spends the first half thinking that I'm a girl – and a cute one at that, one that he may fancy – then halfway through the gig he may realize that I'm a guy and he has to turn in on himself. I'm not trying to give any definitive answers to what it is to be a man or a woman, I'm just trying to provoke questions.' Seduced by melody and the irresistible charm of the front-man delivering it, people began to talk and the message of Placebo began to spread.

Meanwhile Brian began an onslaught of press conferences. However, he was certainly not an interviewee for the uninitiated. He spent the majority of his time verbally brutalising 'lazy journalists' with a flash of venom when they failed to capture his confusingly dichotomous character with justice. When not remonstrating the very people who publicised him, Brian was showering journalists with brazen honesty of the type that even impassive interviewers would wince at. 'Brian would always call me later, asking me not to mention something he'd said on-the-record,' one interviewer remembered. 'I don't remember many bands years later, but Brian I did. There was just no stopping that mouth of his – his band mates had to remind him to be cautious.' On one particularly memorable occasion, with an indignant flash of his silver finger nails, Brian revealed accusingly that his colour change from the obligatory black was down to the journalists who dared to label him goth.

He needn't have been worried as the group was becoming near impossible to pigeon-hole. Fastidiously applying their stamp of personality on the modern music world before the first album had even hit the shelves, they were certainly confident. 'The antidote to Britpop' screamed the headlines on every self-respecting music paper, a status which was about to be cemented with the release of their first studio album.

To create it, they joined with eminent producer Brad Wood, a Chicago born entrepreneur best known for his work with Veruca Salt and Liz Phair. The new threesome left for Dublin to begin the project. Out of this rose a ten title offering of hedonism, euphoria and sexual desire. Songs such as Hang onto Your IQ tell the story of someone plagued by sexual inadequacy, Lady of the Flowers is a poignant and unveiling number that listeners could positively drown in, and Bionic is a tale of throbbing sexual frustration and unfulfilled aggression. Metaphors as appealing as 'You stole the keys to my house … then you locked yourself out' set the dark mood, and atmospheric Nancy Boy was the dangerously catchy hit that would secure them the largest slice of success yet.

Brian and Stefan got a flat together for the recording, and instantly set about making the place a home. The bathroom became a shrine to the art of prostitute calling cards – Brian and Stefan had set to work robbing telephone boxes and adorning the walls with adverts for sexual relief. Papering the walls, floor and ceiling with these slogans somewhat isolated them from Robert, who was never interested in the band's overtly sexual nature. Matters were not helped by the fact that Robert was housed away from the band, sharing with producer Brad Wood.

'We were like kids in a candy shop,' recalled Brian on the Henry Rollins show. 'We didn't even know our way around the studio. We couldn't believe someone had actually fallen for it and given us money to make a record. It was a dream come true – and [the first album] captures that youthful exuberance and joy at being there.'

The youth and vigour he described was evident on the album. 'Brad was as much into electronic music as we were,' enthused Brian, 'and that suited us as we didn't want to make a pure punk record – we wanted to make something that was colourful.' The album was to be dichotomous – it would symbolise the loss of innocence and passage into a feverishly erotic world, yet the backdrop for this initiation included toy instruments, electronic keyboards and the light hearted didgeridoo. A trademark of Placebo's first incarnation, Brian was utterly unashamed.

On the contrary, he admitted to Melody Maker that his favourite toy guitar was the Fisher Price Keytar, containing a memory bank of childrens' rhymes. It was to feature heavily on Teenage Angst. 'These instruments communicate such naivety – you haven't heard those sounds since you were a child, and they trigger responses in your emotional memory,' he revealed. Bleakly, he also stated 'As soon as you pop out of the womb, you start to die. It's the paradox that you begin life but you also begin death. The use of toy instruments enables us to communicate that on a sonic level.'

Brian has also described the song as 'experimental rock crushed into a pop format. The music pulls you in and lulls you into this sort of false sense of security and then hits you in the head with something intense. We like that deceptive quality.' Such hooks were to become a classic Placebo theme. Allowing another glimpse into the world of the younger Brian, he commented 'A song like Teenage Angst is about teenage heartbreak. When you're a teenager you respond to the world around you in a way that's 100% heart. As you get older, in order to stay sane, you learn how to react with a balance of both head and heart. I'm interested in that loss of innocence.'

Come Home was a song about loneliness, frustration and the feeling of being rootless – belonging nowhere. The theme of eternal pessimism is translated in the frenetic drumbeats and the refrain 'Every sky is blue but not for me and you.' In response to the 'brutal pleading tones' of the song live, a reviewer experiencing the full fervour of the song live quipped earnestly 'How could anyone hope to return home after they've been deflowered by a Placebo concert?'

Bionic was equally dramatic. 'It's screaming sexual energy,' exclaimed Brian. 'It's absolutely belting out desire. That's kind of a reflection of the person I was at 20.'

36 Degrees meanwhile was a playful take on body temperature. 'The person concerned is a little cold-blooded,' Brian explained. 'If someone gets too close, they have to push the person away. That's what it means to me.' It could easily have been autobiographical, relating to Brian's times of celibacy whilst battling loneliness and heartbreak in his days at Goldsmiths. His constant pain made closeness and intimacy near

impossible. Consequently the character's body temperature is 36 degrees – 1.5 degrees lower than the standard average.

The seemingly random numbers in the chorus spelt out the telephone number of Brian and Stefan's favourite curry house in East London. The building still stands today but is no longer an Indian restaurant.

Hang onto your IQ tells the story of a mysterious man struggling with sexual inadequacy. The music is harrowing and heart-wrenching and it evokes an almost childlike sorrow – pressing play invites the listener into Brian's dream world, one where loss, longing and self-disgust prevails. Lyrically it symbolises a second chance, urging the audience to fall back on their innate intelligence and unique identity and to be proud of who they are and what they own. The line 'I'm a fool whose tool is small, it's so miniscule, it's no tool at all,' encapsulates the top male insecurity – that of having a small penis and the associated emasculation.

'It's not actually describing my own anatomy,' Brian added. 'That's just the state of the character in the song. He's at a point of such low self-esteem that that's the most self-deprecating thing he can say about himself at that point. Not only am I an idiot, but I've got a small dick and I just feel so disgusted with myself, which I guess I have felt at certain points in my life.'

Nancy Boy was recorded during a time of turbulence for the band. All three members were continually at each other's throats and Robert was said to be irritated by the overtly bisexual theme. 'I would always be apologising to the band for its lyrical content,' Brian had joked. Despite the tension in the studio, and Brian's astonishing belief that it was the one track on the album that he hadn't quite nailed, it went on to become one of the most famous and self-defining moments of their career. 'Sonically, we tried to capture a kind of drug-induced sexual rush; it's got a rising car sound which was meant to kind of reproduce the first rushes of E, and it's obvious that the character in the song is kind of drug-crazed at that moment. There are times in your life when you're so off your head that all you want to do is fuck.' He continued 'It's a celebration and a slag of that behaviour at the same time. It doesn't promote promiscuity but it doesn't judge it either.'

There was also a surprisingly serious message attached to it. He continued 'That line about "Eyeholes in a paper bag, greatest lay I ever had," it's just saying that the drag queen in the song is probably very ugly, but is attempting to reach some kind of beauty, twisted beauty, perverse beauty. I guess it's saying you can be ugly and be an amazing lay; it doesn't really matter.'

In a curious twist, Brian also revealed that the song poked fun at experimentation for the wrong reasons. The satirical double meaning queried why bisexuality had become a fashion statement, the new epitome of cool. 'I'm questioning people's reasons for sleeping with the same sex. In the same way that heroin is very hip today, being bisexual seems to be very chic. It criticises people who think it's fashionable – guys who think that because "some of my best friends are gay" that they are going to try it out, but they haven't actually felt the same desire themselves.'

I Know is one of the more introspective, heart-felt Placebo songs on the album, courtesy of Brian's plaintive lyrics and Robert's debut on the didgeridoo. This describes a time in Brian's life when he fled to New York, distraught after his relationship with his French girlfriend disintegrated. The couple had been living in Paris together, and Brian had fled to escape the pain. 'I lost my home and I fell into a very deep depression. We had decided not to talk to each other but I couldn't bear it anymore.' Unable to resist the temptation, 'I picked up the phone in some phone booth in Broadway and called this person and said "See, I know I'm not supposed to be calling you right now, but I really need to talk to you." The song is a part of the conversation we had over the phone.'

Cloaked in the anonymity of a songwriter, Brian exorcised the guilt of his failed relationship, comprising emotions so intense that they would have been so difficult to face without this form of unconventional release.

Lady of The Flowers, named after French author Jean Genet's deeply homosexual novel of repression, violence and desire, had many meanings. Mainly it focused on the ending of a painful relationship, one which Brian was reluctant to discuss and the same one which featured on I Know.

Finally, Swallow, the most sonically confusing song on the album, begins with incoherent mumbles of agitation alongside a breezy guitar hook. It was a prime example of the ethos that Brian stood for, known as 'Confusion is sexy.' Picture its conception, and you see Brian and Stefan on an LSD trip together, listening intently to the hums of two nearby power stations. 'That buzz is F sharp,' Stefan's technically trained musical ear heard. The recollection of these sounds inspired the early version of Swallow.

Brian later clarified 'It's what happened the last time Stefan and I took acid. At first, you might think it's about losing all your drugs, or maybe it's someone who's so wasted during sex that they forget not to swallow.' He added more realistically 'I don't really know – it was never really written in a state of reality.'

And so Placebo was born, a debut album of just ten songs. All were close to the singer's heart. The finishing touches were put onto the disc and on July 16th 1996, the proud parents saw its first release to the public.

It immediately soared to number five on the album chart, surprising and delighting the group.

However, it wasn't all glamour – the video 36 Degrees was perhaps one of the most traumatising the group had ever experienced. 'Never again!' Stefan assured the media, referring to the painfully long underwater video shoot. The director, Chris Cunningham, had wasted no time in initiating Brian to the world of underwater torture.

Famous for his work with Aphex Twin, Cunningham had infamously gloated on the moment when he truly knew his work had been significant. 'The most surreal point in my life was when I sent out an edit of Madonna's video for 'Frozen' unfinished with a two-minute black hole in it. She called me up in tears at five in the morning and said I'd wrecked her career. I remember thinking, "It doesn't get any better or worse than this." If I never do anything else in my life, at least I'm responsible for wrecking Madonna's career!" On the infamous Molko shoot, he reveals: 'I had him up to his neck in a pond. I love that bit when you've been working for hours and artists are at their most tired. You get really good stuff then. Like, Brian Molko was so cold, I think his nuts were the size of raisins! It's great, I've got him on tape sobbing for future blackmail purposes.'

The chart position of that third single, released on July 3rd 1996, was less favourable, reaching just number 80, but Placebo were not ready to give up. In fact, they were confirmed for their largest shows yet – the Reading and Leeds festivals. Brian took the new attention in his stride, boldly declaring 'After playing to 16,000 people in Paris, festivals weren't going to scare us anymore.'

It was a combination of their appearance at festiavals and the release of Teenage Angst in October 1996 that gave Placebo their first taste of mainstream success. With hints of indie, pop and rock, it appealed to a wider audience than previous more alternative tracks and subsequently reached number 30 in the charts. The video was shot inside a bright red latex box, which caused mirth for the band as they compared it to a vagina. Despite suffering from tonsillitis that day, Brian was happy to fling himself to the floor and mimic falling in typical drama student style. Guilt ridden children displayed hand-written messages such as 'It was me that stole your cigarettes' and black eyes, smudged lipsticks and tears feature in what would become a classic Placebo theme.

The single also featured the Bob Dylan inspired Been Smoking Too Long, with the amusing admission 'I wanted to capture some kind of like moment but maybe it's better if I'm sober!' This sparked an era of emotional vulnerability which Placebo fans were to find utterly addictive. Hug Bubble is the other track on the CD, which uses the karaoke microphone from a children's toy guitar for a haunting feedback effect. The 7' record also includes a previously unreleased demo known as Flesh Mechanic.

Brian explained the title track in sombre terms as a paradox between life and death, innocence and evil. Few would have suspected that this compelling sound would be borne out of Fisher Price children's toys but that's Placebo – they tricked you again.

A tour across the channel began in November 1996. France immediately succumbed to their charms, and an instant chemistry formed between the multi-lingual singer with his penchant for all things French, and the sophisticated and passionate Parisian audiences. They recognised the melodic charms of Lady of the Flowers and its links with French novelist Jean Genet. Just as many of Brian's lyrics were written from an oppressive bedroom in Luxembourg, Genet mirrored his darkest emotions when writing from his lonely cell in prison. 'She stole the keys to my house', Brian lamented, pouring his heart out to an ecstatic French audience, 'and locked herself out.'

The reception was, unfortunately, not quite so rapturous in the notoriously insular North America where the band would be 'coined' while performing. Georgetown Weekly magazine verbalised the country's uncertainty. 'For its time and its place, it satisfies. But, there's this nagging, irrational feeling it might be a fake.'

Yet there was a much darker force at hand – the relationship between Brian and Robert.

'The first date was in New York,' recalled Robert of the US tour, which began on November 16th 1996. 'The atmosphere was super tense and I could tell something was up as Brian was no longer making the slightest effort to be agreeable. I asked Stefan what was going on and if I would be doing the German tour (after the US tour) just before going on stage, and he just said "No, you're not."'

Robert had suffered from depression throughout their 1996 tour. He was also becoming 'increasingly weary of being the focus of Brian's rages against the world.' Brian, meanwhile, perceived Robert to have embodied two of the ultimate sins in the Placebo Bible – homophobia and intolerance.

Professionally they were polished, but personally a million sins lurked beneath the surface. 'People expect that when things fall into place professionally all the voids in your life are going to be filled,' says Brian. 'They're not. That first album was basically made by a miserable band.' The tension was discernable during their first interview for MTV, where Brian effortlessly monopolised the attention and Robert was seen on film rolling his eyes at Brian's viewpoints. 'I did everything I could to gain his trust,' Brian lamented, 'but it was never enough.' Meanwhile, perhaps fatigued by the constant stress, Brian was increasingly erratic in his attitude to press. 'I really don't have time for this,' he reportedly huffed following one 15-minute suspended session with the NME before storming out. The singer confessed several years later, with a wry smile, 'I'm described as an ex-difficult interviewee but that's fair.'

Brian also believed that Robert was consumed with jealousy by the attention he effortlessly commanded as frontman. Meanwhile, Robert alleged that Brian was too impatient to give their relationship another try. Whilst he offered to receive counselling to cope more effectively with the conflicting emotions that fame had thrown at him, he claimed that Brian had dismissively rebuffed him. The spunky singer may have been unduly impatient, but the group was accelerating in speed while Robert was becoming more and more detached from them in their moment of glory. Something had to give.

After tearful arguments left Stefan cowering on the hotel balcony, piggie in the middle as his two bandmates tore each other to pieces, Brian memorably declared 'I want to leave the music business. If this is what being in a band is all about, then I might as well work in a bank, hate my boss, take the tube home, fall asleep in front of the TV, dry-fuck my wife for two minutes and do it all again the next day, five days a week. It's bullshit.'

Indeed, if fulfilling their wildest teenage dreams and playing onstage with David Bowie wasn't a recipe for happiness, something was seriously wrong. The pressure of their conflicting personalities was beginning to spill over into the public domain.

It culminated at the Phoenix Festival, a time which Brian is often loath to discuss. All three ended up camping their tents at opposite ends of the field. Persistent drug-taking and the overuse of certain Class A substances had done little to quell the tension, which was now reaching breaking point. Brian and Robert could barely look each other in the eye. Fortunately the group had invited temporary band mate Steve to the festival to witness their live show. Taking one look at them, the brash Northerner immediately sensed their unhappiness. 'You miserable cunts!' he exclaimed. 'You're in a successful band, selling loads of records and look at you. Look at the fucking state of you.'

His unrestrained honesty set a seed of inspiration in Brian's mind and he made Steve promise to stay in touch. Meanwhile the group was scheduled for a performance of paramount importance – a national TV show on BBC titled The White Room. This was one of their first big shows to a nationwide audience, leaving Brian to later yelp 'My God! I came on TV singing 'What a beautiful ass!' Finally in a dramatic showdown, moments before this critical show, Brian dramatically pulled the plug on Robert, and dissolved the band as they knew it.

He told him the three could no longer be in a band together and it was clear who the unwanted member of their unholy triangle was to be. 'Brian said he couldn't stand to play with me anymore and I said more or less, that the band was not solely his to decide what to do with,' said Robert. 'Incredibly, I volunteered to get therapy in order to be able to deal with the "situation" – him- better to which he replied he 'did not have time for me to sort my head out.'

Brian's version of events was swathed in mystery however. 'To be completely honest about it would make me come across as unnecessarily vicious,' said Brian with a touch of mystery. It was to be the only time his mouth would remain firmly closed in the onslaught of loose-lipped and controversial interviews of the next few years. 'Put it this way, I think he felt very threatened by me. He robbed me of a lot of things, many months when I should have been ecstatic…'

Whatever had happened, all three knew that once they had left the stage at the White Room, the familiar dynamic with which they had courted success would never be the same again.

His contractual obligations fulfilled, Robert duly left and, promising they would 'show him beautiful things,' Brian was joyfully reunited with former band mate Steve. He calmly commented in a fanzine shortly afterwards 'There are no boneheads in my band anymore.'

Steve and Stefan became Brian's two husbands and whilst the marriage was unconsummated, the three assured – and thus sexless, Brian cheekily chided, it was far from the series of bitter fallouts that plagued them in the past.

The original lineup held an undeniable chemistry. All three found their own place within the set-up, bonding immediately over their shared feelings. And so a new phase began – the next chapter in Placebo history.

Chapter 3.

'People want me to be fucked up, but they're too late –
I already am' – Brian Molko.

With Steve in tow, the group embarked upon a new era, but this time spirits were high.

Now featuring a tall silent Swede, a boisterous Mancunian 'wide-boy' and a feminine 'weirdo magnet' front-man, Placebo was anything but ordinary.

Finding two more different bedfellows seemed all but impossible, yet they were to have a unique and infallible chemistry which would carry them far.

On January 9th 1997, before the dust had settled, the band was invited to Madison Square Gardens as guests of honour at the one and only David Bowie's 50th birthday bash. The star packed cast included greats such as The Cure, Lou Reed and Billy Corgan of the Smashing Pumpkins. It was a rock and roll freak show personified. Noticing something special about Placebo, but suspecting they were yet to reach their peak, there was no question in Bowie's mind as to who would fill the support slot's shoes.

As Steve had been on the original demos, the return to the first line-up completed the picture in the group's quest for worldwide recognition. They had also been invited on tour with notorious rockers Kiss – allegedly more memorable for their face paint and rock attitude than any discernable tune – but according to Brian 'It wasn't the same. We just laughed.'

He certainly wasn't laughing at Madison Square Gardens. The New York hotspot held an audience of 20,000 people – Placebo's biggest show yet. They had been due to appear at Bowie's fundraiser for Save the Children earlier that week but due to cancellation, the New York show was to be their first of 1997.

Brian's last show with Bowie on the Outside Tour had certainly been eventful. He'd broken a string and, high on a cocktail of marijuana and Jack Daniels and coke, had thrown his guitar across the stage in indignation. Despite the hiccup, and the mammoth-sized, alcohol-fuelled ego, he'd managed to win over an audience of 8,000 Bowie fans. However at more than double the size and far from Europe, would Placebo achieve the same success at a venue across the Atlantic?

His first meeting with Bowie had been equally nerve-wracking. Following what Brian called a 'toilet tour' of the UK where the largest venue had held just 300 people, he had found himself catapulted into the limelight just days later, when he was bundled onto a plane to play a large stadium show. Understanding their trepidation, Bowie had fortunately gone out of his way to make the trio feel comfortable.

'We came offstage, high on adrenalin, walked towards the dressing room and there was Bowie standing by the door with his arms crossed and his shades on. I'm like "Alright, Dave? Want a cigarette?" That's the first thing I ever said to him: "Want a fag?" He really went out of his way to make us feel comfortable. He's a lovely man and deserves to be hugged constantly.'

Brian also voiced the benefits of getting over his nerves. 'You're always a bit scared of somebody who's so legendary,' he admitted. 'It took us time to relax in his presence but once we did, we found that there's a lot of knowledge and a lot of wisdom to be gleaned from him. He's a very giving person and he's very fascinating to speak to. He and his band were very happy and willing to mix with us. Obviously we felt very privileged.'

'Never lose your spontaneity,' Bowie had told the trio sternly in one of their rare but cherished meetings, with a touch of fatherly nurture. Brian was to treasure this advice from the man he considered his forefather, someone who had secured his entry into the musical world and paved the way for greatness.

Enjoying backstage camaraderie and a wonderful atmosphere, Brian was still nervous about meeting his childhood heroes who would also attend the event, namely Sonic Youth and Frank Black of the Pixies. 'Your hands start shaking and you start to feel like a silly little fan,' he confessed.

He needn't have worried. Backstage wherever Brian went he was said to be the centre of attention, and was often found in the middle of the room engaged in the bizarre task of perfecting fellow performer Dave Grohl's eyeliner.

Other celebrity guests included Naomi Campbell, Prince, Beck, Moby and Bowie's wife Iman, best known for her makeup range designed to flatter black skin tones. 'I got to meet all my heroes, especially Sonic Youth,' recalled Brian. 'I was more nervous meeting them than I was about Bowie. They changed my life. I spoke to Lou Reed for a while and he gave me a big hug. I was really freaked out by the whole thing – it was a really amazing experience.'

Even more special for Brian, he was able to soothe his pre-show nerves with some indulgence of the white line variety. Accompanied by Robert Smith of the Cure and two generous helpings of cocaine, he slipped into a toilet cubicle undetected – or so he thought. It was with less fondness that he recalled their subsequent discovery by a member of NYPD.

Enamoured by the famous clientele, Brian turned his attention towards the sonic output in the hope of delivering something truly memorable for both him and his idols. In a never to be repeated feat, Placebo chose to cover Bowie's 'Andy Warhol' from the Hunky Dory album. One of Brian's favourites as a child, it was a perfect way of honouring the star who had participated in their rise to fame, and of course, celebrating his birthday.

This show introduced Placebo to a whole new audience, many of whom were transfixed by the profound and mysterious melancholy of tracks such as Lady of the Flowers, and equally mesmerised by the powerful punk classics that were Nancy Boy and Bionic.

Serving to increase crowd fever even more, Brian tactically announced his burgeoning friendship with Bowie at the start of Nancy Boy – 'This one's for David, we know it's his favourite.'

'When we arrived, all we could think about was Bowie,' an enthralled European fan breathed after the show. 'We travelled all the way from Europe for him. But as soon as Placebo started, we realised we had a whole new contender for best artist here.'

It was a sentiment echoed by many of the audience and indeed the media. 'One really has to see Bowie to appreciate him,' NY Rock commented approvingly. 'He's a startling blend of man and woman, performing a startling blend of rock and cabaret. He has a presence that captivates and seduces.' It became clear that whilst the glowing praise referred to Bowie, it could just as easily have been about Brian that night.

Placebo was unleashing itself on an uninitiated public, and to enormous effect. One previously dedicated Bowie fan left the arena with only one thing in mind – getting hold of a copy of Placebo's latest album. That's a sure sign the provocative drug was working. What's more, Bowie touchingly returned his praise by affectionately naming Brian 'the daughter I never had.'

As if their stateside adventures weren't enough, the trio returned to find their new single Nancy Boy had earned a number four chart position on home turf. The video was Steve's first with the group and as he was still contractually obligated to Jaguar, his face was blurred out on screen. It was a disappointing debut for Steve, but he was certainly not left out. He used the wordplay of the 'eyeholes in a paper bag' lyric to appear in a Melody Maker photo shoot with a brown paper bag over his face. This settled legal issues, and caused a huge amount of mirth to a pressurised band at the same time.

What was the message behind this catchy cult classic which was slowly infiltrating into the mainstream? 'I don't think I can explain,' Brian smirked mischievously on a BBC TV Interview. 'It won't get shown on telly.' Eventually after much persuasion, the unusually bashful Brian conceded 'It's about getting off your head and feeling frisky.'

Purists shook their heads with disapproval but Brian was keen to prove that it was a concept many ordinary British people could relate to on some level. '150,000 Ecstasy pills get popped every week in London – I don't think all of those are musicians,' he argued later with a wry smile.

Brian would constantly apologise to the group during rehearsals for Nancy Boy's juvenile lyrics, yet beyond the haze of sexual desire, they appeared to have a significant message. They took a satirical look at misogyny and society's obsession with beauty. Phrases such as 'eyeholes in a paper bag' parodied some men's willingness to have sex with unattractive women provided they do not have to look down. It tells the uncensored story of a hedonistic, selfish lifestyle in all its glory, mirroring both its good aspects and its bad ones. Above all, the message is one of overwhelming honesty.

B-side Slackerbitch enjoyed a similar theme. Brian was terrified that the frank refrain 'Slackerbitch, fag hag whore, looks real cute but lips are sore' and the distasteful teasing 'You're an orifice' could be construed as misogynistic. It certainly seemed to portray a vitriolic image of women. Originally due to appear on the first album, Brian had censored it for fear of a public backlash. He'd played it to a number of trusted female friends however, none of whom had found it offensive, and was eventually persuaded to let it appear on one of Nancy Boy's B-sides.

'It is quite horrible, and an exploration into someone's misogyny. The man in the song feels very threatened by women, but at the same time it's very heart-felt. It's angry, nasty, insulting and completely politically incorrect. I'm not afraid to say I've felt some of those things. It walks a very fine line and it's dangerous.'

Brian has also fought against male misogyny, stating 'I was walking around Ladbroke Grove with a girl and two blokes came up to us and said "Are you looking for cock?" That wouldn't have happened if I looked more like a bloke. What it does give me is an insight into how horrible, infantile and offensive men can be. It gives me a kind of anti-role model, encountering male attitudes in the street and in bars that I find completely repulsive. It shows me what I'm not and it keeps me in check as a man.'

Ironically then, it was Brian's feminine appearance that allowed him to experience some of the misogynistic outpourings he was writing about first-hand. He was certainly qualified to discuss the topic.

The single for Nancy Boy, released on January 20th 1997, appeared in three formats. The seven inch vinyl contained a special edition 'Sex mix' of the song – a speedier version – and Slackerbitch. Meanwhile CD 1 contained two other new B-sides, Hugbubble and Bigmouth Strikes Again.

The term Hugbubble is drama student speak for a loveable person, and is a word Brian would later use to describe favourite film director Todd Haynes. The song itself is a dark instrumental which, whilst not one of Placebo's most memorable songs, it certainly fit in with the theme. The recording Bigmouth Strikes Again was a cover version of a song by the Smiths. A tribute album to the group was being launched by the name of The Queen is Dead and Placebo were invited to pay tribute by choosing a song to cover.

'When we got the offer, we were surprised that no one had taken "Bigmouth Strikes Again," so we decided that people must have been scared. We took the challenge because it's such a vitriolic song, we just tried to up the ante sonically to match. We wanted to balance the hatefulness lyrically with hatefulness, sonically.' With Slackerbitch on the same CD on the Nancy Boy single, it seemed clear that this was the perfect single for the listener to vent their frustrations.

He did not think much of his counterparts on the separate tribute album, commenting 'I think the Supergrass one is about the only other good one on there. The rest of it is pretty dire. Bis did The Boy With The Thorn In His Side which is just atrocious.'

CD 2 featured a more light-hearted vibe with Miss Moneypenny and Eyesight to the Blind. The first shares its name with the fictional character in James Bond films. Brian shares wisdom such as 'Shooting guns just makes you horny… all you need to make a movie is a gun and a girl.' The later is a heart-felt retrospective tune about a man suffering a tragic loss.

Brian's appearance on Top of the Pops to perform Nancy Boy was an eventful one. Due to the immense success of the single and the adoration of the audiences they were asked back two weeks in succession. On both occasions, the studio was flooded with calls from confused viewers – half to complain about his gender-bending antics, the other half merely to enquire incredulously as to whether the singer was a boy or a girl. Brian, dressed in a PVC pinstripe jacket, sporting a shoulder length bob and with an eyeliner-painted face as angelic as his voice, took it all in his stride, calmly provoking more confusion than he could ever have hoped for. 'Indifference is the killer,' he remarked afterwards.

The singer continued 'It's funny and it means it's working. When straight boys turn around and say "She's lovely," it's working. What they're doing is responding in an innocent way to what they see, devoid of repression. People who are intelligent or sorted enough to take it how it is won't be subverted by it. But there's a whole load of guys out there who'd like to kick the shit out of me because they think I'm just a poof, and their girlfriends fancy me.'

Provided that Brian remembered to shave, he managed to fool a considerable number of people. When he didn't, his trips to the local shops to purchase black nail varnish attracted a great deal of unwanted attention.

'If straight boys still fancy me even when they realise that I'm a guy, that means I've achieved what I set out to do. I know a lot of boys who fancy me and when they realise I'm a guy are forced to ask themselves a few questions about themselves or at least forced to realise that desire and attraction are not as simple as they think. They may also realise that their first reaction is more truthful,' Brian told G-Spot magazine. 'When I meet people that say they used to fancy me but stopped when they realised I was a guy, I spend about 20 minutes telling them that they do still fancy me but they are telling me that they can't because they're repressed. I hope that by coming into contact with me that they may not rule out the possibility of sleeping with a man. It might just put the seed of thought in their head to be less prejudiced.' Lock your sons away – Molko's on a mission.

Delighted by all the attention, Brian reflected that whilst he hadn't been able to get laid at college, he had fallen into a scenario where he could be equally attractive to both men and women at the same time – and that appealed to him. For a bisexual character like Brian, it was the ideal situation. He was free to pursue flirtations with whomever he pleased and change people's preconceptions of identity in the process. This pseudo-psychologist was certainly able to mix business with pleasure.

Amazingly, he met a disbelieving fan in a pub who hadn't understood the ambiguity. 'That can't be the singer from Placebo,' he told his friend, craning his neck to look closer, 'because the singer from Placebo's a girl!'

Did Brian feel remorseful for all the mischief? Not a bit. 'People's heads are there to be fucked with, but it's kind of playful. It's like that line in Trainspotting when Begbie gets his win on the horses and they all go dancing and he gets off with a drag queen and Renton says: "In the next century, people will stop being men and women and there will be just one sex. People will stop being bi, gay and straight they'll just be sexual." I think that would be a nice world to live in, where people are just sexual.'

Fiercely opposed to categorising his desire, he continued 'If I can challenge people's preconceptions of what a man is supposed to look and behave like at the end of the millennium, then that's extremely positive.'

However perhaps the most infamous story of all concerning Brian's gender was the case of a group of Italian men obsessed with the rock group Tampasm. The group comprised of four fiery-tempered females with a punk-rock sound. Charlotte, a blonde girl in the group, was close friends with Brian and reportedly had a brief romance with him. The group of Italians, who'd loyally followed every date of Tampasm's UK tour, noticed ever-present at Charlotte's side, 'one of the most beautiful women' they'd ever seen. Desperate to get close to her, they began to debate amongst themselves over who would win her heart – or, more likely, the key to her underpants.

The plot that followed was rather like the gender-bending TV show There's Something About Miriam, where a beautiful, busty and outwardly feminine Brazilian transsexual fooled a number of men into competing for her heart. Screened in the UK in 2003, it was a dating show with a difference. The men came close to discovering her secret live on screen on numerous occasions, especially when post-date heavy petting had got out of hand. The proud winner of Miriam's affections was dismayed to discover her sexuality and all of the men on the show clubbed together to sue. With a lawsuit hovering, they were offered psychiatric counselling for their perceived trauma.

In Brian's case, there would be no lawsuits. The group of Italians were mesmerised and ever so slightly aroused. Upon approaching 'her', the men were keen to initiate conversation. Whilst none of them took it further, they found Brian friendly and cordial, and were delighted to have made 'her' acquaintance. In fact, if it hadn't been for a chance import of Kerrang magazine back home the following month, they'd have been none the wiser.

Imagine their surprise opening the pages to discover the woman, known only as 'Charlotte's stunning friend' emblazoned across the Kerrang award ceremony reportage. Not only was 'she' called Brian, she had also won an award for Best Band of 1997. The object of their affections was a man, but

– although surprised and shame-faced – it didn't quell their desires. How could it? Brian's naughty experiments had won again and encouraged this group to be more open-minded.

If that sounded crazy, Placebo were about to step the confusion up another notch by appearing in the notoriously camp film Velvet Goldmine. Taking its title from the Bowie song of the same name, with the lead character modelled on glam rock front-man Slade, it promised to be an ode to all things glamorous.

Brian's favourite casting director Todd Haynes, also responsible for the films Goo, Poison and Dottie Gets Spanked, was impressed by Nancy Boy and called him to arrange an audition. Brian had loved Dottie Gets Spanked, a subversive film about the awakening of childhood sexuality, and the discovery of why some things in society are considered normal and some are very firmly not. Poison was another of his favourites, and was the film adaptation of a Jean Genet novel. Themes of homosexuality, lust and heartbreak abound. In Velvet Goldmine, he promised 'a land where all things are perfect and poisonous', just as in his other films, and an excited Brian couldn't wait to audition.

He had immediately wanted the part of Jack Ferry. 'It was made for me,' Brian pouted. 'He has no words and yet is the precursor to them all.' Unfortunately it had already been cast, but Brian was delighted nonetheless when he won the part of Malcolm, lead singer of the Flaming Creatures.

The film, in which all three participated, was loosely based on Bowie's own experiences with the glam-rock era. Featuring glitz, glamour and 1970s decadence at its best, the movie was a tribute to the era that gave birth to Bowie, Ziggy Stardust and Slade. Arthur is a journalist commissioned to find out the secret behind rock-star Brian Slade's mysterious disappearance. By the end, we are assured that his entry into the labyrinth of mystery is no longer purely for research purposes as he is forced to confront his own desires and feelings about the artist, and to embark on a voyage of self-discovery.

While the group played only minor speaking roles, sandwiched in between a hectic touring schedule, they were visually very memorable. The viewer can witness an absurdly over-dressed Molko in knee high platform boots, top hat, hair extensions and a glorious excess of black eyeliner as he sings the T-Rex classic 20th Century Boy.

Slade, the topic of the film, once declared 'Rock and roll is like a prostitute – it should be tarted up,' and in Brian's case that was an adage that wouldn't go unheeded. His heels were so high that they needed to be seen to be believed. Adopting a comic falsetto voice, Brian laughed

'A nurse would come every morning and go "Time for your bandages, Mr Molko!"' Fearlessly, Brian learnt the pain that women had endured for centuries for the irresistible pleasures of platform heels.

Steve, a macho Northerner, was distinctly unimpressed. 'I looked like La Toya Jackson. I had Jimmy Page's pants on with flames down the sides and big red platforms.' Long hair extensions and pronounced eyeliner completed the picture. Brian groaned later 'We all looked pretty stupid basically.' With great assertion, Steve insisted 'It was the beginning and end of my silver screen career. I'm just not made for it – it's not my idea of fun.' There were to be no squabbles and cat fights over parts, then. His heavier, more masculine stature didn't go unnoticed either. In fact, running down the street in ludicrously high platforms, Brian collided with Steve which cracked his ribs – on the very first day of filming. 'Steve broke one of my ribs the first day,' Brian confirmed. 'Well, I ran into his elbow. I have fragile ribs. We were running down the street in our platforms and I just went "crack".'

Despite these incidents, and Steve's obvious reservations, he and Brian landed a song – covering 20th Century Boy as part of the Flaming Creatures. 'I jumped at the chance of singing in that film,' Brian grinned. 'If Bowie and Courtney can do it, so can I!' However, faced with a formidable audience of Michael Stipe and Ewan McGregor, Brian had last-minute nerves. 'I found myself onstage without a guitar for the first time in my life and not knowing what the fuck to do. Steve had to be my 70s dancing coach. He showed me some moves, lots of leg kicks and ass wiggles.' Despite being self-conscious in the absence of his guitar to hide behind, he soon relaxed into the exhibitionism of the day.

In collaboration with Steve, he would utter lines such as 'We're descending down a bit of a decadent spiral' and 'I don't think there is much to live for these days' whilst chain-smoking and sporting the unmistakable Molko twinkle in his eye.

Meanwhile, Stefan was in the band 'Polly Smalls' with Donna, the lead singer from real-life group Elastica. The location for filming was the notoriously tough Brixton in South London, home to as many gangsters and criminals as Lewisham, Deptford and New Cross. Whilst it was a solution for low-budget filming, the area was not one for hanging around at night at the best of times – least of all for men in platform boots, glitter and hair extensions.

Sprained ankles and implausibly high heels were the least of the group's concerns as they wandered through the ghetto-like area of Brixton dressed as drag queens. 'One night we were outside Brixton Academy,'

Brian recalled, 'trying to find the way in. We were all in full costume, walking around with Michael Stipe and this number 94 bus drives by and Michael says "I dare you to go and get on that bus now." I said "No way! You go and get on the fucking bus, Stipey."'

Fortunately neither party was foolhardy enough to attempt it. Their lack of bravado could easily have saved their skin. It was a fun experience overall and one that encouraged Brian to have further aspirations about acting. 'Madonna's done it, Courtney's done it, why can't I? The difference between them and me is I have a degree from university,' he gloated to Melody Maker.

However, the dust settled, and the star-dazzled actors hung up their feather boas to return to reality. That reality was a bleak one, with the film frequently criticised in the press. Box office profits stood at $1.5m, just a sixth of the $9m expenditure.

David Bowie doubted the authenticity of the film as well. 'It wasn't that I disliked it, it's just that I thought it wasn't terribly successful. The only bits I liked were the gay bits. They were really very well done and you really felt the heart of the director. But I thought the rest of the film wasn't very good. It felt very early 80s to me.' Similarly Brian conceded 'Truth be told now that I look back on it, it wasn't the smartest idea ever, I think we looked really stupid. But so what? It's acting – it's not real.'

However it wasn't universally hated. The Los Angeles Times presented a particularly glowing review, praising the 'riot of colour and attitude' and describing the film as 'a perennial threat to the status quo.'

Brian, ever the patriot of glam, went to equal lengths to defend the film too. He furiously and delightedly corrected one American who disliked their hedonistic adventures. Deep in conversation with industry moguls in New York, Brian skilfully brought the subject round to his favourite film of the moment. One bold music industry rep declared 'That picture sucked – every last frame of it.' With carefully calculated sadism, Brian moved in for the kill, asking 'Is that how you truly feel about it?'

'Hell yes,' he answered. 'Velvet Goldmine was a complete waste of time for everyone involved.'

Humiliating him in an instant, Brian revealed 'Guess what? I was in that film, you fucking idiot! The director is a friend of mine, I worked really hard on all my scenes and we all love how the movie turned out. Sooo…fuck you!' Fending off Brian's middle finger, now just centimetres from his nose, the mogul learned, like many others before him, not to mess with Molko.

Arguably, the disappointing sales figures had merely illustrated Velvet Goldmine's reputation as a successful cult classic, never intended for the mainstream. The lack of reception did not detract from the passion of the director, actors and everyone else that helped to bring it to life. However, the tragedy for Brian was that the film would also seal Placebo's fate for several years, as they fell prey to one glam rock cliché after another.

Despite Brian informing the press 'We like showbiz, flamboyance and glamour, but we're not huge fans of glam rock,' indicating that the love of glam was in appearance alone, and scornfully dismissing claims that they were influenced by an 80s sound, the comparisons just kept coming.

Initially it had been a goth stereotype the band had groaned at, causing Brian to say 'As one as one motherfucker said goth, they all said goth. I stopped wearing black nail varnish because of that. I don't hear anything gothic in our music. I don't see any similarities between us and the Mission or the fucking Sisters of Mercy or, god forbid, the Fields of the fucking Nephilim,' he raged.

According to Brian failing to acknowledge the difference between acting and real-life, journalists had now jumped on board the glam rock band wagon and from that moment Placebo's fate was determined. 'Brian was influenced by Marc Bolan,' one proud author asserted. There were few tangible similarities in musical style, so it seemed safe to presume that the inference referred, yet again, to image.

A journalist from the Independent went on to add 'By writing songs that make proud reference to…feelings of alienation and by throwing in some pseudo-profound, pseudo-rebellious banalities, Placebo serve the valuable function of providing a dress-code to the people who don't fit into the Boyzone clique at school…it's the only reason goth bands exist at all.'

The somewhat patronising article stopped short of analysing the sound, instead branding Placebo as a band for the alleviation of teenage angst. Articles like these would open the door to a series of glam rock and goth rock stereotypes which would continually be reinforced throughout their career.

By all accounts, glam rock involved using makeup for dramatic effect, creating a clown-like appearance and larger than life persona to make a statement rather than for true aesthetic purposes.

Meanwhile in Brian's case, whose subtle and understated hues were a far cry from the war paint of Slade, Kiss or Ziggy Stardust, fans believed it was less of a marketing ploy and more of a genuine reflection of who he really was. Yet Brian was learning that self-expression had a cost – and that cost was media credibility.

Did Brian have sex appeal? Undoubtedly. But was it the primary focus of his presentation? Absolutely not. Furthermore, the best performers excelled at both.

Fortunately Brian's distinctive image both onstage and on the silver screen, whilst not meeting with media approval, did give comfort to his fans. Men arrived at concerts in feather boas, discovering for the first time the joys of black kohl eyeliner and the courage to sport it. For these men, Placebo not only echoed but celebrated the confusion they felt inside. Shameful, dark and long-hidden secrets about identity and sexuality were transformed into assets under Brian's watchful eye at a Placebo concert.

Lesbian couples openly kissed in the corners whilst enamoured teenage girls plastered to the front row barrier debated his sexuality with feisty persistence, usually impishly declaring that their passion for him remained intact regardless of the answer to their hotly debated questions.

Concerts became the 'freak shows' and 'weirdo-magnets' that Brian had always hoped for, with flamboyant men and women finally finding the freedom to express themselves. Brian approved, stating encouragingly 'If you project yourself as a star, then you probably are one already. You don't have to be in a rock band to be a star. You just have to go dancing one night or to a drag club to see how many real stars there are.'

The environment of a Placebo show, where punters could be themselves without judgement, proved addictive and the group soon found themselves bearing the brunt of a terrifying legion of obsessive fans. Some delighted Brian, whilst others terrified him.

The first time he realised the intensity of the devotion he had inspired was when a girl approached him and requested that instead of giving a conventional autograph and signing her sheet of paper, he should spit on it. Reflecting on the event, he recalled 'It's kind of shocking. I got mobbed yesterday. I went out of the venue after the gig and got mobbed by about fifty people, people just thrusting things into my face screaming at me. This girl was like "Will you spit on my piece of paper?" and I have a really bad cold at the moment. So I coughed up this really huge looger for her and I think she was really freaked out by that. She didn't really know what to do with it. Somebody who actually asks me to spit for them deserves something like that I think. It's very weird, there's a great deal of distance between yourself and what other people think you are.'

Another girl who received a hug from the singer was followed down the street by half a dozen screaming fans clamouring to touch her after the event, as if Molko sweat could somehow be transmitted. Brian's cigarette butt and, dubiously, a set list that purported to have a drop of Brian's blood on it from an onstage cut, emerged on Ebay. Astonishingly, people were bidding.

Never before had there been a group with such a reputation for obsessive devotion. However, alongside the harmless rows of Molkettes mimicking faultless glossy black hairstyles were fans who took their adoration to frightening extremes. It reached unprecedented heights and crossed the line into intrusion when Brian arrived home one evening to find a star struck fan on the doorstep of his flat. She'd tricked a security guard into believing she had left her keys at home and now, clinging desperately to the stairwell railings, was refusing to leave. It ultimately required the strength of three people to remove her from the building. 'It's the old mentality of "If you're not gonna love me then I'll make you hate me." They just wanna be a part of your life in either a good way or a bad way,' mused Brian.

Later in a moment of frustration, he told the NME how debilitatingly low self-esteem had left him ill-equipped to understand the situation. 'I started to feel weird and confused about who I was. I found it difficult to relate to myself and on top of that there are suddenly all these people whose lives are so empty that they started to model themselves on me. I just find it amusing that people want to look like an exaggerated version of me.' Considering the Molkettes with their identikit black bobs and pastel pink lip glosses, he said 'it's very strange, and, I'm sure this'll piss a few people off, you have to say "Why don't they just get a life?" To be confronted by a thousand yous, is weird… whatever you do, you're going to disappoint people, because you can't be everything they want you to be. Essentially they don't know who they are. I always knew we'd be a weirdo magnet but…' He trailed off.

He later complained that his words and insistence that fans should get a life had been taken out of context, although the sentiment remained. He just wasn't ready for this mixture of public scrutiny and accusation coupled with unconditional adoration from fans he'd never so much as exchanged a word with.

There was also a dizzying amount of responsibility attached to his role. He spotted fans at his shows repeatedly that he'd also seen in Manic Street Preachers documentaries, some of the same people who attended regularly and sent him heart-felt messages saying "When I listen to your music, I don't have to cut myself as much." Bewildered by representing so many things to so many people, Brian desperately took a step back and embarked on a series of antics which the press would never let him forget.

Perhaps fame should come with a complimentary therapist, because, like many others, Brian was hopelessly unequipped to deal with it. He threw himself instead into a revelry of debauchery, unable to find meaning in the chaos that was currently his world. 'People want me to be fucked up', he announced to Kerrang's Paul Brannigan. 'But they're too late. I already am...'

The drama increased when he was mistaken for a prostitute at a hotel in Nottingham. Mistaking Brian's dramatic post-show makeup for the almost unmistakable signature of a lady of the night, the conservative hotel manager gently intervened. 'We don't have that sort of thing here,' he cautioned him. A by now heavily inebriated Brian did not take kindly to being reminded of the hotel's policy on prostitution and, typically, disaster struck. He went to dramatic lengths to prove his gender, pulling down his trousers while screaming 'Do you want to see my dick?' 'The poor man was reduced to tears,' Brian cackled rather unkindly later.

He also recalled, with a mixture of mirth and horror, an experience in a post-show bar in Austria. Chatting with the bar tender, things seemed to be going well until he became over-affectionate with him, reaching over the bar to give him a hug, and felt something hard against his thigh. Brian takes up the story. 'I thought "Oh hello" then looked down and thought "Oh no." It was a gun.'

Brian's knack for provocation and apparent fearlessness in the face of danger led to many more awkward situations. A mischievous insult directed at someone's wife saw him sent flying across the room at a showbiz event, and without wings. The location was a Spice Girls party, where he had not only chatted up celebrity Victoria Beckham, an ill-advised tactic in itself, but faced broken ribs – hilariously for the second time that year.

'It was all my fault,' Brian conceded wearily, with seasoned experience 'It usually happens when you insult someone's wife and you're so off your face that you don't realize that he's standing next to her. You know, but it was funny, it was just one of those nights. I broke a few ribs getting thrown across the room into tables and chairs.'

After the painful recovery, during which he had to avoid bouts of laughter altogether, he managed to see the funny side of his misdemeanours. Brian's big mouth reputation reared itself again and again alongside his love for hedonism – a lethal combination that would keep the showbiz pages of music magazines and newspapers occupied for the rest of the year.

His attraction to Victoria Beckham did not save her from his acid tongue, as he later reported in the press that he found all five members of the group 'physically repulsive.' 'I have a problem with music that's disposable,' he had added, naming and shaming the culprits with a characteristic lack of diplomacy. He did however commend them for one thing. 'They've made lots of money for the record company, which they can spend on us,' he laughed.

Becoming increasingly loose-lipped, Brian's dangerous penchant for honesty began to emerge, and its ensuing chaos was unveiled. He teased the NME by stating that he had drugs hidden in his underpants and moments later revealed the real reason he loved impersonating women – female toilets had all the more mirrors for indulging in nose candy. 'I love drugs,' he brightly announced, in a casual tone more suited to mentioning he had eaten cereal for breakfast. 'Like most people I've had bad trips on LSD and ecstasy, but that doesn't stop me taking things.'

He added 'I don't have a problem with needles. I've intravenously injected drugs before. You're a bit scared the first time but then you get a bit of a fixation for them, which is dangerous. You like the little skin bubble that it causes and start to play with it. You start thinking that in hospital they don't shove drugs up your nose – they inject you, so using needles is clearer, purer and gives you a better hit.' With a last minute flash of conscience, he added 'I don't recommend it for your readers though.'

The damage was already done however. Brian had been equally honest about his sexual misadventures, claiming at an interview in 1997 that his bedpost notches numbered between 10 and 500. He'd had enough conquests 'to give me an unhealthy sense of AIDS paranoia.'

He told journalists he'd injected speed and crack, sometimes simultaneously. 'It was dangerously nice', he revealed. 'Crack is like a ten-minute buzz, followed by an eight-hour comedown. When I took it I did understand why it was so addictive, because as it hit my bloodstream, I wanted more right there and then. I just get bored when I'm sober.'

Despite jokes that one day he might give up his fast paced life and become a Christian, one suspected that the change wasn't imminent. What was the reason for Brian's consistent overindulgence – other than the pure rush? 'Cocaine makes you talk a lot of shit,' he explained. 'When you're in music biz situations, you have to speak to a lot of people who you don't want to talk to and I find that tiring. Cocaine allows you to talk bollocks to people you don't really care about and get it all over with nice and quickly.'

Meanwhile a scar from drunkenly trying to put his arm through a closed window had sparked rumours of self-harm. Explaining it away later, he mused 'It healed in the shape of a Nike tick' without an inch of remorse.

He hit out at accusations that he was a fake. 'My "partial" homosexuality is not a game of seduction as I read about myself somewhere. I've known since I was very young that I was bisexual.'

The honesty addict continued, 'I can't prevent myself from washing my dirty laundry in public. It's pathological with me. My writing is extremely confessional and definitely shameless.'

Indeed, Brian was unabashedly honest, fuelled by a 'pathological craving' to tell the truth, a sense of youthful bravado and a regular supply of drugs. In fact one thing that he'd once boasted was that the group spent £700 a week on chemical stimulants. As their allowance from the record company was just £140 a week each, the figures, which Brian later conceded were hugely exaggerated, did not add up. The group's cartoon character persona was by now larger than life and beginning to cause serious damage.

Guardian music critic Caroline Sullivan verbalised the problem. Referring to a friend of hers, she recalled 'Here was an individual who, rather than taking an instant dislike to fake debauchee Brian Molko as any sensible person would, actually didn't mind him one way or the other. Then he read a Placebo article and "could never take them seriously again." I don't know what they said to affect him that way, but it must have been considerably more than the usual "we're hedonists looking into an abyss of narcotics and amorality" line of ludicrousness.' Her words highlighted that Placebo were becoming known less for their musical output and more for their extra-curricular activities.

Brian agreed. 'Through my own naivety, I've said too much and yet there's a certain part of me that still wants to be honest, honest, honest,' he agonised. However if broken ribs did not deter him, words could never hurt him and the effects of the brash disclosures in the national press would faze him even less. His management attempted to tone down his disclosures but, ever resistant to control, Brian paid little more than lip service to their warnings. The carefully crafted press release knighting the band as 'the antidote to Britpop' was dismissed as 'bollocks made up by our press people' and the tedium, fatigue and boredom that Brian experienced during interviews was petulantly vocalised. It was honesty on a level some would call arrogant. Whatever the reason for such candour, it was on a scale previously unheard of for a rock artist.

Traditionally, tales from behind the velvet rope have always been coveted – many of the indulgences within are secrets that have never been told. Journalists relentlessly practise techniques to induce interviewees to open up and deliver the scoop of the day they've been searching for, a scoop that will deliver both author and musician a dose of notoriety.

However, they were to have their work cut out by Placebo. When Brian opened his mouth, he routinely forgot every PR rule that had been handed to him. While other artists offered little more than teasing snippets of their life of fame, designed to tantalise, and guardedly exposing no more than they had intended, Brian told stories of his rock and roll lifestyle without pretence. Every journalist wanted an interview with the group, scarcely daring to imagine which sought-after secret they would expose next.

In reality though, Brian defended that Placebo's antics were probably no different from that of many other young males enjoying the first throes of success. The only difference was that the band's indiscretions were in public. The music industry is renowned for narcotics, substance abuse and opportunities for illicit sex, while many young people shamelessly crave success and stardom – could it be the accompanying lifestyle of excess that it offers?

'We were incredibly wild and crazy, we did everything,' Brian defended. 'But it was nothing more than any young man with money, attention and success would do. The only thing is that we'd do it in public and we promised ourselves we'd never lie about it.'

Defiant and unapologetic, he claimed the rumours barely concerned him. 'It's all true and all lies. It kind of contributes to the rock n roll myth. Rock n roll should be badly behaved, it should be dirty, it should be transgressive and amoral. We spent a lot of time diving into the deep end of every rock n roll cliché – it was a baptism of fire and we weren't going to rest until everything possible was transgressed.' So Brian had set upon the lifestyle with an almost competitive ambition to replicate the lifestyle of the greats before him.

His refusal to be candy-coated, insipid or dishonest in his approach had divided opinions. Some cited sheer stupidity whilst others admired his self-confidence and his belief that putting on a front of clean living to be likeable was scarcely necessary when the music, like all good music, would speak for itself.

The headlines continued, portraying Brian as a 'drug-crazed sex dwarf' in a cruel reference to his height and penchant for drugs and insisting that he was a 'drug hoover' with little respect for morality. Even Brian himself confessed he had never been particularly moral about 'desires of the flesh', once again cutting journalists' work out for them. He foresaw every comment in advance and admitted to being guilty as charged.

It also begged the question – was this really Placebo, or merely a stunt calculated to gain attention and publicity? Whether intentional or otherwise, this achieved the goal of multinational press exposure. No matter what means were used to hold the public's attention, there was no denying that it was truly held. However, behind the sordid humour and the jokes about sex, drugs and debauchery lay a powerful message which the group wasted no time in conveying.

One infamous psychological experiment even discovered that

those who hated Placebo with a passion probably had a little more in common with them than they'd like to admit. Heterosexual men viewed pornographic videos whilst a band attached to their genitals measured penile blood flow. Those who expressed the highest levels of homophobia and disgust towards homosexual acts were in fact the most aroused by them, preferring gay porn to straight porn. Indeed, like these psychological experiments, Placebo had a habit of forcing people to come face to face with their worst fears – a facet of psychology some fans found far more interesting than a report of the cocktail of drugs Brian had consumed over breakfast that morning.

Plus shockingly for the media, Brian did have moments of lucidity. In discussion with the Melody Maker about his last holiday, a trip to Indonesia with his brother, Brian revealed a heart-felt affection for animals. Referring to a visit to the local zoo, he recalled 'We were completely tour-fucked and I just lay on the beach for a week. We went to the monkey forests and hung out with the monkeys – that was cool. There were these beautiful little one day old monkeys being breastfed and stuff – that was really sweet. They were quite vicious though and they get into scraps with each other a lot so you have to watch it and keep your hands in your pockets, otherwise they jump on you. They're quite nasty but they hang onto you and climb over you which is cool.'

His time with his brother allowed him to reconnect with his niece and nephew. Brian had instantly adored his nephew Martin from the moment he was born, just a month before Brian turned 18. A drawing that Martin had scrawled for him became a good luck charm and was transported all around the globe. 'He made it for me when he was two or three,' Brian recalled. 'To me, the drawing perfectly illustrates the innocence of childhood, which doesn't suggest anything about the pains to come.' In a public shout out to him, he added 'Remember that wherever he may be in the world, your uncle is always thinking of you and really loves you.' This new tender side to Brian was kept well hidden and might surprise the media, who preferred to type-cast him as a perpetual drug hoover with skin as thick as a rhinoceros.

Brian also adored his niece Clara, who had grown up to become a primary school teacher and relocated to Florida. Meanwhile Martin, a keen guitarist who longed to follow in his uncle's footsteps, eventually earned a place at the University of Nice. Due to their father's home in Monaco, the two grew up speaking fluent French.

The drawing from his nephew wasn't the only good luck charm that Brian carried. The second was darker and far more unusual, given to him by a nameless fan. A Polaroid had been hurled on to the stage following a concert in France, featuring an anguished looking teenage girl scowling with a backdrop of dark purple wallpaper. 'Kill Fuck Die' was the simple message that had been scrawled across the front. 'I still don't know who that girl is and I'll probably won't ever,' said Brian. 'I just hope the physical and emotional pain that is so obvious on this picture has stopped, or at least dulled. The picture and words seemed very disturbing in my eyes, and they still haven't lost their intensity. I keep it in my make-up bag and I carry it all around the world, like a lucky charm.'

He offered a heart-felt message to the fan – 'Remember that wherever you are, you are never alone. This world can be as beautiful as it is ugly. You just have to make the future better than the past. The past is over- it only remains in our memories,' he reassured. His final words were both exciting and promising – 'The future is a gamble.'

However Brian's secret sensitive side was quickly buried again as, refreshed from his break abroad, he began another onslaught of media interviews. This time he used his fame to champion a greater cause than merely the appreciation of illicit drugs. Fiercely political, Brian posed as the Health Secretary for the UK in a special edition of Melody Maker. He made his political debut dressed in a white collar suit cum schoolboy's uniform plus heavy black eyeliner to complete the look.

In spite of his eccentric appearance, he had some controversial ideas for the future of the health service.

'I think it's absolutely bloody appalling!' he stated. 'I intend to remove all the old men – all the jobs for boys. I'll remove the capitalistic attitude towards hospital beds and I'm going to siphon off all the money than the British Government spends on weapons unnecessarily and put it into the Health Service. I'm going to bring the NHS up to the standards of private medicine.'

Brian condoned equality and deplored that prisoners were refused expensive operations in favour of younger patients, claiming that 'social status, age or criminal record should not have any influence on who gets the bed. Whoever is first into the emergency room must be seen.'

Unsurprisingly, drugs did come into it and campaigning for the legalisation of drugs, like idols the Dead Kennedies, was one of his top priorities too. 'I'm gonna set up places around cities where you can go to get your Ecstasy checked before you take it to make sure you're taking only E. Obviously these drugs will be taxed… people are gonna take them anyway and you can't stop them. There'd be help points in every club with nurses to help people who freak out. It's not the Government's place to take choices away from people.'

Other political beliefs included a desire to 'stamp out pro-lifers' and the declaration 'I will never forgive Tony Blair for encouraging all of his party to abstain on the Criminal Justice Bill, which everyone seems to have forgotten about, along with the hole in the ozone layer.'

Brian's bizarre political manifesto would come as a surprise to some who believed his verbal diarrhoea extended only to drugs and copulation. The strait-laced among music fans shuddered collectively at the thought of Brian's plans and thanked God that such a strange individual could never make Parliament.

They had nothing to be concerned about, as Brian had very different plans ahead of him. He was consumed by slowly but surely reinventing his public image.

Firstly, the group re-released Bruise Pristine with what they described as a more 'adult' sound, without the 'helium' vocals that had seen taunts in the past. May 12th 1997 was the release date, letting loose a more mature sound and a reassuringly high budget video. Subversive, erotic and surrealist, director Howard Greenhalgh's visuals perfectly matched the song. With a large cow dripping milk from its swollen and distended udder as couples fornicate around her, milk drips tantalisingly from the walls and ceiling. The models wear lipstick in exaggerated smears across their faces, smears that Brian has boasted were personally administered by the band themselves. The finishing touch to this scene is Brian, in a PVC pinstripe jacket, rocking his Fender guitar. The video is as mysterious as they are, and in the absence of logic, pure emotion takes over for the enamoured fan. The listener falls prey to hypnotic, heartwarming Sonic Youth inspired guitars and rhythms. Placebo had set out to be addictive and for many, this electrifying tune was no exception.

Positive publicity continued when Brian was invited to model for a number of high profile fashion designers. The first was Calvin Klein. Impressed by Brian's edgy, gender-ambiguous image that appealed to alternative youth culture and kept them guessing, the designer asked him along to a shoot. Other celebrities invited included supermodel Kate Moss and Scottish rock singer Shirley Manson from Garbage.

Brian was assigned a suit, which he refused to wear in favour of the female wardrobe options. Photographers reluctantly shot him in feminine attire, but the shoot was never aired to the public. This led Brian to chortle years later 'I never saw the pictures. I think they decided to humour me and then just put it in the can.' However this was to pave the way for other lucrative fashion deals in the future, and the prognosis for Brian was looking good.

Meanwhile the group was unleashing their brand of rock on a new and previously uninitiated audience – Finland. Speaking from Helsinki following a heart-stopping performance at the Provinssirock festival on June 13th 1997, Brian gave viewers another dose of his challenging and refreshingly brazen honesty. 'Hey shithead!' he called at a passerby with the trademark frankness for which he is both adored and reviled, 'Haven't you ever seen a TV camera before?' His ego temporarily satisfied, Brian confided to the amused interviewer 'At the moment we're financially stable but mentally very unstable.' He had just put into words what an entire nation had been thinking.

'So you weren't unstable before?' asked the journalist with appreciable scepticism.

'Yes of course!' he countered without skipping a beat – 'but even more so now.'

He paused for thought. 'We wanted to be a significant and successful band on a global level. It doesn't happen overnight and it doesn't happen without sacrifices. If our sanity is at risk because of it, so be it.'

The channel followed this with a clip of Brian simulating fellatio on Stefan during the guitar solo of Nancy Boy, to a myriad of hysterical screams. This group knew how to put on a show. However, there were sure signs of the instability he talked of. 'I really desperately wanted to be rock n roll,' he revealed to one magazine. 'I was tearing wallpaper off the walls and waking Steve and Stefan at six in the morning, having panic attacks. We took our souls and bodies to an extreme, and then realised we couldn't do it anymore.' Emerging slowly from the abyss, he revealed 'Drugs and alcohol are just an extended version of running away... it was time for detox.'

Before that could happen, once again disaster struck. Brian was scheduled to play the Scottish festival T in the Park that July. His mother had decided to make an appearance in the audience, travelling from Dundee. Nearing 60, she was having hearing difficulties and was determined to make the most of seeing her son live before the problem became worse. Brian was thrilled by her presence and in typical drama student style looking forward 'to stepping things up a notch' and showing off.

He realised his parents would never share his passion for the rock and roll lifestyle, groaning 'They hate it. To them it's all sex, drugs and butt fucking and that's all. They don't see the art of it and they don't really understand the basic need for creative expression.' Nevertheless he was hoping he might win his mother over, if only for the day.

Alas, this was not to be. From the beginning, the event was doomed to fail. It had been pouring with torrential rain, the group had played badly and there were technical difficulties. Seething with frustration yet remembering Bowie's advice never to lose his spontaneity, Brian contemptuously kicked the amplifier during a frenetic guitar solo. The audience began to boo and the cracks had truly started to show. However it was what was to happen backstage that truly made a mark in what Brian was to describe as 'the worst day of our career.'

The next day, on July 14th 1997, Brian made the front page of a national newspaper – and for all the wrong reasons. Picturing a snarling Brian on the front cover, the Sun's bold headline shrieked 'Rock-star thug beats up fan for wanting a photo.' Unfortunately for the band, today the music was the last thing on reporters' minds.

'Rock-star thug Brian Molko whacked a terrified fan over the head and pelted her with stones at the T in the Park festival yesterday,' the article stormed.

Sophie Patterson, then 22, and author of the critically acclaimed fanzine Lives, Loves and Lipstick had been backstage to chat with the band following their performance. Sophie, who reportedly began her journalistic career writing reviews for an Oxford University newspaper, had interviewed Brian twice in the past. They had come to blows when she had spoken to his ex-girlfriends and subsequently boasted about his penis size. 'She actually went to the trouble of speaking to people I used to sleep with and writing about the size of my dick in a fanzine. Now I really don't appreciate that,' Brian groaned. She had also written potentially defamatory articles linking Brian to feisty red-head TV presenter Sarah Cawood, who at the time hosted the Girlie Show.

Although the friendship between the two could quickly have turned sour, things had apparently remained on good terms until that day. The Sun quoted Sophie as saying 'Suddenly he flipped after I asked to have a photo with him. He slapped my face really hard and then poured a full pint of beer over my head. Brian was calling me every name under the sun, saying I was a fucking bitch and a stupid cow. He was shouting "Fuck you, don't ask me for anything when I'm at a gig." I was really upset and crying – I don't know what I did to deserve it.'

Brian was confronted by Sun reporters who witnessed the alleged incident, while a musician friend of Sophie's egged her on to "kick the little fool in the balls." Surrounded by a celebrity crowd including Big Breakfast presenter Denise Van Outen, Brian fled the VIP bar with Steve at his heels. They returned moments later where, from the safety of a 6-foot wire fence, the two allegedly swore at Sophie and a Sun reporter and pelted them with rocks. 'He came back and started throwing rocks at my head,' Sophie continued. 'I asked him to stop but he wouldn't. I had no idea this guy was so violent.'

'He portrays this feminine image on stage, wearing girls' clothes but he's nothing but a brutal thug.'

Ironically just months before the incident, she had written in her fanzine 'I'd never write anything to piss anyone off. [Brian] is the most peculiar guy I've ever met. What stories can I tell about Placebo? Oh there are plenty, but obviously some things are best kept secret. I'm not a bitch who dishes the dirt on every pop star I meet. If I wanted to do that, I'd be working for a sleazy tabloid.'

Evidently for her, the story praising Brian's anatomy and the subsequent revelation to the Sun about the T in the Park altercation did not fall into this category. Following the report, Sophie publicly denied that she had made the claims to the Sun, rubbished suggestions that he was a thug and said that rocks had not been involved.

In her version of events, faxed to Melody Maker magazine afterwards, she had greeted Brian and he had responded with a curt 'Get lost!' Sophie then admits squirting the back of his head with a water pistol in retaliation. Taking up the story, she added 'Brian's anger exploded. "So you think that's fucking funny, do you?" he yelled and threw a whole pint of beer over Sophie's head. "You can go and shove your fanzine up your fucking ass!" and gave a middle finger hand signal before sticking his tongue out.'

Sun journalists Dominic Mohan and Matt Bendoris witnessed the end of the altercation and followed Brian out of the backstage area where, from the safety of a gate, he and Steve began to shout at her. 'Both band members, acting like a couple of schoolboys, threw stones and mud from behind a metal gate at a reporter and shouted insults,' said Sophie.

This was a slightly different version to that of the Sun and Placebo's management responded with a third version of the story in an emergency press release. 'The band were in the backstage area enjoying a quiet drink. It was while the band were talking that Sophie Patterson took it upon herself to interrupt them. Unsurprisingly, she was asked to go away. Ms Patterson, who is known by the band and management for her dogged determination in pursuing the band, did not take to this kindly. She decided to fire a water pistol at Brian Molko. He again asked her to go away, but she continued to fire the water pistol in his face.'

It continued 'Brian reacted – he threw a small amount of beer towards Patterson. With hindsight, this was probably not the best course of action, but it was the sum total of her alleged assault.' The statement ended with an apology to Sophie if she had 'got a little wet.'

Despite the public apology, Brian's reputation had been tarnished. Close friends the AC Acoustics allegedly assured Sophie that whatever had occurred between them, Brian was 'too out of it to remember anything.' Sophie's hopes that the two would kiss and make up were dashed. A subsequent report appeared in the Sun, making the feelings of one member of the media only too clear. 'Sophie's only crime was having the bare-faced cheek to ask his lordship for an autograph. I could have wrung his pretty neck… he looked relieved when a burly minder led him away before I could get to grips with him.'

Around this time, Placebo had been receiving death threats, a disturbing pattern that was to continue for the next couple of years. Security was tightened around the group and Sophie and her friends were banned from the V97 festival in Chelmsford, an act which she claims was due to Placebo's management. This remains unsubstantiated. Yet the claims of violence and thuggery couldn't have been more incongruent with pictures of a diminutive Molko dressed in a demure pair of leopard skin tights and a thigh-skimming dress, every inch the angel, just one month later.

Whatever the real story behind the endless saga, Brian's reputation had taken a near terminal tarnishing – and it would take a monumental effort to rebuild his public image. Grimacing, he hoped to put the whole harrowing experience behind him. 'The whole thing turned into a nightmare,' a shamefaced Brian revealed to the Sun. 'I don't even want to think about it.'

Steve was more willing to elaborate. 'Brian was out of his nut on drink when that happened and the whole thing dogged us for months. The girl that was at the centre of it all turned out to be a complete nutter. She followed us all over Europe after that and we had to employ minders to keep her away. We couldn't get out of Scotland fast enough.'

The bittersweet parting shot that was their departure from T in the Park that night had been traumatising, but the group were determined not to let it ruin them. Furious by the events of that year, Brian allegedly refused to take part in promotional campaigns.

'The petulant star has infuriated his record company by refusing to speak to the media,' the Sun reported. This perpetuated the difficulties, leaving many to believe a series of vicious rumours in the absence of any genuine press report to counter them. However, given the destructive stories in the press, it was little wonder that Brian was reluctant to open up.

'Nobody was talking about the music,' a wounded Brian recalled with barely disguised frustration, 'which is what we're trying to redress now. I don't do interviews on my own anymore because people focus on me and my psychology and my sexuality and my image and it's like "Hold on, excuse me – there's two other people in this band. Let's talk about some fucking music for a change.'"

Placebo were by now very misunderstood. Their biggest assets seemed somehow lost in translation. Whilst waiting for a linguistic expert to be their saviour, presumptions continued. Damning reports emerged in the rare moment that attention shifted away from cross-dressing and Brian's favourite brand of eyeliner – Rimmel, for those who were wondering.

His voice was described as 'an unearthly wail' (The Guardian), 'a voice like a dehydrated crack in the Nevada Desert, in a pitch normally set aside for aliens,' (Dazed and Confused) and 'an open invitation to take the piss.' (the NME). Kinder journalists, better versed in the art of diplomacy, reported a 'transatlantic whine.'

Brian was also criticised for his honesty. Whilst the listener might sympathise with the cartoon like depiction that began to be synonymous with Brian's life, the onus was also on him to shift the focus back onto the music. It was becoming increasingly difficult as the first question on everyone's lips was 'Tell us about the drugs and showbiz parties.'

Unquestionably, Placebo marketed themselves as a freak show, and duly came under criticism for it, but was that the full story? Was Brian responsible for the caricature the media had spawned? He argued that he had never set out to become a role model to troubled teens, let alone lead them astray. He did not see himself responsible for 'a wave of white pasty faces' anymore than he did for encouraging drug use. Plus to him his cheerful name checks of class A drugs were no more irresponsible than the revelations of pop favourite Rihanna. The outwardly wholesome Barbados-born singer declared in one interview that 'carbs are the enemy' and confessed that slimming was the most important priority for her. Placebo's message meanwhile was simply to 'be who you are.'

The group urged their audience to leave their inhibitions and insecurities at the door and not to be concerned with how they fitted into the shallow preoccupations of wider society. 'Our music is for people who feel they're square pegs in round holes,' he remarked. 'I've always felt that way about myself.'

Despite the press having a field day where wicked rumours and tales of sleaze and seduction were concerned, the one thing they could not do was pigeon hole the group. Compared to Geddy Lee, Babylon Zoo and Slade – claims that were met by Brian with snorts of derision – journalists tried desperately to unveil the mysteries of their distinctive sound.

Two of Placebo were brought up in a country where as far as TV was concerned, popular music simply failed to exist. The third's love of rap was the polar opposite of rock and the cacophony that resulted was certainly unique. Brian had an equal fondness for passionate blues singer Billie Holiday as he did for notorious rappers Public Enemy. The group's combined musical interests spanned classical, rap, rock and soul. Fans felt that they imitated few, yet were silently influenced by many.

What's more, their musical repertoire was astonishingly varied and as paradoxical as the message they represented. Whilst some songs embodied Sonic Youth's atonal rhythms, they could still pull out a breathtaking heart-rending ballad to lie alongside it. Placebo's appeal lay in their ability to be multi-faceted, from the punk-rock of Nancy Boy to the melodic melancholia of Lady of the Flowers. Placebo could even write a great love song, although reassuringly it 'is always twisted.'

What is more, no social group was immune from Placebo's charms – from the outwardly conventional 9-5ers to the Goths and glam rockers kitted out in feather boas – from teenagers to the elderly, all appeared at their shows. This was a group with divergent backgrounds, from desperately poor working class to upper-crust high society, vast musical tastes, extensive record collections and an array of emotions and sonic styles, each different from its predecessor. Yet all of the group's paradoxes fitted together.

In their keenness to dig the dirt, perhaps the media had missed the most intriguing scoop of all. That was that Placebo could never be labelled.

Chapter 4.

'We left a trail of blood and spunk across the country – at that point we realised we had to calm down a bit' – Brian Molko.

Somewhere in the heart of otherwise tranquil Bath, a party rages on into the early hours of the morning. As dawn breaks, while the rest of the town are awakening, this small group are partying. Couples are fornicating almost without reservation, the floor their playground, free from inhibition as conversation rages on above them. The centre-piece of this clandestine gathering is none other than Brian Molko.

Detaching himself from his anonymous partner, he retreats to the privacy of the bathroom, recoiling in horror at the haunted face staring back at him from the cracked mirror. Did he use a condom? Did he cum? He can barely remember. Staring down at his trembling hands, he can barely recognise them as his own. His guitar stands broken in the bath, a poignant symbol of months of self-destruction. His hands are vibrating, yet he picks it up nonetheless and – as if to make amends – begins to play.

This unlikely setting was the first day of recording for the group's second studio album, Without You I'm Nothing – or at least according to the popular press. The details of their decadent three-day orgy, printed in Select magazine, were certainly news to the band. All three vehemently denied the claims, offered alongside a headline in Select magazine entitled 'Placebo – The Filthiest Band in Britain?'

'If you did all that, why would you brag about it in a magazine?' Brian asked incredulously. 'It feels like we're some sort of vending machine for filth.' Stefan broke his characteristic silence to add 'Everything I was quoted as saying was made up.'

So what had really happened when the group closed its doors to the public? While their careers were gathering speed, the negative side of fame was also becoming increasingly prominent. Brian had received explicit death threats on his answerphone, had regularly been attacked by the jealous, the homophobic, and the inebriated, and wearily wore the tag 'The fag your girlfriend wants to shag.' By now better known for his vices than his voice, the stream of negative press against Brian showed few signs of slowing down, and the trio's personal lives entered into meltdown.

To make matters worse, Brian was already smarting from a breakup with the petite and androgynous actress Liza Walker, best known for her appearance in TV serial London's Burning. The beauty had also appeared in a number of high-profile films such as the Jungle Book and Hackers. The former girlfriend of pop star Chesney Hawkes, Liza clearly had a penchant for musicians. Meanwhile Brian loved the fact that Liza looked like him, believing sexual attraction to be 'narcissistic'.

The two were like-minded, sharing many interests, but most importantly they were passionate about each other. Brian felt he'd fallen in love. However the euphoria was to be short-lived, as his constant travelling made a successful relationship near impossible, and he struggled with maintaining fidelity.

'My love life is practically non-existent!' Brian moaned to Kerrang. 'The job doesn't really allow it. Monogamy is a concept that I've really struggled with… but the nature of your livelihood makes it very difficult to keep relationships going, regardless of whether or not you're shagging like a rabbit, just because you're never there.'

Devastated by the break-up of his relationship and still deeply in love, the crestfallen Brian was forced to relive the mistakes of the past year. The last traces of alcohol had trickled out of his system, to be replaced with a surge of pure regret for his over-indulgence. He had paid for it by losing the love of his life.

Despite the rumours of an orgy at the recording studio being unsubstantiated, Brian did concede that in every wild rumour there lies a grain of truth. 'We dove right into it,' Brian confessed. 'I'm not going into detail, but it was pretty wild. I won't say that I didn't like it. Part of me was disgusted and the other part was fascinated – it was like I was watching myself doing all that crazy stuff.'

He had experimented with groupies, got into brutal fights with their boyfriends, and enjoyed a cocktail of drugs, illicit sex and infidelity. Now he had to face the consequences those events had reaped on his personal life.

'I used to be quite a nice person, but rock n roll eroded it,' he sighed. 'When you realise how you behaved like an asshole, you take your pillow, hold it over your face and try to smother yourself.' A sensitive type, he had resorted to anti-depressants part way through the tour to soothe the pains of the past. However he had grown to loathe Prozac, feeling that it robbed him of his personality and stifled his creative expression. 'By the time I came off tour, I was in such a fragile emotional state,' he confirmed. 'I was just fucked up. I'd taken my soul through the blender, and I really didn't know who I was anymore. I was disgusted with myself.'

In that moment he realised there was only one way to battle the self-loathing and the identity crisis, and prescription drugs were not the answer. Immediately returning to the studio, Brian poured his heart into his music, locking himself into a 'subterranean room with no windows for two months' and along with his two equally dedicated bandmates, began to pen their second studio album.

In the privacy of Real World Studios, Brian waved goodbye to the drama and decadence that the previous year had catapulted them into. He had become weary and all too aware of the relentless media spotlight and the hurtful headlines, although he understood why he was the central focus.

'We left a trail of blood and spunk across the country,' he acknowledged, unwittingly creating another one. 'We realised that we really had to calm down a bit.'

A multitude of mischievous recollections had flickered through his head, but none that he was willing to share. One thing was for sure, he knew from experience that he didn't want to be saddled with the title of Evil Rock-star of the Year. Sexiest Rock-star of the year might have been better, and as he had won both the Male and Female categories in the Melody Maker awards that year, pictured lounging on a burgundy velvet chaise longue, it was quite fitting.

The good news was that Placebo and their exploits had attracted the attention of a big-name producer. The group duly switched their contract to Virgin Records that year, signing an all-important five album deal. Steve Osbourne was chosen as their producer, whose other claims to fame included albums for New Order, Suede, the Happy Mondays and KT Tunstall. Whilst there was a harmonious atmosphere, it was to be a decision the trio would ultimately regret. Brian felt their relationship with Steve lacked the right chemistry and that the ensuing sound was overproduced. 'There are sounds on there that we have no idea where they came from,' he was to lament later.

However, one aspect that there were no disagreements on was the album's theme. 'The first album dealt with sex, drugs and rock n roll.' Brian ventured. 'Crazy sex, wild sex, sex on drugs. On Without You I'm Nothing, we're dealing with the after-effects of that.'

He continued 'The first album was a sexual record packed full of youthful vigour and lust. The new album is introverted, more of a post-coital depression – the comedown. It deals with an ever prevailing heartbreak and loneliness. The morning after is usually more analytical than the night before, and it's often more painful…'

Chortling that he had tried to stay away from the notoriously difficult subject of relationships but failed, he added 'There's a stream of melancholy that runs through this record. Our professional lives were really together but our personal lives were kind of falling apart. We felt ourselves being pulled in a very vulnerable, fragile romantic direction.'

Guilt-ridden and heartbroken, Brian had engaged in psychodrama, acting a role during his passionate performances. 'Sometimes it helps to invent a character and let that character do what you wouldn't normally do,' he mused. 'Like an actor who lives out things not as himself, but in a role. A character is adopted.'

Role play aside, there was one thing he was adamant about – Placebo were no longer the filthiest band in Britain. 'I want to get rid of this comic strip character that England has stuck to my back,' the singer raged. 'I'd like people to know that we are not international hedonists; we are not that vulgar image anymore. I believe it's called growing up.'

Proclaiming himself older and wiser, Brian was anxious for Without You I'm Nothing to portray that. One of his favourite tunes from the new album was Brick Shithouse. Lyrically hinting at the perverse jealousy of the Oedipus complex, it is strongly influenced by PJ Harvey and borrows the harrowing line 'Don't you wish you'd never met her?'

The song, along with much of the album, is a psychoanalyst's dream, featuring confessional states in abundance. 'A disembodied soul floats overhead, observing the living,' Brian interpreted. 'It's a ghost story about someone watching his lover make love to the person who killed them.' Perhaps this feverish product of Brian's imagination is unsurprising. He had confessed to the NME months earlier a desire to be invisible, an astral projection that could spy on others undetected. 'I'd probably watch my loved ones having sex and get a hard-on,' he had revealed.

You Don't Care About Us is a dichotomous track, where an upbeat melody collides with a grief-stricken message from the mouth of an ex lover. It recounts how Brian is criticised for failing to save a dying relationship, much to the surprise of fans who believed Brian's was the narrative voice. Written just two weeks after he ended a course of anti-depressants, its creation represented a return to form and a confrontation of the demons which caused him to suffer so greatly.

'You Don't Care About us is directed towards me, written from the point of view of someone I used to be in a relationship with,' Brian recalled. 'There's a line in it that goes "You're in the wrong place, you're on the back page" which is often what I used to do. I used to imagine the end of relationships just as they were starting. That's the way I used to conduct my relationships. I think I'm quite a misunderstood songwriter – all the bile, vitriol and wickedness people think is directed by me towards other people, but they're often directed from other people towards me and I'm being extremely self-critical.'

In his desire to create a painfully honest album, Brian had adopted self-deprecation on a level many would find nauseating. He was ready to counter the vitriol of his detractors and to his fans he wore jarring vulnerability better than a designer dress. 'It may seem like I'm being arrogant, but I'm actually eating humble pie,' Brian confirmed. 'I'm cutting open a vein and letting it bleed for you.'

Some might find it hard to believe that the happy-go-lucky singer who 'struggles with monogamy' before declaring it a losing battle could actually have a heart at all. On the contrary. The media quickly caught on and labelled him a 'tart with a heart,' a badge he allegedly wore with pride.

For those in any further doubt as to his heart's existence, Ask for Answers is a poignant reminder of its presence. Looking at the scrutiny that has surrounded his public life, the image that has blown up out of all proportion, Brian vents his frustration in this gently healing number. It pleads for unfound answers, and cries 'Dog boy, media whore, to the hell you take me for,' in a nod to those who detract him. Few could have realised the impact stereotypes might have on an outwardly cruel but inwardly sensitive character like Brian. One of the most intense songs on the album, the world seems to stop for a few moments during these entrancing chord sequences.

The title track meanwhile, influenced by the Sandra Bernhard movie of the same name, seems to most accurately represent Brian's 'pathological desire to lay myself naked and bare' for the sake of art. He revealed 'It's a romantic title, but also a very desperate one. It's about the impossibility of love.' When asked whether for him love was nothing more than an impossible dream, he retorted 'Absolutely not. I'm a hopeless romantic.'

With compelling tales of strange infatuation, Brian's rich lyrical poetry magnetises the listener. With its harrowing minor chords, it conveys a deep longing that prevails to the point of irrationality – a universal emotion that resonates regardless of who is listening.

Despite being immensely personal, it is a song that has meant a lot to many people. At Reading Festival one year, a couple chose the stage before start-up as an unlikely location for marriage. The song they chose to seal their love in the unconventional ceremony was none other than Without You I'm Nothing. 'We laughed,' Brian remarked in response. 'We couldn't believe it. I always thought there was a deep irony that many couples make love to this song, but it talks about a relationship that is falling apart. I found that deeply ironic. It's very depressing but people sing it as proof of their love.'

The cover image of the album speaks of a similar theme, with twins symbolising an intense and all encompassing relationship that few outsiders can hope to understand. Most importantly, the song is a message from the band both to their devoted fans and to each other, all of whom form the final pieces in the puzzle that decodes success.

Allergic to Thoughts of Mother Earth is one of the earliest Placebo songs on the album. It was previewed frequently in 1997 live sets featuring different lyrics. The title was changed from Allergic to Thoughts of Mom for fear of offending Brian's mother although the turbulent parental relationship is part of the subject matter for the song. One of the punkier, more rock fuelled offerings and perhaps one of the few tracks that are not motivated by love, Brian speaks also of political connotations. He poses the question of environment versus religion, stating 'It is me having a go at Christians for not giving a shit about the environment because to them their rewards will always be in heaven, so it doesn't matter that we're using this place as a garbage tip.'

He continued 'When I first started writing songs, I had to shake the sceptre of Jesus out of me so I wrote a lot of "I'm angry about God" songs.' Despite getting much of this out of his system in his teenage moments of wrath, the inspiration for Allergic 'crept up' on him. Ultimately, it was Brian's way of expressing that 'Mother Nature is stronger than you and Mother Nature will have her own back.'

The Crawl is a song written with the help of Brian's guest confidante Paul Campion, who became a partner in crime in the studio to ease the pair's mutual bouts of insomnia. The two sat up long into the night penning the verses. The lyrics, hinting at prostitution, have a strikingly dichotomous nature with lines like 'Your smile would make me sneeze' yet 'I would pay to have you near.' 'The idea I had was of hating someone so much that you get allergic to them – their smile irritates you and makes you sneeze,' Brian evaluated with a wicked smile of his own. It also encapsulates the theme of many passionate affairs, where love and hate can often appear simultaneously.

Indeed, Placebo is dichotomous by nature, matching teasing femininity with concerts fuelled by aggression, testosterone and masculine exuberance. Their shows combine designer dresses with down and dirty punk-rock. Yet the two themes are surprisingly competent bed fellows and the same might be said of the themes in the Crawl.

Meanwhile My Sweet Prince refers to the tragedies of fatal romance, hopeless love and heroin addiction. Also intensely dichotomous in nature, elsewhere on the album he refers to himself as a tart, yet here he is a prince. To continue the paradox, he recalled his delight at having successfully placed 'fuck' and 'baby' in the same verse. The song provides both tenderness and aggression and the contrast of raw sex mixed with tender romanticism. Brian undertook the gruelling task of devising one anthem to express them both. From the man who, in accordance with Sonic Youth, has adopted the slogan 'Confusion is Sexy' as a mission statement, we wouldn't come to expect anything less.

The story behind My Sweet Prince was a closely guarded secret concerning a period that Brian is often reluctant to discuss. The singer had experimented with heroin on the previous tour, although it was a brief flirtation. Having a self-confessed romantic nature, it seemed inevitable to Brian that he'd succumb to its mysterious charms eventually, but he quickly saw the light. 'When it's a choice between heroin and friendship, heroin and creativity, you make that choice pretty fast,' he recalled.

Pioneered by his protective band mates, Brian recovered from the period but wrote the song to honour the devastating effect the drug had once had on his ex partner. While he had recovered from addiction quickly, his girlfriend had been far less fortunate.

'There was quite a big tragedy in our lives that occurred while we were demoing the record, and it had to come out. It just vomited itself forwards. It's about two romances, a romance with a substance and a romance with a person and they both ended very, very tragically.' Elaborating, he recalled, 'One day, someone wrote a message on the wall of my room: "My gentle prince, you are the only." The relationship ended disastrously because the person in question is almost dead.'

She had attempted suicide following the breakup of her impassioned relationship with Brian. His lipstick smudged message on the mirror had haunted Brian from that day forward, and he was determined to express that pain in a song. Whilst the girlfriend survived, and is aware the song is about her, the two no longer have contact and he is unaware of whether it helped her.

Whilst heroin might have destroyed their relationship, this song –

like Without You I'm Nothing – is one that lovers sing to each other to demonstrate their love, few suspecting the sinister meaning behind it.

Every You Every Me is more upbeat, with a vibe that couldn't be more different from the sad, slow melancholia of My Sweet Prince. Brian had initially pledged to name the song Heavy Metal Petting Zoo and was wounded when his more conservative management refused.

Telling the story of a tart with a heart, whose relationships frequently degenerate into chaos, the light-hearted and tongue in cheek lyrics are its highlight. Like the Crawl, the words were written by Brian in collaboration with Paul Campion. 'It's about a lot of people – probably everyone who's had the displeasure of sleeping with me. I want to stress that I said displeasure,' Brian chortled.

Summer's Gone has never been played live to date and Brian once told a journalist who enjoyed the song that it was his favourite simply because he was 'old.' It might seem that the group had a low opinion of it, Brian's relationship with it being one of disdain, and it was rarely discussed within the press. Its biggest failure according to Brian was that it was overproduced.

Scared of Girls tackles male inner misogyny, a theme tackled in Slackerbitch and Nancy Boy before it. 'Scared of Girls from the new album is a self-disgust song with an "I'm-ashamed-of-who-I-am" kinda vibe. One of the lyrics is, "I'm a man and I'm a liar" – spoken from the point of view of someone who doesn't feel very happy about themselves.' He added: 'I wanted to know whether the men who behave like whores do it because they love women, or to the contrary, because they hate them, fear them.' With an added twist, he revealed 'I got through without much respect for myself. Ultimately I considered myself as an object.'

More tales of low self-esteem are in store in Burger Queen. The song is a fictional account of a gay goth who is addicted to hard drugs and same sex liaisons and the life of hell he faces living out these fantasies in small-town Luxembourg. Brian placed himself in the context of his character's isolation, as he comes to terms with living in a society who will never fully tolerate or accept him.

Like all Placebo songs, it does have a trace of the autobiographical. 'We spent our teenage years locked in our rooms playing music. Like many boys that age, I dreamed of becoming a star,' Brian recalled. 'A city like Luxembourg can be stifling when you are seeking to create an identity. I felt isolated – there was no place where I could express myself.' The song recalls being a voyeur to the type of life to which he can never belong. Like many classic Placebo themes, it features sadness and despair but with a tinge of unmistakable optimism.

Evil Dildo is the secret track at the end of the album. When the world goes crazy, what is Placebo's response? Put it in a song. That logic gave birth to a dark instrumental, featuring an ode from a stalker. It might not be the most flattering declaration of love Placebo have ever received, the product of a furious outburst by a woman whose voice is disguised by a karaoke machine – but it's certainly the most interesting.

Unfortunately, hopelessly unprepared for fame, the distinctively-named Molko had neglected to become ex-directory. While Stefan received more innocent calls, mainly 12-year old Swedish fans begging to know when he'd return to play a gig in his home country, Brian was far more of a weirdo magnet. After one particularly insulting voice recording, Brian resolved to put it into a song.

With a characteristic attitude to his enemies, he recalled thinking 'Fuck you, we're going to make some money out of this by turning it into a song.'

The refrain at the end of the instrumental claims 'I will fuck you up the arse, and then I will sneak into your room… and cut your cock off, and stuff it in my mouth, and chew it off with my little teeth.'

The last two songs, along with Allergic, were first written and recorded at a Leipzig recording studio in 1996, whilst the majority of the others were penned at Real World Studios. Towards the end of the sessions, Brian had abandoned efforts to find chemistry with producer Steve Osbourne and instead returned to Phil Vinall, the man responsible for Nancy Boy. The two found instant camaraderie and, with most of their hard work done, entertained themselves by screaming into a toy parrot.

At around this time, fuelled by the relief from pressure, Pure Morning was born. It was an unexpected surprise or, in Brian's words 'a little gift from the Gods' delivered during a final B-sides session. Yet it was instantly adored, so much so that the band's management insisted on it appearing on the album. Complete within 24 hours, Brian had little time to think about the meaning of the song, which had 'instinctively vomited itself forwards.'

'The lyrics were off the top of my head, a first take thing, so I wasn't even thinking about the significance of them. After that I realised it's a song about friendship – celebrating friendship with women. It's about that point in the evening when the sun's coming up and the rest of the world is waking up and you can't go to sleep, basically, and you feel like a complete asshole because you're coming down. And it's at that point you feel like your life is the least sorted ever and all you really crave is for a friend to put their arms around you and make you feel better. That's the pure morning.'

The lyrics hint at a cheeky love serenade, a passionate love affair mixed with strong friendship. The song details Brian's appreciation of women and in particular, two women who lived on different continents in London and Tokyo, both of whom had meant a lot to him. He also clarified 'It's about that strange situation you get when you've been up all night and your body feels like shit in the morning. In comes your friend, she makes you a joint and you fall asleep quietly. It's the song when you can't feel your flesh anymore.'

So Without You I'm Nothing is indeed a psychoanalyst's dream, filled with stories of self-disgust, failed relationships and songs so intensely vulnerable that listeners' hearts will stand still and their very souls will tremble. The album was to make an immeasurable impact on fans worldwide for whom music was indeed the universal language. A portal of dark emotions, the experiences described in the album seemed devastatingly relatable and true to life, soothing the pain, frustration and hidden desires listeners could not bring to the surface in everyday life. To hardcore Placebo addicts, it was one of the most meaningful, compelling and criminally addictive albums in history.

Satisfied with the new material and filled with promises that the unexpected Pure Morning would be the first single, the band left the studio and returned to London to unleash their new album on a feverish public. An invitation into Placebo's, extraordinary no-holds-barred world came in the form of an exclusive show for fan club members only, situated at the Colchester Arts Centre in Essex. The venue was centrally located just a short one hour drive from London and 400 fans gathered eagerly, breathless with anticipation at the unveiling that was to follow.

Clad in burgundy trousers, wearing a T-shirt fittingly depicting a dragon in memory of his darker heroin-fuelled days, and sporting curly hair – the casual style he had adopted during his voluntary imprisonment at the studio – Brian strode on stage. Chain smoking Marlboro Lights, and introducing the new songs with the velvety transatlantic accent his fans knew and loved him for, he was met with rapturous applause.

'I was surprised by the slow songs,' a self-confessed punk-rock addict James Pasquali announced, 'and I was even more surprised to find that I liked them. This band persuaded me to take a chance and step out of my genre.'

He wasn't the only one to be surprised. Shocked yet captivated by the mixture of new and old material, which shared only the singer's distinctive voice in common, new addictions were forming that very night.

The positive response made light of a difficult time for Brian as vicious rumours circulated that he had impregnated a teenage girl. The account has never been proven. The allegedly underage fan had threatened to have him arrested according to popular belief, when he told the press 'My stalker is bringing the police [to a show] to arrest me. That's probably the worst trouble I'll ever be in.' Fortunately for Brian, the event in question passed without incident and there was no pitter-patter of tiny Molko feet.

He turned his attention to the new single Pure Morning, which would be released on August 3rd 1998. It was directed by Nick Gordon, a passive man by nature who was only too happy to take a back seat to Brian's creative direction from time to time. Brian was able to command creative control for the first time in his career in what he referred to as the 'necessary evil' of video production.

The video depicts a suicidal man perching on the window sill of a top floor building. While his bandmates look on helplessly from below, distraught passersby and policemen gaze skywards in terror. Steve and Stefan are promptly handcuffed and arrested whilst a policeman rushes to the scene to save Brian. Just as he grabs out for him, he jumps, to a collective wince from the audience. In a surprising turn of events, he finds his feet and begins to walk down the building 'like an angel' and remarkably free from injury. Noting a successful collaboration between himself and Gordon, Brian laughed 'It's nice to see the fruition of your stoned imagination come up on TV three weeks later.'

Coincidentally the pained and depressive look on his face was no role play. Nursing the 'mother of all hangovers' that morning and totally unequipped for a 9am start, the white pallor and depressive demeanour was entirely authentic.

Brian had a stunt-double for the shots walking down the building, not wishing to break an all-important Molko nail. Kitted out in black nail varnish, and the distinctive neck-length bob, Brian's doppelganger relentlessly performed the more dangerous shots.

Interviewed on a German TV show, Brian quipped 'I had it figured out – for 5,000 Deutsch Marks I'll walk down the building for you – no less!' The song itself was an electronic and altogether more melodic offering, seeing the group use a loop for the first time ever, and the visual accompaniment corresponded perfectly with its fast-paced sound.

The single became the sound-track to Lexus car adverts, whilst it was also responsible for Placebo's name hotting up on US shores. Across the Atlantic, the group was receiving as many as 2500 radio plays per week, a mean feat for an English based group in no hurry to break America. Brian was to later demand to an Albany waiter in mock horror 'Why is Pure Morning not on the jukebox?' They accepted their warm welcome by the USA both graciously and in good humour.

The two CD set featured several new B-sides for collectors. Mars Landing Party, a French rhyme, was perhaps the most notorious of these. The product of another relaxed B-sides session with Phil Vinall, it comprised a short, explicit French rhyme that was lyric-wise ludicrously dirty and sound-wise ludicrously innocent. The words translate to: 'Kiss me, put your finger up my ass, an unknown presence, an ambiguous presence, until I can't take it anymore.'

'We were in a particularly cheerful mood when we recorded it due to chance rehearsing,' Brian explained. The pressure of finding the perfect tracks to line the album had ended, and a more relaxed work ethic had taken its place.

'It's just a good dirty joke,' Brian added. It was a way to mix Girl from Ipanema and Je T'aime Moi Non Plus. We sent them into space and it became a porn story.'

Needledick was another B-side, with a bug-like character sporting a tiny penis being the inspiration. He was modelled on 8-Ball comic strips that Steve had introduced the group to during their friendship.

The dust had barely settled on Pure Morning, which achieved a number four spot in the UK charts, when another track was released – this time You Don't Care About Us. The accompanying video, directed by John Hillcoat, took place in the London Aquarium.

Using the theme of heartlessness to get political, it features the group, captured, tagged and eventually facing the unpleasant prospect of becoming shark food. Brian is shown attempting to escape the clutches of uniformed officials courtesy of some expert writhing perfected in his drama-school days. Eventually however he loses the battle and is plunged into the water. The group's wardrobe is more prominent than in previous video shoots, with Brian in an 'I'm Evil' T-shirt designed to put out the message before his detractors could, and with Stefan sporting a pair of shiny leather trousers – perfect for underwater mayhem. Their outfits were clearly unconventional swimming costumes.

The group has shared mixed feelings about doing a video with an underwater theme. After the trauma of 36 Degrees, all three had promised each other they'd never agree to one again. However, they were persuaded. 'We thought it'd just be special effects,' a wounded Stefan recalled. Unfortunately it was freezing cold water for the trio as they found themselves cast into the ocean again in the name of art.

The single, released on September 28th 1998, featured two new songs. Ion was an instrumental that was to introduce the group's live shows that year, and 20th Century Boy was a studio version of the T-Rex track Brian had sung on Velvet Goldmine.

Despite requests to put 20th Century Boy on the album, Brian had been resolute. 'We'd never make that version for ourselves, just for the fun of it. We did the cover because it was needed for the film. We don't even own T-Rex records but naturally it was a song we'd known for many years. We listen to it on the radio. We've never been T-Rex fans though.' By this point in his career, Brian was understandably fearful of perpetuating a cliché about glam rock dinosaurs. A compromise for the stubborn Molko was to allow it to appear on the You Don't Care About Us single instead.

With two singles under their belts, they were ready to take on the world with a brand new tour. The band embarked on a series of extensive UK dates, culminating in two nights live at Brixton Academy on October 24th 1998. Again Brian graced the stage in a dress – this time a black and white John Richmond creation, which he urged fans not to copy.

By this time Placebo had built up a large and loyal fanbase and the roars of approval were deafening. The set had something to engage even the most seasoned and cynical of listeners with Slackerbitch rearing its head for the first ever live version.

After concern that the lyrics would appear misogynistic, Brian took on the unenviable role of the person at which the song is directed. However on the day in question, infuriated by the release of the 'Filthiest Band in Britain' article, Brian decided to let loose on the song's real purpose.

'It's been said that we are the filthiest band in Britain, but it's not true,' Brian began. 'This song is not about us,' he announced to the tune of deafening cheers. 'It's about you.'

After the show, emotions were still running high. 'Absolutely butt fucked is the only way to describe how we felt about that article,' he sighed afterwards.

Suffering for the sake of one's art and with a candour that would make even the hardest-hearted blush, is a strength that few possess – but Brian had risen to the challenge and he hoped to survive the backlash. However he knew his limits, and Slackerbitch was wisely left off the album in anticipation of the Misogynistic Sex Dwarfs headline that was sure to follow.

After wowing the UK from Liverpool to London, the group set off on their first major US tour, beginning on December 1st 1998. Aside from a short spate of shows in 1996, this was to be the first chance to demonstrate to American audiences exactly what they were capable of. 'We weren't meant to go over to the US until next year,' Stefan recalled, 'but some of the most important radio stations have jumped on the track and we're plunged into the nightmare scenario of trying to break America.'

First, the band narrowly escaped arrest for indecent exposure after urinating on the highway, then their baggage went missing, rendering a show in Denver impossible, and their accommodation turned out to be a series of cheap and seedy 'fuck motels' with undeterminable stains adorning the walls. The horrified group left several of these moments after arrival. Nevertheless, despite the inevitable strife, all three were determined to make their first major US tour a roaring success.

Arriving in the smallest town of America's smallest state, Rhode Island in Providence, they prepared to initiate themselves on an unsuspecting audience of several hundred demanding locals ready to pop their Placebo cherries. However the December 2nd show was not without event. 'We can't seem to kick the habit of breaking the lighting rig wherever we go,' groaned Brian of that night.

This show closely followed a performance at Mama Kins in Boston, a venue owned by Aerosmith, but which – according to Brian – 'is a bit of a toilet.' They were scheduled to play a show with heavy rock group Rancid and it was evident who the audience had come to see. 'Everybody is a Rancid fan,' Brian groaned, 'so we end up playing in front of about 20 people after having played in front of 2,000 in Paris.'

Still battling with severe jetlag, the group travelled to New York – not to its cultural heart, but to the small town ambience of Albany on December 4th 1998. The tour bus was beginning to irritate the group due to a clock that raucously rang out the hour with train sounds, which appeared to be permanently attached to the wall. However, the hotel was to be even worse. On arrival, they found a singles dating society for the over-40s congregated at the bar, sperm on the walls and a breathtaking stench of mould.

'We're in a hotel that charges hourly rates, has spunk on the walls, with 45-year old divorcees and singles in the bar trying to cop off with each other. We get on the phone straight away and book ourselves into another hotel,' Brian recounted.

The new hotel was next to the airport, and inconveniently located as far from the city as they could get, but it fitted the band's minimal budget. The theme was of an English country inn – not very rock and roll. According to Stefan, it was 'relatively spunk-free' – until Placebo arrived, of course!

At the hotel, Brian proceeded with an onslaught of press commitments. 'It's such a weird place, America,' he told one interviewer with his usual trademark of unbridled honesty. 'We came straight from playing in front of 2,000 Parisians, with crowd surfing and total mayhem to playing in front of 20 people in Boston. I mean, not only can a band be pretty big in the UK and Europe and come here and be totally unknown but they can be huge on the East coast of America and be nothing on the West coast, or huge on both coasts but mean fuck all in Oklahoma, Kansas or Iowa. It's just such a huge country. Breaking it could take forever.'

With that sentiment, Brian acknowledged the alienation he suspected he was going to experience on a long tour promoting an album he feared was too homosexual and too subversive for the majority of the American public.

Brian had gleefully commented that at least they were not playing the conservative Mormon state of Utah, but things were still going to be difficult. 'Our gear was flown in from Chicago to Denver and then flown back again,' a mortified Brian announced. He was incredulous that the equipment would not make it in time for the next show. Adding insult to injury, he added 'It seems we've probably pissed everyone off in Denver. Serves them right for living so high up.'

That was just the beginning. The cancellation of the Denver show on December 11th 1999 was an unexpected downer, though the group then managed to get an unsuspecting local radio DJ fired by letting loose a string of profanities live on air. However, there were calming moments. In Chicago the previous day the band witnessed Chaka Khan live. Steve in particular relished the opportunity to be inspired by her strong voice and equally strong attitude.

Los Angeles saw a low-key but productive show on December 13th 1998, which offered networking opportunities with contemporaries such as Hole and the Foo Fighters. The group was also photographed with cross-dresser and comedian Eddie Izzard. The night was a celebrity-studded affair that later led Brian to chuckle, when questioned about his bad behaviour, 'I don't really abuse audiences – I'm not Courtney Love.' However, whatever he'd witnessed on tour thus far, the final show was to be the big one.

It was December 15th 1998 and the group was awaiting a sound check at New York's Irving Plaza. Still feeling the after effects of a long-lasting 26th birthday party, and blighted by policies of painfully brief ten-minute sound checks, Brian's thoughts were dominated by morbidity. His dreams of the previous night had been of persecution, obsessive fans and men with guns, perhaps sparked off by the previous year's close call in Austria. The reality was not so far from the truth, as Brian was to find out.

It was a Christmas show with a difference. Surrounded by support acts such as Kid Rock and Limp Bizkit, who were offering masculine rock anthems at their extreme, Placebo were unusual bed fellows for this line up. The Velvet Goldmine director and one of Brian's earliest inspirations Todd Haynes was to be there that night, but his presence was among the only support the group would elicit.

Kid Rock's show featured 'puerile entertainment' at its best, with a dwarf rapper and a giant pony who appeared on stage with him, alongside a collection of scantily clad blonde strippers from a nearby nightclub.

After witnessing the absurdity of this show, Brian was ready to take drastic action. 'How we were expected to go onstage after a band that had strippers and a rapping midget on a pony, I'll never know. It forced me to change into a dress, put on too much makeup, and set myself up for an evening of being called a faggot.'

The first disaster took place when Limp Bizkit's frontman, Fred Durst, leapt on stage to introduce the group. Brian's tour manager requested that he leave, unaware that organisers had asked for his presence, and the war of words began. 'Fred Durst just jumped onstage and started insulting us,' Brian claimed. Angered that he had been upstaged, Fred invited the crowd to join him in a chant of 'Placebo sucks,' which was the last straw for the band. 'Our manager was furious and he chased him out of the building because our tour manager was about to kill him. So we were saying to Kid Rock, "Sort your mate out", and he was going, "He's not my mate, man." People used to say I have a knack for provocation, but now it seems like I don't have to try,' Brian grinned in reflection.

Undeterred, he arrived on stage and introduced the group as ego-cocks in frocks without strippers, ponies or vertically challenged people to offer before beginning the ill-fated set. In no time the stage was showered with bullets and drenched with beer. Even worse, bottles of urine were hurled on to the stage. Realising they were no match for a huge gathering of several thousand drunken Americans, all three made a speedy exit.

Stefan had a more diplomatic memory of events. Whilst sources of support were few and far between, those that the band did have were more than appreciated.

'I thought there would be more abuse than we actually got,' Stefan declared. 'The reaction was actually quite the opposite. We were having redneck football players standing in the audience going, "Brian, I love you. I love you." The contradiction was kind of strangely beautiful.'

For the remainder of the audience, fired up by Fred's relentless chants of 'Fuck Placebo,' something the grudge-bearing rocker would repeat on his return to Irving Plaza three years later, the show was over.

Brian recalled 'The next day Howard Stern got Fred Durst on the phone on his radio show, and he was saying, "Fred, you're a fucking dick." Kid Rock was on the show going, "The guys were cool, I don't know what Fred's problem is."'

Rather than being angry, Brian had actually relished the attention, thriving on the negative publicity. 'My best weapon is my mouth,' he explained, 'and I've got a microphone!' Realising all too well that his voice could humiliate an audience in an instant if he applied enough quick wittedness, Brian strived to get the upper hand. 'When things get that confrontational, it often gives you an extra push, an extra desire to overcome.' Eyes sparkling with new-found fervour, he added 'an extra fuck you.'

So Placebo had both delighted and offended, perhaps in equal measure, and had received both love and hate in abundance, but notably never indifference – and that was just how they liked it. They'd tried their best, made their mark and had established a small but devoted cult audience all over the USA in preparation for their return. Shuddering at memories of run-down motels, little did they know that a few short years from that time they would be returning in style and commanding five-star hotel suites in the country, a far cry from the sleazy joints that had been their introduction to America.

Whilst achieving notoriety in the USA for the ever-popular 'weed song,' the UK were awarding them with equal respect. On February 16th 1999, Placebo was delighted to find they were performing at the Brit Awards. Pure Morning had been nominated for the Best Single category, and the group also made an appearance with very special guest Mr David Bowie. Brian and David's voices harmonised for a show-stopping performance of Without You I'm Nothing.

Brian recalled the night as by far his most treasured memory. 'The two of us playing guitar and singing in harmony with each other – that was a real "Pinch me, I'm dreaming" situation. We weren't too bad – we were in the right key at least,' he said cheekily, 'but we could never really get the lyrics right.'

No-one could have anticipated a band as unconventional as Placebo at such a mainstream event, but sparks were flying on the night. This collaboration was clearly meant to be, and was set to repeat itself on Placebo's return to New York just a month later. Far from the altercations and hostilities of their previous Irving Plaza show, the audience were behind them 110%.

The new US tour was to be with Stabbing Westward and saw them targeting areas they'd never ventured into before – Cincinatti, Detroit, and the dreaded Utah (Salt Lake City) to name but a few. Yet again sparks flew in Boston, when Brian's guitar strap broke mid-song, leaving a shame-faced group to start all over again. Finally, Brian set the stage on fire during Pure Morning, by flicking a cigarette butt into the amplifier. 'Stop it!' Brian exclaimed helplessly as flames and a thick cloud of smoke rose from the stage. Despite almost killing his band mates and fans, Brian was able to see the funny side of it. As security doused the fire, Brian chimed in 'a friend with a fire extinguisher is better.' As a parting shot, Brian advised the expectant crowd 'Keep your sense of humour.' Whilst it wasn't quite the advice Bowie had offered to 'keep your spontaneity,' it was welcomed by this Boston audience.

Brian certainly had a lot to be smiling about, when he discovered his boyish brand of looks were captivating top models. Fuelled by certain class A unmentionables and an above average level of bravado, Brian claimed to Select magazine 'If you walk into a room and tell yourself "everyone wants to fuck me", everyone will want to fuck you.' He later winced 'I've discovered that's not true.' However, he had certainly had his moments.

At the Brits, he had been relentlessly pursued by British supermodel Caprice. Despite towering over Brian at almost 6ft tall, she took a liking to the rock-star, who reached her breasts. Making no secret of her unusual crush, she approached him at an after-show party where alcohol was flowing in abundance and inhibitions were discarded just as freely, to make her move.

Brian took up the story. 'It was very flattering. She came up to me and said, "I've heard a rumour about you, and please tell me that it's true." Basically, she'd become quite obsessed with a certain part of my anatomy; someone had told her – falsely, I add – that it measured in the double figures. It was like being chatted up by a 13-year-old girl; she spent the evening sitting in the corner with her mate, pointing and giggling behind her hand. And she's the archetypal beauty for men around the world! It was far more fulfilling to say no.'

He added 'The buzz I got from turning her down was far greater than the buzz I would have got from sleeping with her.' Perhaps puzzled that as one of the world's top models, she'd been turned down, Caprice withdrew with her tail between her legs. It was to be another feat of irony for the man who just couldn't get laid at college. It was an event that Brian vowed to place in his memoirs and even his autobiography should he decide to write one.

Placebo returned from the event to even better news – that new single Every You Every Me had achieved chart popularity, hitting Number 11. The video had a simple theme, depicting live shots from the group's show at Brixton Academy the previous year. These shots captured the pure, raw essence of what being at a Placebo show was all about. It also introduced a typical Placebo fan to the public. Showing countless elated faces in the audience – eyeliner and colourful flowers in hair all intact – it featured a lesbian couple kissing and cuddling to the sound of their favourite group and crowd-surfers making their way over the barrier.

However, a second version of the video had also been made. Placebo had received a request from the makers of blockbuster teen film Cruel Intentions, who were keen for Every You Every Me to appear on the soundtrack. Letting the press into the unusual decision-making process of whether their track should appear in the film, Brian revealed 'We watched it on the tour bus. I said "If he doesn't die in the end, if it's a happy ending, we don't do it." It's quite perverted and manipulative, so the theme of the song fits in quite well.'

A dark tale of sex and seduction adapted from the popular film Dangerous Liaisons, it might have been even better matched if Brian had had his way and the song had been named Heavy Metal Petting Zoo.

They accepted, subsequently causing some embarrassment to the ever-fickle Brian who now believed 'the film was actually quite shit.' However, the dark and confessional nature of the lyrics undoubtedly seemed to correspond with the twisted love triangle depicted in the film. Perhaps the sympathetic could see some of Brian's 'tart with a heart' persona in the outwardly cruel and inwardly torn Katie Holmes – it's difficult growing up. It achieved a multitude of publicity for the group and ultimately it was to be a decision neither party would regret.

Following its success, the band was inundated with invitations to perform the hit live on shows in Australia, France, the UK and many others. One of the most memorable of these appearances was TFI Friday, a British comedy, entertainment and music show that took place each Friday evening on C4. It was hosted by the controversial ginger-haired presenter Chris Evans. There was no love lost between the two, with Brian boldly declaring a year earlier, 'Chris Evans is a wanker and I will never go on his TV show!'

Remarkably, despite these harsh words, he agreed to take part – on the condition that the wardrobe department kitted him out with a 'Hypocrite' T-shirt. It had been a ploy to raise laughter, increase press attention and above all deflect criticism, denigrating himself before his enemies had the chance to get there first. The message spoke for itself, a cheeky invitation to accept him for who he was, or not at all.

'That way I pre-empted anyone slagging me off,' Brian confirmed. 'It was like I was saying "I'm fully aware of what I am."' Here came the punch line – 'It also went well with my designer skirt.'

Chris's people had a different story, claiming that he would only allow Brian on the show if he wore the aforementioned T-shirt. Whatever the truth, the show was on the lips of amused showbiz reporters and columnists for weeks.

Meanwhile the tour continued, benefitting from the new found popularity of the single, and exploring territories new. They performed their first ever gigs in Ireland including a show at Dublin Olympia on August 27th 1999 and a stint with David Bowie at the HQ Club on October 10th 1999. The audience were again supportive, displaying their loyalties in a unique way. 'Many have mascara-smudged the word "Fuck" on their foreheads, honouring a previous Molko scam,' reported the NME. 'Girls with tiaras and tall blokes in black camisoles are in happy accord, loving this opportunity to parade their style.'

Not everyone had warmed to the Placebo charm, however. The group had been scheduled to play at the Imola festival in Italy on June 20th 1999, but it quickly emerged that the programmer had made a tragic mistake. 'We were scheduled just before Metallica,' Brian revealed. 'See the problem yet? We did, when we stood onstage. Metallica fans want to see Metallica – we're far too gay for those people. We quickly changed the set list and skipped all the slow songs, but couldn't even get to play. We got fruit, beer and all sorts of things thrown at our heads.'

However Brian stubbornly refused to remove the melancholic Lady of the Flowers, and was pictured leaving the venue with a beam of untroubled defiance. The protective arm of his tour manager Steve Chapman reassured any nagging doubts the show had prompted in Brian's mind. Their look and sound was not for everyone, and perhaps not compatible with thousands of heavy metal fans in black lipstick, but they had enjoyed pushing the boundaries.

More boundaries were abused at their first show in Singapore, where local law forbids the impersonation of a female by a male. This did not bode well for Brian. However, he found a solution by kitting out the far more masculine Stefan in a bright red dress. Some might say it was an act of unforgivable disrespect, ego and arrogance, yet for Placebo their behaviour was justified. 'What we do doesn't actually stray into the world of drag, so in that case we're not actually breaking the law,' Brian said. 'What we represent is clothing freedom, basically, as opposed to putting on a wig and singing Judy Garland.'

Another unusual occurrence was that Luxembourg too had awakened to Placebo's charms. The band was invited for two shows, commencing on June 29th 1999. Yet far from a proud expat, for Brian it was payback time. Brian and Stefan had an opportunity to get their own back on the teachers that had 'ruined their lives' throughout their formative years. Any perceived humiliations were more than recompensed in kind, as security were instructed to eject their ex-teachers from the arena just as they had ejected the two from the classroom all those years ago on account of bad behaviour. That bad behaviour looked set to continue well into adult life. Brian noted 'It was that student-teacher relationship getting reversed – we sat them down and went "uh-uh-uh-uh!"' Brian smiled wryly, waggling his finger in a remonstrative gesture.

He also recalled his conversation with fellow ex-pupils less than fondly. They would chide 'You're all grown up now!' and Brian would respond 'Yeah, so fuck you!'

No-one from those days could have anticipated that Brian and Stefan would even be on speaking terms, let alone sharing a stage. Hitting back at their scorn, Brian said of his classmates 'I was obviously born to do this job. It makes me richer and more popular than those fuckers will ever be.'

Brian remained traumatised at the cruelty of his peers though. 'I still have nightmares about returning to school and repeating my final year,' he had once confessed. 'But it's great: I remember halfway through the dream I left college years ago, and walk around insulting everybody.'

Standing now before an audience of familiar faces at Luxembourg's local ice rink that evening, Brian was to perform and in doing so, regain the control he had lacked in his earlier days – those he thought he had left behind 12 years previously.

The show got off to a fast-paced and energetic start with the electric Scared of Girls. As he prepared to launch into a new song, Brian noticed the crowd chanting. 'It's not a football game,' he teased, his voice laced with sarcasm. 'It's not the Luxembourg Red Boys – it's a fucking gig, you know what I mean?' he had chided in an exaggerated Anglo-American accent with hints of Liam Gallagher.

His one moment of fury took place when he caught sight of an unauthorised bootlegger and gave an infuriated message to security, one that was all too clear.

'I've just spotted a bootlegger – he's over there. Turn the fucking tape off and surrender it!' Brian ordered security. As the audience screamed in hysterical approval, he continued his message to the unsuspecting public. 'You're not making money off my ass, baby!' he sneered. 'The only ones that make money off my ass are these two. So put it away, unless you want to leave without a head – and without a video camera!' With a sneer, he turned his back to the crowd and let security do their work.

He smirked, revelling in the new found power. It was Placebo versus Luxembourg and for once Placebo seemed to be winning. For Brian and Stefan it was definitely payback time, though they had also been busy enjoying introducing a virginal Steve to what they described as 'the wonders of Lux!'

Brian was in the mood for taking prisoners yet again that day when a disrespectful fan threw a shoe onto the stage mid-performance. Without skipping a beat, his face twisted into another sneer and his voice loaded with vitriolic sarcasm, Brian growled at the perpetrator. 'You won't be getting this back,' he taunted. 'See, we collect shoes. So you can hop home – and while you're hopping home, you can whistle this tune to yourself.' Thus it was with a smirk that he entered into Teenage Angst.

As climax neared, Brian ripped off his bright orange velvet shirt and dove into the audience, giving the crowd a very personal re-introduction of the boy they had incorrectly dismissed all those years ago as a nobody and a failure. His return had only reinforced to his followers that the stars around Brian burned brighter than ever.

The group then appeared at T in the Park, Scotland on July 11th 1999. Whilst their last experience there had left them fleeing with embarrassment, Brian was determined to show that he'd grown up. He was back with a different flavour. 'We won't blow it this time,' Brian assured the Sun, their former feud for the time being forgotten.

'The last time we were at T in the Park it was the worst day of our career. We didn't play well and the sound was terrible. Then the incident with the fan blew up. I don't even want to think about it. We're determined to give it our very best shot this time around,' the singer assured. They did, but – Brian being Brian – the show did not pass entirely without incident. Feeling the full force of Molko's acid tongue, he had retorted 'Sorry I'm late onstage' – which would have been more amusing had he in fact been tardy – 'but I was getting a blowjob from Gay Dad backstage. It's not just his music that sucks!'

Astonishingly, Cliff, the lead-singer of Gay Dad, was onstage later that day but made no mention of the barbed provocation. He had felt the full force of Molko's acid tongue, but told Melody Maker the next day that there were no hard feelings. 'People were saying that there's some kind of hate campaign between me and Brian Molko. Not at all. I think they're brilliant.' Continuing the good humour, he added 'All I can say is, "Brian, take your false teeth out!" He has false teeth. That's one of those showbiz secrets I'm not really supposed to divulge.' Finally, someone's sense of humour was on the same wave-length as Brian's tireless mischief.

Not everyone was so happy to bow down to the insults. This was demonstrated that festival season as Brian proceeded to insult an entire audience at Milton Keynes's Big Day Out on July 10th 1999. This time Brian sparked up a rather dull festival by reporting 'Sorry I'm late – I've just been backstage getting a blowjob off Marilyn Manson – he gives the best blowjob I've ever had!' Smirking girlishly about his 'pretty lips,' Brian was faced with a crowd whose jaws had visibly dropped. If that wasn't bad enough, he went on to dedicate Bruise Pristine to '18,000 crimes against fashion.' According to Brian, it took some time for the penny to drop. When it did, bottles of punters' urine were hurled at him, making rather more close contact than he would have liked. He completed the set in spite of a rising number of boos. Once again, poor Brian was attracting attention for all the wrong reasons.

His personal life was proving equally difficult after the singer began an ill-fated relationship with a French musician. The tall and glamorous Benedicte, an aspiring singer, was stunningly beautiful, and someone Brian would go on to describe as his ideal woman. However, trouble was afoot as the two rarely saw each other due to Brian's hectic promotional schedule. She lived in Paris, whilst Brian on the other hand had no emotional home. Even worse, the two were also reported to be competitive with each other – Benedicte craved the life of the stage too, later becoming the front woman of the mixed gender rock group Melatonin. Brian admitted to being 'elatedly happy' in love, but increasingly struggled to fit the other complicated elements of his life around it. His relationship, sadly, was failing.

He consoled himself by developing a close friendship with unlikely companion Marilyn Manson, also known as Brian Warner. He famously accompanied him to Camden based fetish club the Torture Garden, to 'freak out some Goths.' Little and large, the two Brians seemed to get on exceedingly well. They shared a similar sense of perverse humour and Marilyn returned Brian's blowjob jokes with the same rumours in kind. Responding to these claims, Brian chuckled to Kerrang 'I don't know about that, but I do come up to his waist!'

Brian told Melody Maker that he appreciated Manson's Machiavellian tendencies and his ability to successfully manipulate the press. The singer's innate sense of ruthlessness also appealed to him. 'If he insults you in public, it's an expression of approval and affection. He's got this reverse humour thing which I find hilarious,' Brian enthused.

Another event which perhaps aided in warming Brian's wounded heart was a Belgian festival that saw him perform with REM. 'It was the end of the world this year, the Nostradamus one,' Brian recalled, referring to superstitious and unsubstantiated claims that the world would end on a specific date and time that year.

'I tell Michael Stipe this and he's like "Great, man – it gives me a new way of introducing the song tonight." So just before [REM song] End of the World, Michael said "I was talking to Brian from Placebo, and he informed me it was the end of the world today. Are you listening, Brian? Did we fucking make it or what?" My heart was glowing,' revealed Brian. Cheekily, he claimed he was not so bothered about the end of the world if it meant that he didn't have to play the gig. Shockingly, he got away with his brazen honesty.

Both the small-town ambience of Luxembourg and the huge festivals of mainland Europe were long forgotten as Brian found himself in a recording studio putting the finishing touches to the new single, Without You I'm Nothing. On this occasion however, the group had secured a recording slot with David Bowie. The hugely successful collaboration between the band and Bowie had been appreciated enormously at the Brit Awards and working together to develop it into a song now seemed not just an ideal, but a necessity.

The single, due for release on August 16th 1999, was to feature the twosome harmonising yet again, plus a variety of remixes of the song. Stefan was elated recalling watching Bowie perform his vocals from behind the glass screen and thinking 'Fuck, that's Bowie!' He added 'It was magical. I can't say it's a dream come true because I'd never even dreamt it, but after the fact, I must admit it was one of the most thrilling and unforgettable moments of my life.' The track was to appear on gay soap Queer as Folk in the UK, yet another validation for the group.

'We're going to lock Bowie's wife in the boot of a car and confiscate all his cigarettes until he does a vocal for us,' Brian had cackled years earlier. Whilst no one could promise such foul play had not taken place, Bowie's eagerness about the group spoke for itself.

Brian jokingly told Cream magazine of a second collaboration between the two that no-one had quite been aware of. 'He wrote the song Little Wonder after me. He wanted to call it Little Wanker but he changed it because he didn't want to offend me.'

Whilst Without You I'm Nothing would achieve only moderate success, reaching Number 79 in the UK charts, it immortalised a successful partnership. It was an auditory souvenir of a great friendship, and Brian and Bowie were to be allies for life.

Meanwhile, the tour was slowly winding down and coming to an end. After a whirlwind of success, a spate of chaotic travelling and a fulfilled goal of spreading the Placebo message worldwide, fans could have been forgiven for believing that they'd reached a level of utopia.

However, like any good rollercoaster, the climax was dizzying and ultimately sickening. What was once pleasantly chaotic became relentlessly tiring and the cracks of a highly pressurised year were already beginning to show.

The pressures of the tour had brought both pain and pleasure in equal measures. For every hedonistic high was its corresponding tragic low. Televisions were flying out of hotel room windows and Molko confesses to 'ashtrays finding their way to reception via the lift.'

Pure Morning had reached Number two in the charts in South Africa and a mammoth tour with Garbage and Orgy was planned to celebrate. However, the exhausted group was in no mood to rise to the occasion. During this tour, bassist Stefan had fallen off the stage and broken his wrist and Brian, by now heavily sedated due to worsening insomnia, had fallen asleep for 14 hours in a crippling position. Far from being concerned about his ability to play that night, Stefan was consumed by the personal consequences, sighing 'It's the hand I fondle my tool with.' Meanwhile, Brian woke up with compressed vertebrae in his neck and found the slightest movement near impossible.

With one band member's wrist in a sling and another unable to move his head, the group was in trouble. At a loss for what to do, they began to take out the anger, fatigue and frustration on the audience. Brian's big mouth became larger than ever as the pressure intensified, and music industry workers were left aghast at queries of whether they had given blowjobs to reach their coveted positions and if so, how many.

Moments like these had culminated in disaster many times before, such as when Brian appeared onstage in Australia declaring 'I hate this fucking place and I'm never coming back!' As with all hysteria, it reached moments of hilarity as well, with Brian once grabbing an audience member's mobile phone and mercilessly goading the unfortunate caller, courtesy of the fact that he happened to be named Archie. His candid honesty and child-like temper raised some smiles among the grimaces.

However it did little to quell the feverish anticipation of a growing number of Placebo fans across the ocean that were compelled by his gigs and craved more. With all five continents getting their fix of Placebo, it had to be at some cost.

The V festival was the band's final show of 1999, but for Brian it was not to be. Just hours before his scheduled appearance, doctors ordered him to cancel over fears that his voice would not last the session. It would be the first cancellation ever for the band. The poorly singer was hospitalised with severe tonsillitis, which left him fed by a drip and unable to swallow.

Unfortunately for Placebo, they were replaced at short notice by Kula Shaker, who had come up against the group in a Battle of the Bands for unsigned acts in 1995, which saw a tiebreak between all three participating hopefuls. The group had announced 'Sorry Placebo fans, but Brian Molko has gone for a very long wank!'

Deeply disappointed by ending up in the emergency room, Brian issued a repentant press statement. It claimed 'I would like to personally apologise. I have contracted a severe case of tonsillitis and if there was anything that I could do to get myself well and get up on stage I would. Unfortunately, the golf balls I have grown in my throat appear to be stronger than my resolve. If it's any consolation I am very depressed about not being able to see James Brown for two nights in a row. We promise somehow to make it up to you. Be sure to wrap up well and wear a scarf at all times. All my love. Brian Molko.'

Whilst devastated at missing the show, he was simply unable to make it. It was time for the group to say goodbye, recharge their batteries, and anticipate the next moment of glory to the tune of a thousand fading screams.

Chapter 5.

'The road to excess leads to the palace of wisdom – for we never know what is enough until we know what is more than enough' – William Blake.

Live at Reading Festival just 12 months later, Placebo was back with a vengeance. 'Our thoughts compressed, which makes us blessed, and makes for stormy weather,' Brian sang.

As if on cue, the heavens opened, and a thunderclap sounded – God playing his giant amplifier in the sky as a signature of authoritative approval. Brian's ultra-religious mother would surely have approved.

Yet religious experiences were the last thing on Brian's mind. The front-man gazed out over his audience petulantly, arms outstretched and pointed skywards as the rain descended. The downpour spelt relief for the crowd of dishevelled and feverish onlookers in their masses. The fever had finally broken.

The tone of the performance was a million miles away from the chaos of the Without You I'm Nothing tour, which had ended with Brian on a drip in hospital with 'pus being dragged from my tonsils with six-inch needles.' It had been an eye watering experience, and one that came with guilt as the band had never missed a show prior to that date.

After months of falling out of every showbiz party, pallid skin and ferocious acne mirroring his poor inner health, it was time for one serious rescue mission. The singer had been abusing his sanity without reservation to keep up with his party lifestyle and the experience at the V Festival had been the last straw. Teetering at the metaphorical cliff edge, the troubled singer had finally chosen life.

Determined not to let history repeat itself a second time, he began the long road to recovery. The singer was formally off the guest list.

The newly matriarchal Brian began to cluck in the press like a harassed mother about the virtues of wrapping up warmly – he didn't want his fans to go through the agonising pain of tonsillitis that he had.

Desperate to settle down and develop roots, he had purchased an accommodation in East London, much to the despondency of the owner of Notting Hill's Market Bar, who insisted that Brian was one of his best and most frequent customers. According to rumour, Brian's drinking habits could make or break the pub economy, rather like songstress Amy Winehouse's recession-defying binges at the Hawley Arms in Camden. Brian was keen to distance himself from that reputation, and instead ensconced himself in his new home.

Finally having a permanent place to decorate and call home had grounded Brian. If he was honest, he thrived on the gritty atmosphere and urbanite creativity of the east end and it was an area he quickly warmed to. Despite that, he largely resisted the temptation of wild nights out. Would his new home keep him out of mischief? Only time would tell.

The equally docile Stefan had taken to sanding his own floorboards during the group's time off – far from the decadent parties of the past. Placebo had temporarily become very respectable – even, some might say, boring.

It wasn't a charge that concerned the front-man much. Rather, he felt it was time to end his relationship with the press altogether.

His desire to escape the 'media circus' and pass through London unobserved led Brian to make drastic changes in his appearance. He adopted a short haircut, grew an uncharacteristic beard and barely wore makeup at all. His jet black mane, the product of regular trips to the hairdresser, had faded to a more sedate brown. He was truly incognito, blending in with the capital city crowds and looking almost normal.

There was another reason for his desire to blend in – he had offended everyone from small town Britain to Midwest America and journalists around the world had voiced the desire of those around them to give Brian a slap. This had translated into real life violence on many occasions. 'We just got sick of running into the same people and hangovers and getting into fights. People were trying to beat us up on a regular basis.' He added, perhaps a little untruthfully, 'I really don't know why.'

'People were mistaking clones for me. These poor kids came close to getting a riotous beating,' the singer grimaced. However, due to his new appearance, Brian no longer faced any such threat. He had once shared an underground train with a gathering of unsuspecting goths who were on the way to a metal festival but escaped without injury by over-zealous admirers. 'I was able to pass through incognito because I simply wasn't pale enough,' Brian laughed, relishing his golden brown tan, the signature of a recent holiday in Nice. 'They'd look at me, think "Is he?" then decide, "No, it can't be, not with that tan."' Brian simply chuckled silently at the irony, and turned away.

As much as he'd enjoyed a blissful break, it was soon time to go back into the studio. After rest and recreation, the group locked themselves in rooms with no windows and just the news channel CNN for company, determined to create the perfect third album.

Unlike previous clashes with 'arrogant' producers, there was a calmer relationship with Paul Corkett, a fellow insomniac who was happy to take a back seat to Brian's invincible ego. 'It's like Paul has no ego, which is quite incredible, and we have three huge ones, so he balanced things out!' Brian chuckled. 'He became our friend, collaborator and partner in crime.'

To add to the sense of calm, Brian's relationship with Benedicte was slowly improving too – despite occasional arguments, a permanent relationship was a stabilising influence for him. He was now firmly off the radar where one-night-stands were concerned and had also developed a great sense of self-respect for someone who had once considered himself a body to be objectified.

Even studio time had become a strife-free vacation for the band. It was a luxury that the three thoroughly appreciated. 'You need to take a break from time to time to sellotape your brain cells together,' Brian remarked in conversation with Kerrang. 'For a while we became cartoon characters and we needed to become normal people again. You need to be able to get back to normality so that when the time is right you can be a proper rock-star again.'

As well as turning down groupies, all three were entertaining themselves by playing ping-pong. To fans of their previously hardcore lifestyle, this was horrifying news, tantamount to hearing that they'd spent time in the local bingo hall with a gathering of pensioners.

The change wasn't mere speculation, either – Brian's new lifestyle seemed to be real. Disbelieving fans learnt via a letter in FHM magazine that Brian did in fact 'turn down shags.' A group of girls who had spent time with the band backstage were to be disappointed, describing Brian as disinterested and uncommunicative. Whilst Steve had played a game of the band's beloved ping-pong with the girls, Brian had allegedly been 'moody' and, declining all offers of extra-curricular fun, had simply retired early to bed.

Finally, if journalists caught a cunning glimpse of Brian popping pills, they would also be disappointed to learn that vitamins were his new drug of choice and that he was more likely to be sampling herbal remedies than speed capsules. He had also begun to supplement his diet with spoonfuls of vinegar – a foul tasting instant remedy for hangovers and voice failure. Class A substances were banned from the studio and the tour after Brian and Steve had a huge argument over which one of them had stolen cheese from the refrigerator. It prompted them both to put a little more water in their wine.

During the studio time, there was just one big party – to celebrate the birthday of Skunk Anansie drummer Mark Richardson. This provided a rude awakening that the group's capabilities in the partying area were not as great as they had once been. 'We partied like it was 1997,' Brian reminicised. 'None of us made it into the studio the next day. Me and Steve looked at each other, and went "Oh shit. The party's over, isn't it? Fuck!" The old habits reared their ugly heads, but we're pushing 30 now.'

It was a surprisingly clean-living Placebo that had descended on the recording studio that year, faces glowing with golden tans, ready to create the 13-title CD that was Black Market Music.

'We christened Black Market Music in an ode to bootleggers. We know our fucking album'll be straight on the Internet,' Brian had groaned.

Describing it as forbidden fruit from the tree of knowledge, he suggested an illicit vibe to the CD, one of 'something that should be kept under the counter.' However, the name had not been their first choice. 'It was a toss-up between Haemoglobin and Black Market Music, but we didn't want American DJs to go "This is Place-bo with their new album Homo-goblin and the first single Tasting Men"' he grimaced.

The new album featured dark and angry moments but benefitted from a less egocentric perspective and, in direct contrast to the hugely popular Without You I'm Nothing, looked not inwards but to the outside world for inspiration. Taking a break from what he deemed to be self-indulgent navel-gazing, Brian began to look to a whole new musical style. Even in the throes of success, the band was refusing to adhere to their tried and tested formula.

The subject matter was equally diverse. 'It's quite a dark record on a lyrical level. It's still about falling in love, there's quite a lot of religious imagery and a smattering of politics.' If the first album was about sex, and the second about love mixed with post-coital depression, the third was all three of these and yet much more.

Perhaps unusually, Brian turned predominantly to his political beliefs for linguistic lubrication. A fervent supporter of old-Labour policy, the singer was passionately inspired by political happenings during their time in the studio.

As a result of over-exposure to CNN and the daily broadsheet newspapers

– their only contact with the outside world during intensely focused studio time – they read about the anti-capitalist May Day riots. What had started as a demonstration against the war, with a festival like atmosphere, had quickly turned destructive. An alleged £50,000 of damage was caused in McDonalds, as rioters rampaged through Trafalgar Square. Windows were smashed and local residents' cars broken into.

The formerly peaceful protest descended into utter chaos, requiring an expanded police operation at a cost of £1 million. Those who were not fans of cheap fast-food eateries might say that destroying McDonalds was an excellent choice, or even a stroke of genius, but the police's attitude was one of far less tolerance. It saw several receiving jail sentences for the violence, including – ironically – an Eton public schoolboy turned activist. This appealed to Brian, possibly because the boy's privileged background was not unlike that of his own, making his rebellion that bit more surprising.

To him, the crowd's actions were far from mindless destruction – they had a specific message to convey. The plinth of Winston Churchill's statue was daubed with anarchy symbols and graffiti, screaming the words 'Reclaim the streets.' Brian was delighted that the youth were asserting their rights, but it was this slogan that captured his attention most avidly. He began running through the studio, declaring 'Dope, guns, fucking in the streets!' in reminiscence of the old adage by White Panther. Someone in the studio, rumoured to be Brian's then girlfriend, remarked 'That's your chorus!' and a new song was born.

The song in question was Spite and Malice. 'You opened up the papers and saw that green Mohican painted on Winston Churchill's statue and it was brilliant. I would have loved to have gone down to the police station where the guy that did that was held, bailed him out and shook him by the hand and said "Well done, motherfucker!" That was so inspiring.'

Whilst Brian was safely holed away in the studio and unable to rescue courageous protesters, he did manage to write Spite and Malice in honour of the movement. This lesser action probably caused his mother to breathe a huge sigh of relief.

'It's like the Public Image Ltd song Rise,' Brian elaborated. '"Anger is an energy." As you approach your 30s you start to look around and get more interested in politics and the world makes you angry. We've still got heartbreaking love songs on the album and full-on old school Placebo punk but rock is getting extremely pedestrian. I think kids are gagging for albums that will piss their parents off again. John Lydon said that rock music is about creating generation gaps and we believe in that. There's still so much to get angry about.'

Unfortunately, despite a passionate slogan and no shortage of anger, there was a creative block and a black hole in the vocals where the chorus should be. Determined to deliver something extra special, Brian called in legendary friend and acclaimed rapper Justin Warfield of One Inch Punch. It wasn't the first time the two had worked together, with Justin previously creating a remix of Bruise Pristine. Delighted with the result, Brian was confident that Justin could provide just the right vocals.

Fans of the band reacted with confusion on learning that a song was to feature not only Brian rapping, but a special guest direct from the genre. A past fracas with Limp Bizkit at New York's Irving Plaza had left Brian with distaste for a lot of rap music, dismissing it as having a 'negative sports-metal vibe.' He believed Korn and Limp Bizkit were in this category, bravely declaring that not only did they incite violence but that they were boring.

'I find that kind of music extremely negative, homophobic and chauvinistic,' he said. 'We've dealt with difficult emotional issues and intense emotions, but there's always been a strain of positively and optimism within that, which those bands lack, really. Also our music has a variation, whereas Korn, Limp Bizkit and Kid Rock are extremely repetitive. I find it gets a bit boring after two songs.'

His suspicion about the negativity of these acts was proved dramatically correct when a girl was killed in a stampede during Limp Bizkit's show at Roskilde Festival on June 30th 2000. Onlookers claimed that Durst had incited the crowd's violence and refused to call a halt to the set when audience safety had become compromised. This culminated in several injuries and the trampling to death of a teenage girl by an increasingly aggressive crowd. Even more tragically, she happened to be a fan of the rapper many believed to be responsible for her passing. To add insult to injury, the parents of the deceased teenager then claimed in the press that Durst had offered to attend the funeral and help with costs but had provided a fake telephone number. Whatever the truth might have been, it infuriated those who believed he had abused his authority and ignored opportunities to diffuse the violence.

Brian wanted to convey that rap music could channel aggression positively. He wanted Spite and Malice to stand for anarchy, individuality, human rights and peaceful protest – far from aggression for its own sake. He also wanted it to contribute to the war against homophobia and, despite Justin's deceptively masculine appearance, that was one cause he was very happy to represent. He consequently jetted in from LA to put the finishing touches on the song. The love between them was clear even years on, with Justin declaring passionately on his Twitter account 'When Placebo is on, I believe them to be untouchable.'

Back at Reading Festival that year, Justin had joined the group on stage to pair his resident rap tones with Brian's contrastingly feminine vocals. Defying those who stereotyped him as a macho man, he also visibly engaged in some playful onstage flirting with Stefan. From the audience's roars of approval, it seemed that taking a sonic chance had truly paid off for Placebo.

What's more, it wasn't the only politically themed rhyme to pack a punch on the new CD. Haemoglobin, possibly one of the most alternative and least accessible in sound and content, became a firm favourite nonetheless. Declaring Billie Holiday as the 'best singer of the 20th century' it was natural that Brian should choose to portray a version of her song Strange Fruit. Her tragic tale dealt with the plight of lynched slaves hanging from the trees in America.

As Brian's version was not autobiographical, unless metaphorically so, he did come under fire for his courageousness and audacity in feigning understanding of something he could have no personal knowledge of.

However, to Brian, the challenge was worth the backlash. The song invites the listener inside the mind of a black man in the deep South awaiting his fate. 'Where Billie's walking around observing fruit [dead slaves] hanging from the trees, we've actually placed you inside the man's head,' Brian explained. 'It starts off with him hanging from a tree – he's in a state of resignation. In the second verse, he gets cut down and that resignation turns into confusion. And by the third verse, that confusion has turned into anger and a lust for revenge. It's a simple moral thing, prejudice breeds prejudice and violence breeds violence. We started this band in our early 20s and now we're getting towards our 30s and you look at the world around you a bit more. And it touches you, what people are prepared to do to each other for religion, for land. Violence still exists. There's a war every day, people getting murdered every day. If you watch the news, you get affected by that.'

More broadly speaking, the message hits out at mindless intolerance in all its forms. It could refer to homophobia, bullying or jealousy and points at how – in the race for survival – the mind of a victim can all too easily become the mind of a killer. Above all, the message is abhorrence of mindless intolerance in each and every form.

Passionately condemning slavery, injustice, organised religion and above all humanity itself, Blue American first took shape during a troubled moment at home when Brian was playing his acoustic guitar. He had been watching a documentary on the trials and tribulations of first-time authors struggling to get an elusive publishing deal. It was at this moment that he created the line 'I wrote this novel just for you, I'm so pretentious, yes it's true' which Brian described as an attempt to insult himself before his detractors could get there first.

The irony was not appreciated by Guardian music critic Caroline Sullivan who chided after a live performance of the song 'Eventually he speaks. "This is a song about a sub-species called Americans," he says in his apple pie East Coast accent – no I don't get the logic either.' However, the 4,000 fans at London's Brixton Academy clearly seemed to and the show went on.

Best described as '3.5 minutes of pure self-disgust American style,' the buoyant sounding melody was miles away from the depression and self-resentment that inspired it. Astonishingly self-deprecating, Brian explained 'The person in the song is at such a low point in his life emotionally that he's started to hit out at everything that is a part of him. He's attacking his parents, his culture, his culture's history, self-help, psychiatry. It was written when I wasn't in a particularly good mood.'

He continued 'The person is … just disgusted by the fact that he is a human being, a human species, which is the most destructive on this planet, and everything he touches turns into garbage – war, violence and garbage. The person in the song is hitting out at his culture and the fact his country could be responsible for racism and cruelty.'

Thematically it is similar to Allergic – covering the arrogance of the human race's penchant for self-destruction. Brian expanded 'Human beings are the only species on this earth who turn everything they touch to junk. I find Darwin's theory of evolution very interesting, that all other species adapt to their environment and human beings are the only ones that have adapted their environment to them. Therefore we are the most selfish species living on this planet. I think that since this interview began there must be at least two or three species that no longer exist.'

Brian had no shortage of anger this time around. Yet veering away from the political side of things, Peeping Tom has a personal touch reminiscent of the Without You I'm Nothing album. Brian portrays a lonely character who spies on the object of his affections through binoculars while she undresses. He invites us into this person's world, encouraging a sympathetic view of a pervert. Spying on the one he loves is the only way that he knows how to express his love.

'When it comes to human emotion, I firmly believe that nothing is black and white,' Brian remarked. He empathises with the character's humanity and innate wretchedness, believing that it does not necessarily make him evil. Instead of reacting with anger or disgust to this character's deviations, he looks inside his mind and discovers that in spite of all his failings, he too is merely human – and inherently fallible.

'I try to place the listener inside the emotions of the voyeur himself and try to portray the character in a sympathetic manner – to show the love he has for the person he spies on,' Brian continued. 'I look at the fact that this person is the only ray of light that exists in the voyeur's life.'

He was at pains to point out that he was not the character in the song. Yet should we assume that Brian himself is a pervert? 'Haha!' Brian chuckled. 'In every reputation there's a grain of truth – a tender pervert perhaps.'

Subversively, the song encourages listeners to come face to face with all that they despise. Like a paedophile, a voyeur is ostracised from society, and can be tragically misunderstood. An American news article recalled a particularly brutal vigilante attack on a paediatrician – a customer had mistaken his job title, proudly displayed on the wall, as a reference to paedophilia and promptly shot him dead. Conversely, Peeping Tom encourages an open mind into the whys and wherefores, and the healing of a pervert.

The theme of voyeurism could also work on another level, investigating not only how Brian is perceived in the media, but also the public's unrestrained appetite for sleaze. Why do fans have the voyeuristic urge to peep into someone else's mind frame in an interview? Why is the world discontent with letting the music speak for itself?

For someone who has claimed that a live show is worth a thousand interviews, this song could encapsulate precisely the feelings that Brian has towards the press. Beyond that message, the song is filled with an universally relatable pathos and sadness, and features a haunting piano melody that was Brian's own creation.

The front-man had begged Stefan to teach him the instrument, but found himself disappointed at his refusal. The bassist instead insisted that Brian must find his own style – and consequently the song was borne out of an experimentation that was uniquely his own.

Meanwhile, Blackeyed is a return to autobiographical style, reaching away from political anger to exorcise a different kind of anger – that of Brian towards his parents.

He had shared a fraught and faltering relationship with his family most of his life and the frustration had to come out. Venting his sorrow at hailing from a broken home, Brian echoed the beliefs of self-help author Oliver James on parents – put simply, 'They fuck you up.'

Talking to Alternative Press, Brian grimaced 'My dad tried to dissuade me from pursuing artistic endeavours. He ignored me for most of my life, and then wanted to be my friend when success came along. He studies the songs more and I think he probably gets the message.'

Slave to the Wage is a Bob Dylan inspired number, offering a message in no uncertain terms about the pitfalls of the rat race. It encourages listeners to chase their dreams and not become another cog in the giant wheel.

'If you want to work in a bank and that gives you a hard-on, go and work in a bank. But if that's not what gives you a hard-on, don't be afraid to explore what you want,' Brian asserted. Whilst it's slightly bizarre to suggest that any job should be sexually arousing, his message is clear.

Yet he had never had a conventional job aside from shredding paper in an office one summer, the monotony of which had prompted repeated masturbation sessions in the staff toilet. Critically speaking, he had never been caught in the rat race, searching for a far away freedom - what knowledge did he have to tell others how to avoid it?

However he has had his own demons to confront. Stereotyped as a lazy rich kid, he also had more experience of the working world than his critics might give him credit for. Coming from a privileged yet unhappy background, he felt pressurised to gain a socially acceptable job. With a deeply religious mother and a workaholic banker father, there was no question in either's minds as to how Brian would turn out. Yet he was unhappy with the prospect of following that path.

Having witnessed his brother fall into a conventional, materialistically blessed yet very unfulfilling role as banker, the artistic young man was determined to do something different. He'd witnessed his family falling apart, and had first hand experience of the loneliness of flitting from one city to another in the name of his father's work. Indeed, the past continued to plague him even in his adult life, with terrifying nightmares of childhood haunting him to this day. He faced the oppression and indifference of loved ones towards his endeavours and broke the mould in spite of it all. Being forced into two incompatible directions had enabled him to forge his own identity.

This song had a profound effect on its listeners. On the Black Market Music tour, those who had grown equally tired of the rat race arrived at after-shows, telling Brian they had found the courage to seek a different job as a result of his words. Meanwhile Brian is still breathing a huge sigh of relief that he waved goodbye to his early days as a lowly shredder.

In the next song, Passive Aggressive confronts Brian's feelings about God and turns against the religious side of his background. The song hints at mental disorder and explores dichotomous states within it, roaring 'It's your fault that God's in crisis, fuck him, he's over.' The paradoxical title is complemented by the sound, with a gentle start and a dramatic crashing chorus. Lyrically it begins with depression, despair and inertia, yet it culminates by rising into pure anger and venom, making it truly worthy of the duality of the title.

Commercial for Levi continues the theme of more complementing differences. Would Levi's sue? No, the song marks the honour of the longstanding Placebo sound technician of the same name and the day he saved Brian's life.

One night the singer had been enjoying a meal in a restaurant prior to a forthcoming show in Milan. Unsurprisingly, he was drunk throughout and had at one point jumped onto the dinner table, making the shame-faced crew very relieved when it was time for them to leave. Some in his party had shuddered in embarrassment, exclaiming that the concert had not even begun yet.

The scene bore an uncanny resemblance to the aptly named Italian painting Feast in the House of Levi by Paolo Veronese, featuring a hedonistic drunkard and some dwarfs at the dinner table.

If the crew had hoped leaving would diffuse the tension, they were sorely mistaken as, upon leaving the restaurant, Brian's antics only intensified. Spying some fans, he leapt atop a Fiat Uno car and launched into a drunken rendition of Nancy Boy. 'It all breaks down at the role reversal,' shrieked Brian, oblivious to the crowd of puzzled onlookers, the shocked stares of the fans, and – even worse – the owner of the car, who was approaching fast.

He waved his keys angrily, prompting Brian to run into the street to make a quick getaway. As he dashed between two parked cars, Levi pulled him to safety just before he fled into the path of a fast approaching vehicle.

Narrowly escaping death was a profound experience for Brian and one for which he remained ever grateful. 'If I was a Samurai, I would have to follow him around for the rest of my life and take care of him until I saved his life,' observed Brian of the ancient Japanese tradition. 'But my little payback for that is to put his name in a song.'

As well as a touching sonnet to the man who saved him from almost certain death, the song is also a cautionary tale of the dangers of metaphorical death. It features a blend of lyrical filth and melodic innocence, as it plays out its warning not to be seduced by the perils of excess.

Tales of 'spunk and bestiality' curiously accompany an almost childlike melody, which resembles a built-in lullaby for an infant's toy, in classically confusing Placebo style. Ultimately, the tell-tale story gives thanks not just to Levi but to all those in his life who saved him from falling from the metaphorical cliff-edge.

The remainder of the album features themes of love. 'It's about relationships that reach that point of familiarity breeding contempt,' Brian said of Narcoleptic, which deals with the all-consuming cocoon withdrawn into during a love affair.

Meanwhile Special K captures the chemical rush and elation characteristic of falling in love. It captures the feeling of 'looking across a crowded room, falling hopelessly in love in one second and knowing that your life will never be the same again.' The theme seems strangely optimistic for a man who used to preach the impossibility of love.

However, as with any Placebo song there is a twist, and if you were looking for the downer, you wouldn't be disappointed. There is indeed a comedown, a brutal falling to the floor after love has run its course, because 'what goes up must come down.' There is also a drug element, comparing the rush of illicit substances with the rush of being 'head over heels in love.'

The song was said to be inspired by Brian's turbulent on-off relationship with girlfriend Benedicte, whose presence had caused Brian to 'fall in and out of love ad nauseum' since their earliest days together. The pain of stormy break-up was brought to life and partly exorcised in that song.

What better way to convey all of this than with references to the drug ketamine? It served as both a horse tranquiliser in modern medicine and – back in the 1950s – as a drug for astronauts embarking on space journeys. It was used in the latter to create an illusion of anti-gravity. As a recreational drug however, it could spell trouble. It cripples the bladder muscles over time, leading in extreme cases to permanent incontinence. The street name for this rather unpleasant drug – Special K – became the title of the song.

Brian's greatest concern over the meaning was that it should be associated with Corn Flakes. Fans shaking boxes of Special K cereal in time to the music became a regularity in the front row of some of his shows. 'It's not about a breakfast cereal,' Brian blushed. 'In our recording studio we had a mascot – a box of Special K. I left it there one morning on a desktop and it stayed until the end of recordings.' As for the drug, whilst Brian had taken it once in his college days, his thoughts on it were widely documented – 'Never again!'

Days Before You Came is another intense but ill-fated love song. It mimics the Abba song Day Before You Came, although the subject matter is much less cheerful. It explores the concept that 'love and drugs are one big pillow' and that listeners can anaesthetise themselves with both, becoming dangerously dependent.

Finally, Taste in Men became the group's first single. Initially an electronic dance track intended to confuse those who thought they had pigeon-holed the Placebo sound, it gradually took on a new guise and became more than anyone in the group could have imagined. During the studio time, the group had excluded themselves from almost all musical influences, with the exception of one – NIN. Listening avidly to 'Wish', Brian sought to make Taste in Men 'that nasty, that unlistenable.'

Lyrically, it centres around the pain of obsession, loss and unrequited love.

Mirroring the intensity of a jilted lover in desperation to win back his or her partner at all costs, it describes that emotion with a throbbing bass-line. Brian recollected 'The person is suffering from obsessional pining and feelings of torment – the kind that follows you from the moment you wave up to the very moment you go to sleep. It's ever-present, it's right in your face and it affects your ability to function or do anything properly. It's a kind of pain that absorbs every aspect of your personality and every molecule in your body and the person is so desperate that they are willing to do anything possible or change themselves in any way to win this person back. Sonically I think the sound reflects that pain.'

This is the song that claimed the most attention in the subsequent press campaign – and not all of it good. 'It's deadly boring,' one fan complained in the Melody Maker. Not to be dissuaded, Brian hit back, claiming that the negative press from both her and four other featured fans was 'a fix.' Yet for Black Market Music, the backlash was just beginning.

A third album is a critical make or break time for most artists and Placebo was receiving more mixed reactions than most. Why did so many people dislike Placebo? Was it, as journalist Sylvia Patterson reported in the group's first full-length interview to publicise the new album, because Brian is 'an unlikable twerp with a paranoia complex?' Or was it merely the band's uncompromising attitude to honesty that had everyone's feathers so ruffled?

The passage of time hadn't curbed Brian's acid tongue, and on his comeback he was prepared to be as unapologetically frank as ever. As just one example, the singer wasted no time in devising his own personal 'shit list' live on German TV. With the mischievous grin for which he is renowned, only ever leading to mayhem, he unveiled the top five Placebo pet hates. These included Phil Collins, Sting, Simply Red, the Backstreet Boys, 'because they can't have it their own way' and last but not least Limp Bizkit. Whilst their fans shared the mirth, some new and perhaps more conservative listeners were taken aback. During the same TV show, Brian proceeded to strike the interviewer playfully with a sword, chiding 'Merry fucking Christmas!' when he asked for a gift.

During the remainder of the interview, the group took the opportunity to let loose some 'dirty German words' with the exception of Steve who joked that he 'could barely speak English.'

So that was Placebo – knowingly offensive, unshrinkingly unapologetic in the face of criticism and tenacious in their refusal to paint a saccharine sweet appearance for the benefit of political correctness. They'd rather whip out a crack-pipe in public than lie about doing so. Indeed, they're not for everyone. But for the fans who chose to partake, the experience was of a drug that they would never forget.

Journalist Sylvia Patterson, on the other hand, didn't like Brian one little bit. NME published a front-page feature to coincide with the release of first single Taste in Men on July 16th 2000. The article claimed that Brian had 'pinned NME to the wall with one glassy eyeball entirely filled with hate.' Ironically, the claim followed a statement by Brian saying that was not enough love left in the world. The article attacked his male-pattern baldness, dug up rumours that one-hit wonder indie brats Daphne and Celeste had declared him 'ugly into the realm of the beast,' and alleged that the front-man was 'paranoid and delusional to the point of mental illness,' – unfortunately for Brian, not once did it mention thoughts on the new album.

Fans were left unaware of what it contained, though they now had a far more intimate knowledge of the back of Brian's head. In fact, the persistence of referring to his hair was to catch on, leading Brian to demand that subsequent interviewers avoided the subject altogether. Radio DJ Ewan McLeod recalled 'I was warned that if I mentioned his hair then our interview would be terminated at once.'

Patterson also claimed that Brian was 'programmed to dismiss, to patronise, to bully and to misinterpret, in as rude a fashion as he can muster.'

She criticised him for believing he was subversive in a climate where multi-million selling boy bands openly declare themselves to be gay. She also appeared to condemn homosexuality, stating that for homosexuals to have different rights to their heterosexual counterparts was 'exactly how it should be.' However, one had to question, if the NME felt that vehemently about Brian's impotency in the musical world, what the validity was of placing him on the front cover.

The publication, like many others, thrived on sensationalism, and Brian's disarming honesty alongside Patterson's barely disguised hatred for the singer provided that for both parties. NME certainly sold a good deal of copies that week.

As the critical third album's release date approached, it simply became fashionable to despise Brian Molko. It wasn't exactly the start the singer might have hoped for. However, remaining undeterred by the hate campaign that surrounded them, the band embarked on their UK tour. It would coincide with the album's release on October 9th 2000. A friend of Brian's from Goldsmiths College contributed to the visual projections onstage and the two worked closely with one another to create an amosphere that they felt embodied the subversive nature of the songs.

What ensued was dark, intense and not for the faint-hearted. Yearbook photographs of the band and their Luxembourg classmates flashed up onscreen during Blackeyed, with unsettling and subversive slogans on them. These included 'Daddy is my lover,' and 'Mommy smokes crack.' It was hard to say whether these slogans were matched to pictures of particular people for a reason or if it was a random association. Rumour had it that they referred to real-life drug and incest scenarios affecting his school pals. Stefan's photograph aptly said 'Most likely to be gay,' whilst Brian took responsibility for the most sinister slogan of all, 'Mommy died in childbirth.'

Incidentally Brian's mother was at one of the shows, held at the Glasgow Barrowlands on October 8th 2000. She clapped her hands in time to the music from her vantage point at a platform at the back.

'Sorry, mom!' Brian chuckled, with a small hint of sincerity after dropping yet another profanity in classic Molko style.

Other visuals included a man with binoculars spying through the window at the object of his affection, an unsuspecting teenage girl undressing. Commercial for Levi, meanwhile, was transformed into a sea of colour – violet, shocking pink and magenta adorning the band's Elevator Music logo.

Brian was inspired by Bill Viola when bringing the visuals to life, claiming 'We wanted to come up with messages that you might be able to see in an art gallery as well. I like the idea of watching a little bit of a film, something quite unsettling and abstract enough for the individual to make the connection between the song and the visual – and them themselves.'

This was perhaps the group's most social tour, with all three posing for pictures and autographs after the shows. Only one incident made the papers when Brian was slapped in the face by a livid fan. She approached him with a bootlegged poster, which was all it took to incite Brian's fury. Firstly it was illegal merchandise procured outside the venue, from which the band could not profit, and secondly he was infuriated that such posters usually chose 'the worst picture they could find' of him.

He bluntly refused to sign the poster and in the face of persistence, ripped it in half and flung it underneath the tour bus. By now in a flood of tears, the girl reacted. Whilst Stefan rushed to retrieve it for her, she slapped Brian in the face, a veritable crime of passion.

Throwing his cigarette butt behind him, the singer left, uttering a string of profanities behind him. The signing session was well and truly over.

The following week he took it in his stride, cackling mischievously as he recalled the event. He had put his behaviour down to an unfortunate overdose of absinthe. However, the Molko collective were undeterred by the power of the green fairy, a drug that most definitely did work. In fact, fans became increasingly obsessive in a tour that was more aptly named Black Market Madness. One girl was pursued by half a dozen eager fans that chased her down the street, clamouring to touch her. The reason? The girl in question had received a hug from the front-man. More than ever, Brian was gaining the reputation of most desirable yet mouthiest and most unattainable rock-star.

Despite the glitches, the band's on stage performances were free from drama, with the addiction of performing now serving the function to Brian of 'a greater high than any drug.'

The Guardian summed up the Halloween show, one of two at London's Brixton Academy, that would end the UK tour. 'It's Halloween so it's fitting that the evening's main attraction is a petulant succubus wearing a tight purple suit and nail varnish. If you hadn't seen Placebo before, you'd assume that Brian Molko's garish outfit represented an effort to get festive for the night of the undead. You'd be wrong... Molko wears outlandish clothes and makeup whether he's playing to a sell-out crowd or washing the Porsche.'

The report confirmed that Placebo would never quite fit in with the mainstream – but for a string of ardent fans this merely made their presence all the more compelling.

The group had also been invited to perform at the newly opened Millennium Dome. It would give them the chance to showcase their new material in front of a wider audience than ever before, and it was an attempt to conquer that elusive accolade of mainstream popularity. It was something that, until now, they had always lacked. The show was by invitation only, with no official tickets made available, and featured a selection of renowned artists such as Coldplay and Madonna.

Brian was reluctant to play the Millennium Dome for political reasons. He felt that every homeless person in the country could have been housed for the exorbitant cost that was spent on creating it.' It was a Catch 22 situation whether or not to play,' he recalled. Ultimately they chose to do so but took the opportunity to deliver a damning message about the effects of the Dome, making audience members aware of the conflict they felt.

Continuing the political theme, Brian then appeared in Marie Claire magazine as one of the celebrities to lend their signature to a Drop the Debt campaign. He invited readers to pay attention to the chains of debt that affected third world countries and the high interest rates imposed by the West. Brian was fiercely opposed to injustice and he became interested in playing charity concerts, despite criticism that it was 'unfashionable.' It certainly wasn't in keeping with Brian's previous image.

Regardless of their own political leanings, fans did not doubt that Brian's heart was in the right place. Critics would argue that the socialist values he embodied were out of place and decidedly 'uncool' in a rock and roll climate yet the impassioned singer persisted with them nonetheless. Some said Brian was doing it to raise his profile, while others claimed it was a genuine calling.

Indeed, as the privately educated son of a banker, Brian's interest in this type of political activism might well raise a few eyebrows. His earlier life, whilst not necessarily luxurious, would have been very comfortable. As someone who had never had a full-time job or experienced the hazards of poverty, was he in a position to understand the pains of the lower class? Perhaps not, but he certainly wanted to.

Third world debt wasn't the only good cause Brian had been involved with. He stumbled across a protest fighting for the rights of gays to hold civil partnerships whilst on a promotional tour of Madrid. Despite eliciting little acknowledgement from the authorities and being photographed looking miserable on the march, Brian was determined to make his presence felt.

Political zealour aside, Brian's reception at the Madrid concert, held on November 11th 2000, was an unprecedented success. The show culminated with Brian flinging himself headfirst into the drum kit, much to Steve's trepidation. Fortunately he managed to catch the tiny singer, and – wrapped up in the music induced elation the two shared – he lifted him up for a tender embrace.

Next came Italy. Placebo had always shared a complicated love affair with its Italian audiences. The group's first major introduction was in 1999, headlining the notorious Imola festival. Amongst a group of hardcore Metallica fans, who allegedly failed to appreciate the soft centre that the group embodied in tender-hearted ballads such as Lady of the Flowers, Placebo did not fare well. They simply weren't dark hearted or metal tinged enough to capture their attention. They were no match for the gathering crowd at Imola that day, who clearly craved the headliners, Metallica, and voiced their frustrations by filling the stage with broken bottles. According to Brian, some of those 'hit me in the balls.'

Snorting at the effects of the ill timed, ill placed, introduction, Brian was nevertheless heartened by the true Italian fans that emerged in their thousands to cheer him on at subsequent shows.

Further success at TV shows and press events healed Brian's wounded pride and, when the time came, he was more than ready to return to Italy. In Milan on November 8th 2000, he was met with rapturous applause for challenging a fan and telling him to turn off a video camera otherwise he would 'personally come down there and shove it up your fucking ass!' Sadly his techniques were less than effective, because several of the songs appeared on YouTube just days later. However, Brian's big mouth was back.

The audience appeared to have enjoyed their first Black Market encounter, yet how would Placebo fare at the elegant San Remo festival a few months later? On March 2nd 2001, the group duly arrived for a two song set.

From the beginning it was clear that Placebo and San Remo were a terrible mismatch. With a sedate atmosphere from the outset, the annual festival featured sombre 'businessmen in suits and their mistresses in ball-gowns.' It certainly wasn't the environment with which one would expect Placebo's music to be associated. Stefan reported uneasily 'We knew full well this was going to be the biggest and probably most influential TV performance of our careers.' A live show witnessed by 15 million households, it was clearly a situation where absolutely anything could happen.

Had programmers set up these unlikely bed fellows with the sole intent of causing a stir? If they had hoped incompatibility would lead to publicity, they weren't mistaken. In full awareness that his performance was going out to millions of families, Brian donned a tight leather suit as he prepared for the show in his dressing room.

Playing to a demanding and expectant audience in formal evening wear seemed pressurising enough but the band had suffered little sleep due to their relentless promotional schedule.

Nerves were raw from the start and as organisers asked Brian to mime to a recording instead of performing live, frustrations began to build. Brian was angered at being asked to mime and simulate playing instruments to a taped track – why, he wondered, was he even there? Memories of an earlier New York show and its strippers, midgets and ponies flashed through Brian's mind, but he was too fatigued to see the funny side. Yet again, he was failing to meet with his audience's approval. In a gesture of anger and contradiction, he began to play up the visual side of his image as compensation.

Striding onto the stage in his skin tight leather outfit, Brian was met with both amusement and derision as he began to 'play.' Lifting a middle finger to the camera sardonically was the first sign that he was not amused. Then as the song came to an end, he held his guitar above his head and repeatedly smashed it into the amplifier. For a second there was a shocked silence before San Remo began to boo and jeer in a fashion most unsuited to their formal appearance. Brian stalked off the stage without the luxury of a single clap.

Stefan recalled Brian's guise onstage as 'the most scarily provocative stance I've ever seen.' As a result of it, the band was speedily escorted from the building and left to wait for the arrival of their van. 'Is there a fucking circus going on here?' Brian asked incredulously, as police officials dragged him from one corner of the street to another. Security guards took advantage of his diminutive size to manhandle him while the rest of the crew went in desperate pursuit of their vehicle. 'Get these people away from me,' he implored in a pleading tone, as his brother, who had travelled the short distance from his home in Monaco for the show, watched helplessly behind him.

Brian could then be heard snarling 'Fuck off' at video cameras, pushing a hand with middle finger raised in front of the cameras to prevent them from filming. Filled with contempt, indignation and – at times – visible fear, Brian finally found his transportation and was allowed to leave.

However, there was more trouble in store at the group's prestigious hotel that night, as they were denied entry to the restaurant due to their eccentric choice of attire. Meanwhile, Brian noted that John Lennon's son Julian gained entry in jeans and a T-shirt. Humiliatingly confined to drinks in the lobby, Brian stayed silent but more than one television was hurled from a bedroom window in indignation that night. Despite a newly demure image, the public clearly hadn't seen the back of the old Placebo yet.

A nation was in confusion, and for Brian the painfully high hotel bill for damages was the biggest confusion of all.

On March 31st 2001, just a few weeks after the ill-fated show, Placebo was welcomed back, this time in more appropriate surroundings. In front of an ever-demanding Italian audience that evening, the group remained in high spirits for their first ever show in the northern province of Perugia.

Three songs into their set, technical issues emerged concerning the safety of the barrier. Believing there was instability, the officials put a stop to performance for a little over an hour.

The devil finds destruction for idle hands, as the old adage goes, and never more so than that night as the band were celebrating Stefan's 31st birthday. Inebriation ensued and by Brian's own admission, by the time the group returned, they were 'very, very drunk.' Their first song, a new and poignantly striking ballad, was Leni. This saw a drunken Molko allegedly playing the piano with his fists, slurring the words and forgetting many of the lyrics. He also repeatedly yelled 'Bitch, bitch' during the chorus.

Slave to the Wage was naughtily but perhaps fittingly dedicated to an Italian ex-porn star turned politician Cicciolina. Meanwhile the next song was dedicated to Elvis Presley with the inflammatory remark 'He wouldn't have played Perugia.'

It was an example of the cheekiness that some adored about him, yet inevitably to a furious audience who were probably equally drunk and had been kept waiting, it was an insult that would have been sorely received.

The set ended prematurely to comply with the venue's licensing laws. It had comprised of just ten songs, due to the combination of time constraints and the one hour delay that had already taken place.

An enraged audience tossed bottles at the stage, demanding that their much-loved band come back immediately, but all in vain. Sheepishly emerging from the stage door a short while later, Brian was brave enough to sign autographs for the large collection of fans that had gathered there.

Several cries of 'fuck you' were exchanged, with Brian pulling one girl's hair and simulating a blow job with his finger before sticking it defiantly in the air to another. Finally, history repeated itself when he was slapped in the face by an infuriated audience member, seemingly a frequent occurrence in Placebo land. It was alleged that a hysterical Brian later clung to Stefan's legs whilst pleading forgiveness. However to the public he was wholly unapologetic and Italy joined the ranks of those with a desire to punch and slap Brian. For the first time the source of discontent was not merely his acid tongue, but the music.

While this was a barely forgivable performance for Perugia's public, it was perhaps inevitable that such a situation had arisen. Months of pressure and taking physical and mental limits to the extreme, plus a frustrating delay had all been factors in what had happened.

Nonetheless, the embarrassed and slighted Brian was horrified, consoling himself with the words 'Everyone can be a bit of a dick sometimes – the difference is that I'm a bit of a dick in public.'

Recovering from the shame, Placebo moved on and set their minds to more productive matters – namely the promotion of new single Special K.

The video – in Brian's eyes yet another evil to be transformed into a work of art – was loosely based on the plot of the film Fantastic Voyage. A miniaturised Brian commandeers an equally miniature spaceship on a journey inside Steve's body. 'That's the only way he'll ever be getting inside me,' the drummer cackled on Germany's Viva TV.

The video wasn't all laughs though, with Brian 'being suspended from the ceiling, being spun around, turning green and continually losing my lunch.'

However, as an artist, he was willing to suffer for the end of the finished product. According to the Italian media, the masochism of the video almost earned him forgiveness for the chaos that was Perugia.

Indeed, the video achieved instant popularity – not just in Italy but across the world. However, there were complications with radio play. Whilst allowing many of Eminem's controversial lyrics, Radio 1 censored the word 'stash'. Also, owing to explicit drug references, the single was deemed unsuitable for the conventional two-disc format for release. A special edition one-disc version was created instead, with double the songs of the average disc.

The record company told a different story, claiming that the action was taken to combat the two-disc format which was considered a 'rip off' and not cost effective to the fans.

However, all previous and subsequent releases retained the original format, pointing to issues with the awarding body. The single had been released in Australia first, followed by the rest of the world on March 19th 2001. Alongside remixes such as one of Slave to the Wage by Daniel Johns of Silverchair, two new tracks were unveiled.

Leni is a futuristic S & M love story told to the tune of a haunting piano, and Little Mo is a more upbeat number dedicated to Elvis, who Brian christened the King of rock and roll.

These songs were not destined for B-side anonymity forever – in fact they were added to the live set in a variety of countries. Luxembourg was one such country. Brian's return to his childhood haunt saw a greater following than before, this time commanding an audience of 5,000 people. Concerts took place on April 14th and 15th 2001.

Tickets were signed for fans who needed posterity with the touching message 'Fuck Lux!' – Brian's own trademark reminiscence of a country in which he felt he had already spent far too long.

Their antics and honesty mimicked that of their Japanese tour. Brian revealed 'They didn't have us back for years. They were scared shitless!' However the tour, which had began in Tokyo on January 15th 2001, had been a positive one.

The band travelled from London with Kerrang magazine, a flight which saw Brian wander through business class roaring 'Hello, my lovelies!'

oblivious to the rows of sleeping passengers and believing that they must be in a pub. Quite what resemblance a crowded aeroplane cabin had to a pub one could only speculate.

Only one thing was certain, and that was the fact that Brian was definitely not sober. Having consumed 'dodgy Spanish sleeping pills' alongside a cocktail of alcohol, he was in for a long night. His unpredictable reaction aside, the tour was hugely successful in both Tokyo and Osaka, where Pure Morning – with its celebratory references to the Japanese population – was performed in abundance.

Brian's attentions had by this time returned to his first love – movie making. He collaborated with counterpart Nicholas Elliott who had produced a French adaptation of Burger Queen for a 1999 single. Elliott directed the short film 'Sue's Last Ride' whilst Brian was its creator and executive producer.

The mysterious low-budget film features long instrumental sections from one of Brian's favourite groups, the Dirty Three, although it remained an experimental film with no official DVD release.

Rumours also began to circulate that Brian would be producing and narrating a documentary about the Dirty Three in Australia, although time constraints on tour ultimately prevented it.

The next single, Blackeyed, also saw a more cinematic territory for the group. When director Vanessa Jopp was looking for a band to provide the soundtrack to German movie Engel and Joe, Placebo was one of the first groups she approached. Brian recalled his meeting with her fondly, remembering that she had 'positive vibes' and that he was happy to lend a song to the project.

Engel and Joe is loosely based on the real life story of Christiane F, an infamous German celebrity with a book and film to her name, who had battled intense heroin addiction since the age of 13. Her story chronicles her life from the first ill-fated dose after a David Bowie concert to the life she found herself living afterwards. She was forced to sell her body to make ends meet, rapidly became homeless and lost all that she held dear in her desperation for yet another hit. It took the tragic loss of close friends to overdose and the indignity of their deaths on the street to provide a much-needed wake up call for the teenager.

The book documented the trials and tribulations of a young girl forced into under age prostitution, homeless and violence all before the age of legality. It offered a story many would not have thought possible on the streets of sedate and upmarket Berlin. The sinister tale was made available in several languages including Dutch, French and English. It was also adapted as a film, which provided the inspiration for Jopp's subsequent movie. That of course was where Brian came in.

Feeling the plight of the teenager, he was happy to help with the new film which had a similar plot. In her version, Joe is a runaway teenager also living in Berlin, who suffers violence and abuse at the hands of her mother's boyfriend. She falls in love with a friend and becomes pregnant but is soon faced with financial destitution in a world of fantasy without fulfilment. Like Christiane F, her life becomes one of drug abuse and prostitution. Their names featured the sort of gender ambiguity of which Brian would have been proud, with Joe representing the female character and Engel the male one.

The two actors, Jana Pallaske playing Joe, and Robert Stadlover taking the part of Engel, were just as interested in finding a compatible soundtrack to the movie. Due to Placebo's connections with David Bowie and the dark nature of the lyrics and subject matter, all felt that Blackeyed was full of promise for the film.

A video was created from festival footage, including excerpts from the movie intercut into the plot. Joe is placed within the show, where clever editing techniques see her jumping and moshing along with the rest of the crowd from a front row location. In reality, she had not attended the festival at all.

A drama occurred when a camera man captured some private chemistry between Brian and the leading lady Jana, some of which made the final cut. 'Fuck off, no way!' Brian screamed indignantly at the close of the video. Far from being the playful banter it seemed intended to convey, Brian was reprimanding a photographer who had been filming illicitly outside of shooting time, when camera work had been prohibited in all forms.

Brian's irritation led to speculation that some intimate kissing scenes had been captured without his prior knowledge. Any unwanted scenes were edited at Brian's insistence, amid rumours of a passionate affair. Whether Brian's concerns were merely the invasion of his privacy or whether he had a little more to conceal, no-one knew.

Regardless of the truth and the inevitable feverish gossip, the video was immensely popular with German audiences, introducing Placebo into the public eye as far as alternative music was concerned and securing their success on the subsequent tour. Shortly afterwards, the band was invited to the film's premiere where they appeared alongside the rest of the cast to rapturous applause. As for the real Christiane F, she is now a mother in her 40s, trying to get her life back on track, but requiring daily methadone supplements to this day.

Brian was in a position to understand her pain ever since he had dabbled with heroin himself – and ultimately discovered that his lust for life and desire to maintain a successful career had won out.

The trio had also set their eyes on other collaborations during the tour. For the first time, Brian had been able to meet the woman he claimed to have worshipped since the moment he first heard her music. The lady in question was the glamorous singer PJ Harvey. The pair's meeting was photographed in Australia where the two had a promising discussion with a view to working together in the near future.

Far from a mere penchant for beautiful and talented women, Brian seemed to have a genuine rapport with the artist, whose emotional vulnerability had inspired much of his earlier work. Brian was rapturous in his idolisation of her, saying 'I've been in love with PJ Harvey for years now. She's my heroine – a source of inspiration. Her records are so passionate that they get confronting. The emotional nudity of her albums made me want to make music with emotional depth.'

While Brian had such adoration for his own musical idols, how did he view his fans feeling the same? Did his infatuation with PJ Harvey lead to understanding of how fans felt about him? The earlier Brian might have dismissed those who emulate his style – in a previous NME interview, which may well have quoted him out of context, it was documented that he told imitators to get a life. However the 2001 response was a more diplomatic one. 'Imitation is a natural phenomenon and the highest form of flattery,' he said.

It might have been overwhelming for Brian, in the wake of unresolved self-esteem issues and battles to establish his own identity – to be faced with the responsibility of thousands of Molkettes. Having not being entirely confident behind the excess of lip liner and mascara, it seemed that Brian was finally beginning to fit in to his role. Moreover, gigs were no longer just a stepping stone to success and discovery, but also a way to get political and make sure his voice was heard against injustice.

Gone were the days when the band would each down a bottle of whiskey before the show. Brian's vocal range was ever increasing and fans believed shows were becoming more accomplished, in a term the group affectionately refer to as 'tighter than a vicar's dirt box.'

Brian also strongly believed that image was now taking second place. 'Our image is strong, but if we didn't have music even stronger to back it up, we'd be in a Milli Vanilli situation,' Brian said with the type of candour that did not spare the failed artist's blushes. 'If that were true, we wouldn't be making our third album. People enjoy being transported to an alternative reality, to see something that's larger than life. With Placebo you get the whole package, passion and honesty, the communication of emotion, and you get a strong image and powerful music as well. That's why it works – all the elements are in place.'

Brian's acid tongue continued though, leading to one embarrassing moment with a Portuguese interviewer who asked him to describe the new album. 'Well, it's on a round thing called a CD, and it's got 12 songs on it,' he jested, cue one very red-faced presenter.

However the joke was on Brian at an exclusive acoustic concert, a gift for the group's French fans. At Paris's MCM Cafe, he started off the show with a bizarre saxophone version of Taste in Men. Some questioned Brian's ability to bring up his talents as school saxophonist pupil due to the lack of practise and it raised a few giggles from the audience. A similar show was also put on at Belgian venue FNAC on June 2nd 2001, comprising of slow versions of old favourites such as Teenage Angst and Special K.

Brian was dressed for cabaret on both occasions in a smart black suit designed for him by French fashion designer Agnes B. With a successful clothing and makeup range in Paris and London, she had developed a close friendship with Brian. She adored his first album and he was equally transfixed by the elegance and modernity of her designs. Both were enthusiastic about the idea of working together. She custom designed his ideal outfit for the extra-special cabaret shows where for once image was everything. The two later appeared on French TV with each other to celebrate the fusion of music and fashion and the occasion inspired platonic kisses and hugs all around.

Fashion wise Brian also appeared on the front cover of Les Inrockuptibles in a special feature starring him and designer Xavier Delcour. Brian reminicised over his first time trying on his mother's makeup and voiced his desire to create a world of clothing freedom. 'If women can wear men's clothes such as trousers, why can men not wear skirts?' Brian asked. 'For a long time women have benefitted from clothing freedom and it's time to take that back.'

Aside from his appreciation of French fashion, Brian dominated yet another Les Inrockuptibles cover when he interviewed Robert Smith of the Cure. In his new journalistic guise, he asked his friend and idol some burning questions about his career and musical inspirations. Brian was finally getting to walk in the shoes of the media personalities who reviled him.

Shortly afterwards, Placebo embarked on one of their most memorable shows yet – Germany's Hurricane festival, which took place on June 24th

2001. Audiences were to be left stunned by the group's openness and naked self-expression.

During a performance of My Sweet Prince, the content of which was close to Brian's heart, and which had taken on a combination of profound meanings over time, the singer dissolved into tears.

Mesmerised by his fearless display of vulnerability, the crowd screamed for more. In response, Brian flung the microphone down, put his head in his hands and began to cry yet further.

He also sobbed during several live performances of Leni, which depicts a failed S & M relationship. One such performance saw Brian's hands shaking like a leaf as he was overwhelmed by sheer emotion.

The band tirelessly promoted their message of freedom, self-expression and courage to be yourself, but fatigue had crept in as the 18 month tour drew to a close. That was something that Brian's tears had emphasised.

By this time, Black Market Music had reached the number one spot in eight different countries. In Turkey, a country renowned for its stern attitude towards homosexuality, the locals began to warmly embrace Placebo, an indication of their significance in fighting for gay freedom.

However, it wasn't all good news. Brian's political campaigning had attracted the attention of Nicky Wire from the Manic Street Preachers, who was furious. 'I hear Brian Molko singing politics and it makes me embarrassed to be a musician,' he spouted. 'This bloke who suddenly decides that rioting in the streets of London is cool. Fucking hell! I'm a one man political party against asinine cunts like him.'

Whatever the reason for this attack, the vitriol wasn't shared by many of the group's fans, most of whom supported him as much as ever.

Brian's feelings on Nicky and the band were unknown, although he did have a legendary fascination with ex-band member Richie. Brian had gushed that the musician, who had mysteriously disappeared years ago and is now assumed dead, was 'the most beautiful man in rock and roll.'

Brian continued his political endeavours with added fervour, undeterred by Nicky's words, and his appearance at the Budapest Sziget festival, on August 7th 2001, was to be one of the biggest shows of activism for the group yet.

Fighting back against the mayor of the city, who he had perceived as homophobic, Placebo performed an extra-special acapella version of All Apologies by Nirvana, giving particular emphasis to the lines 'Everyone is gay!'

His unexpected burst of song created waves of approval as the crowd roared ecstatically. 'Thank you very much, ladies and gentlemen, we are Placebo!' Brian yelled before delivering a message in no uncertain terms.

'It came to our attention that the organisers of this festival had to sign a contract with the mayor of this district to say that they would not promote anything that has to do with homosexuality, which as far as we're concerned is a bunch of fucking bullshit! So this is for the mayor of this district, the homophobic twat that he is!'

It was a sinister introduction to Blackeyed. Whatever Placebo did and wherever in the world, they were guaranteed to make their political feelings known.

The tour was now almost over and colder nights were drawing in for the band as they returned to Europe. Brian recalled that the Belle and Sebastien penned book the Winter Lady as an inspiration for their next tour. It features a woman who follows the sun all over the world and in doing so achieves eternal youth. If she goes to a cold climate, she will begin to age straight away. Brian longed to schedule a tour that would follow the sun, despite trepidation that naming it this would taken him into the 'realm of the cliché' and the dreaded 'Sting territory.'

Sadly, following the sun isn't always practical or possible and it was to a cold and inhospitable climate that the band returned for their two final Black Market Music shows, at London's Brixton Academy.

On October 24th 2001, as the lights dimmed and both band and fans relived the past year and a half of adventure and emotion, it was time for Placebo to take a much needed break. With reassurances that they were not going anywhere in the long-term, Brian walked off stage for the last time and began to contemplate the next stage for Placebo.

Chapter 6.

'Six months off for bad behaviour' – Brian Molko

The band had finally stepped away from what they saw as the 'crazy media circus.' As the last chords rang out on the final show of their intense, tumultuous world tour, it spelled the end of an era – and fans were anticipating a very long absence.

Those in the backstage area at that time would have come across an absinthe-addled Molko drenched in sweat, but full of renewed promises for the break of a lifetime and a fourth album to match. Brian was quick to dismiss rumours of a split, but the passion of 4,000 fans could not be pacified. The streets around Brixton Academy were filled with tearful girls of all nationalities reminiscing on the delights of the hedonistic Black Market Music tour, knowing in their hearts that their love affair with the notorious Placebo was temporarily about to end.

Little did they know that they would be confronted with their favourite star just a few short months later. Desperately in need of a break but already on the brink of boredom, Brian had arranged a special DJ set in Athens. Appearing at the centrally located Horostasio rock club, Brian took to the decks to see in the New Year with his Grecian fan base.

Although he had used numerous after show parties to informally sharpen his skills on the decks, his DJ debut would nevertheless come as a surprise to the majority of those who knew him. His only publicised show had been at Brixton Academy in 1997 when he took to the stage following an electric Prodigy concert. Despite his lack of experience, stage fright was the last thing on his mind.

Brian's defiant cries of 'Dance, motherfuckers!' rang out across the club and caused a few cultural misunderstandings with the locals, some of whom produced contradictory signs of their own. One such sign, spelling

'I'm not a motherfucker!' in indignation, got the thumbs up sign from Brian. He also shook his ass to Destiny's Child, showing his appreciation for the song Bootylicious. Brian had always been willing to confess his penchant for cheesy disco tunes, formerly confessing that he listened to Abba and Britney Spears. Among his favourite Britney tunes was the sultry 'I'm a Slave for You.' This came as no surprise to the close friends who had come along to support him, but was more of a shock to hardcore gothic music addicts.

Not content with playing at the Horastatio, he also appeared at the Barfly in London's Camden Town on January 18th 2002. He took to the floor in the small club, which was packed to capacity, just a few weeks later. Fans could enjoy a very up close and personal set on the cramped dance floor.

Whilst it was a night to remember, it turned out to be far from a one-off. If the date at the Barfly was like a drunken fumble, his next project was to be a multiple orgasm all-nighter. Fans were stunned to learn that Brian had gained a long-term residency at the Camden Underworld and would perform every third Wednesday of the month. The residency was for an indefinite period or, in the diplomatic words of Bizarre magazine, 'until they get struck off.'

It was no ordinary club night either. His limited experience as special guest DJ at Brixton had somehow transformed and reappeared several years later as a doctors and nurses fetish club. First inspired by a Halloween party called Bloody Merkin, the theme was a jaw dropping combination of innocent sexuality and stomach-lurching blood and guts.

'We wanted to do something slightly fetish around the whole doctors and nurses thing that a lot of us played as kids – that innocent reawakening of sexuality,' Brian grinned. 'So we've provided a playground of exhibitionists and voyeurs, somewhere for people to cut loose because there aren't any rules.'

Brian had amorous intentions, wanting to get down and dirty with an uninhibited crowd, and he knew that at the Underworld he could find one. The first club night opened its doors on February 20th 2002. Dress code was strictly medical, with only 'pregnant nurses' guaranteed free admission to this experimental night of music and fetish, In spite of that, the club's debut was sure to be a roaring success.

For the under-18s in the crowd, entry was not possible at all. However, staff hadn't bargained for their loyalty, tenacity and ingenuity. As a large line formed outside the club, determined minors prepared to get inventive to gain coveted access to the dance floor.

'I borrowed my sister's ID,' chuckled one anonymous club-goer. 'When the bouncer looked at me quizzically, saying it didn't look like me, I just said it was me without makeup.'

While the dress code was medical, a wave of hard rock fans disregarded this advice entirely, undeterred from arriving in a familiar sea of black. One affronted clubber argued with security guards that Brian could never have suggested such a dress code and consequently the dance floor became a mixture of white PVC nurses' uniforms and all-black leather ensembles. In this unusual mix, one theme that had certainly been adhered to was fetish.

Overjoyed to learn that they hadn't heard the last of the group, fans impatiently gathered at the club, all eyes on the stage. Brian took to the stage over an hour behind schedule for dramatic effect, dressed in a blue surgeon's uniform streaked with blood-stains. He also donned latex gloves as he strode towards the decks.

The onstage set comprised of a maternity ward, a make-shift operating theatre – concerningly surrounded by an abundance of alcohol – and films and slide projections of a medical theme including 'Britannia Hospital' and 'Doctor in the House.' Humorous, sexual, dark and mysterious, it had a unique vibe.

Brian's rather ambitious plan to give birth to a live human being during the evening turned out to be impossible and impractical, but that didn't prevent the collection of followers and clubbers from having a great time.

His other aspirations for the evening included a human version of infamous game 'Operation' and performing an actual operation onstage which he warned 'could get quite disgusting – but it's meant to be that way.'

The debut night was like no other. A small selection of friends and followers comprised the audience and, away from the concert scene, rapturous applause was more muted. This made for a more relaxed evening with the ambience of a private party, where Brian could blend in with the locals.

The musical sound-track to the evening included the Avalanches with their hit tune 'That Boy Needs Therapy.' Brian shook his head from side to side psychotically to mimic the lyrics 'He's a nut, crazier than a coconut.' The confusion and ambiguity of the song, plus its indisputably medical theme, hinted at dark sexual practises and the thrill of the unknown. Brian also played Peaches, a girl who could 'scare him and know that I like it.' These artists were followed by Add N to X, Talking Heads, the Sneaker Pimps, NIN and the bootylicious Destiny's Child. The ass-shaking dance Brian had indulged in for his Greek fans was a one-off, destined never to be repeated, although this did not deter him from enthusiastically bounding around the dance-floor. Hardcore fans unaccustomed to Beyonce's saccharine-sweet brand of pop either recoiled at disgust at Brian's pop princess demeanour or joined in, abandoning their reservations to cheer him on in delight.

'We're all huge Abba fans,' Brian had revealed to the media the previous year, breaking his followers in gently to the idea of him being a disco queen. 'We love to shake our asses and listen to Abba in the kitchen at 4am. Some of our fans hate pop music,' he had revealed gleefully, 'and we laugh thinking how horrified they'd be at what pop enthusiasts we are at heart.'

Morgan, a member of Placebo's tour crew also made an appearance for a teasing and intimate topless dance with the front-man, whilst Mark Beaumont, a follower Brian was to describe as 'the only decent journalist from the NME' followed suit.

There was another reason for Morgan's appearance than mere entertainment. As much as he might enjoy being Brian's plaything, he was more than that – indeed, he had inspired the entire night. The previous month, Brian had taken a short holiday in Spain. He had been using his time off to produce an electronic project there under an anonymous pseudonym. Many loved it but few suspected it was the work of Placebo. Brian had spent his days teasing friends by playing it and listening to their unsuspecting comments.

There was an opportunity for hedonism in Spain, which didn't mix well with the group's arrival at a peaceful health spa in the midst of rural tranquillity. Disaster was bound to happen – and it did. In these unlikely surroundings, Morgan found himself separated from the group when he passed out unconscious at a taxi rank in the early hours of the morning. A local good Samaritan drove the heavily drunk invalid to a hospital where he woke the next morning – disorientated, confused and on an intravenous drip. Peeking at his discharge sheet, Brian – who found the matter hilarious – christened his DJ night after the saline drip that had saved his companion's skin that night. The seed of inspiration was borne, and on his return to the UK, Brian put in a request at the Underworld for residency.

Due to its limited financial prospects and the reality of barely breaking even, the club was not for profit but merely a way for Brian to let loose and have fun with his fan base. Whilst he had limited and somewhat dubious technical ability, Brian enjoyed being the centre of attention as much as his audience enjoyed indulging him and he knew how to bring the attitude, atmosphere and enthusiasm for a great night.

The club was repeated the following month, this time to a larger number of clubbers to whom word had finally spread. All were reluctant to end the evening, cursing the Underworld's lack of late-night licensing. Brian teasingly informed the disappointed crowd that had they been in Spain, 'we could have gone on partying all night!'

Backstage, Brian continued to show a different side to himself. Fresh faced, makeup free and surprisingly sensitive, he was far from the prima-donna that could be seen at his concerts. Turning to a new friend in the tiny, overheated dressing room – a million miles from his spacious VIP room at shows – the newly bashful Brian asked the girl's opinion on Black Market Music. 'Some people didn't like it,' agonised Brian. 'What did you think?' A little inebriated, his eyes glazed over, already disinterested, as his enraptured audience began to rave on the plus points of its music.

Throughout the evening, Brian showed a possessive side, clutching a bottle of absinthe that a fan had given to him with the words 'It's mine!' when friends showed interest. No-one sampled the miniature green fairy that evening, as it was going home to be retained – perhaps for the next night of mayhem.

Also backstage was Brian's new girlfriend Helena, a photographer of Vietnamese origin, along with Som, the Sri Lankan lead singer of melodic rock trio My Vitriol. Brian had always been enamoured with the latter, claiming in Kerrang that he was the male rock-star most worthy of the title 'gagging for a shagging.'

He duly participated in Som's DJ night at the Barfly to show his amorous appreciation just a few weeks later. When Come Home was played, Brian – who initially took a background part in proceedings – visibly perked up, beaming with pride and strutting around the decks. In total drunken revelry, he soon commandeered the stage, leaving the original line up to pale into the background. Som took it in good humour and the 'Gagging for a Shagging' nomination even more so. He found this hilarious when questioned, and, slightly embarrassed, was reluctant to divulge whether he returned the sentiment.

Brian also made a guest appearance at another friend's concert – this time to support Nicola Sirkis of Indochine on February 21st 2002. The attraction between the two was indisputably mutual this time, as Sirkis had warmly remarked that Brian had 'a great ass' in conversation with the French media. However above all, the two shared a respectful friendship, and it was this that was celebrated when the two were photographed embracing fondly as he took to the stage. Wowing Parisian audiences at the Elysee Montmarte in the heart of the city's quirky sex district with an eclectic track list and all-white outfit, Brian was received warmly by the crowds there.

He also flew to Majorca with his friend Jeff Automatic, who had been responsible for his appearance at the Barfly. Jeff owned clubs in London and Barcelona and had made it his ambition to party around the world. Brian was only too happy to help with his hedonistic plans, and appeared for one more night of fun at the Casino Royale on March 2nd 2002, which few of his fans knew about.

He had then been due to re-appear at the Underworld to continue his residency. Raving about his stint there, he had enthused 'I'm lucky to know a person like Darren Emerson, who plays at Underworld. He's the best DJ in England, if not the world. As you can see clubbing is still a big part of our lives. You get that happy feeling and it's cool to mingle with other people.' However the Underworld's love for Brian was sadly no longer reciprocated. The finicky star had cancelled numerous months in a row, and staff had become increasingly agitated by his conduct. Whilst Introvenus had been set to continue for some time, this was sadly not to be and Brian's March appearance at the club was his last.

However, fans who surmised that there may have been pressing reasons for Brian's prolonged absence were not mistaken. The month of May revealed tragic ones.

4Scott was a charity concert for 'legendary plugger' Scott Piering, a publicist who had tragically died of cancer during the band's recording of Slave to the Wage. More than just a plugger but a valuable friend and confidante, Brian was left devastated by his death, lamenting 'We felt his presence in the studio during the recording and there's so much we could have asked him if he had still been here.'

It was not just Brian who had been aware of his potential, tragically cut short when he died at the age of just 53. The British Radio Academy set up the 'Scott Piering Award' in his memory and a charity fundraiser was arranged for the benefit of cancer sufferers. Artists such as Embrace, the Stereophonics, Teenage Fanclub and of course Placebo teamed up to pay their respects to the icon and his legacy in a concert simply known as 4Scott.

The sense of tragedy surrounding the event increased still further for Placebo when drummer Steve's much loved grandfather passed away the night before the show. Visibly fighting back tears, Steve soldiered on out of respect to his friend. It was a sombre moment for the group, with all three members mourning the poignant loss of someone who had been such a vital part of their career.

The Scala in London's Kings Cross was the venue for the memorial, which took place on May 24th. All the groups paid respects using the highly emotive and universally understood language of song – which no-one could relate to more than Piering. He had been passionate about all the artists he had worked with, devoting his time to ensuring their chart success. Up until his last hours, he had been dedicated and Placebo now wanted to repay that dedication.

Boasting acoustic versions of old favourites Haemoglobin, Slave to the Wage, Special K and Teenage Angst, Placebo's set was a success. Haemoglobin was chosen as the Placebo song to appear on the charity CD produced of the night, seeing Brian mouth the words into a megaphone. Launch Music summed up the set with 'You either love or loathe Molko's vocal style.'

Brian next collaborated with electro group the Alpinestars, who had previously produced a phenomenally catchy remix of Taste in Men – his talents were clearly in safe hands. The two groups had initially met after sharing a recording studio in London. The Alpinestars inhabited the lower ground floor of the studio complex, while Brian stayed in the flat above. The eccentric front-man was prone to borrowing his neighbours' washing machine and so he and the Alpinestars became firm friends. On the basis of these meetings, it was speedily decided that Brian would be the perfect candidate to play the Carbon Kid in their latest song due to 'his angelic face and voice.'

After several meetings to confirm he suited their conceptual vision, the two approached him. Brian was happy to help and the vocals were complete within an hour. At that point Brian, satisfied with the creation, confessed to spending the rest of the day in the pub! The working atmosphere was a 'blissful way of working, with no pressure.' Perhaps he could not be blamed for the momentary spell of laziness because thus far he had experienced the busiest holiday of all time. 'I really liked the single,' Brian grinned cheekily on Viva TV, daring to don the same blue tracksuit as in the music video – 'because I didn't have to do anything. They wrote the lyrics and did all the production, and I went to the pub.'

After providing the vocals in true angel style, perfectly embodying the concept of the Carbon Kid, there was a video to accompany it. This was infinitely more hard work, seeing Brian run up and down the corridor of UCL University in Euston to the point of exhaustion.'I had very sore legs afterwards,' he lamented, shuddering in memory of the pain. 'All my muscles ached.'

His perseverance wasn't too surprising though – from enduring hypothermia inducing temperatures in 36 Degrees to potential mind numbing boredom in 12 hour film shoots for which they had just a walk-on part, Placebo were renowned for testing their limits in the name of art. The same location accommodated a Girls Aloud shoot promoting Kit Kats, but unlike his counterparts' more placid shoot, Brian wasn't afraid to get his hands dirty when he became the Carbon Kid, a full blown computer driven athlete.

This video features two Brians in fluorescent tracksuits, who begin a frantic chase along a corridor as part of a computer game. The Alpinestars are competing with each other with simulated Game boy technology to see which Brian will be destructed first. Appropriately then, the song concludes as the one in an orange tracksuit – who could easily be mistaken for a neon-clad London Underground worker – falls to the ground and suffers an unfortunate untimely death when he is flung from the top storey window of the building.

What was it with Placebo and their tendency in every music video to perform confusing stunts on the top of perilously high buildings, fans wondered. The song was released as a single shortly afterwards, and came highly recommended in the media for its catchy verses and quirky vocal accompaniment.

As this tune hit the clubs, Brian was simultaneously rekindling his UK DJ career. He caused a wave of horror among the non-Londoners of his fan base by headlining a club suspiciously named 'Popstarz.' The pop-allergic were reassured to find that this was in fact a renowned gay club in the capital with a coincidental name, and in fact with no Westlife or Fame Academy clichés in sight! However, as with all self-respecting gay clubs, it wouldn't be without at least the tiniest trace of Kylie Minogue.

Brian had shared the decks with Indochine and My Vitriol – the latter session which he commandeered, leaving the original and more bashful headliners in the background – and had presented his own fetish night. He had partied in Majorca, Athens and Paris. Fans had enjoyed Brian's idiosyncrasies, such as beaming proudly when his own song Come Home was played and forming part of the dance floor. They had appreciated his collaborations and the insight they had received into his musical tastes. However, the reality was that the group had to return to the studio. The Underworld staff had been upset with Brian's perceived indiscretions, allegedly booking a last minute holiday on his arranged night and informing promoters at the last moment. For this reason it was perhaps a relief for all concerned that his stint with DJing was over.

Brian now had to confront the real reason he had taken a break – to 'reacquaint myself with normality' and to avoid the inevitable fate of 'disappearing up my own arse.' It was time for some rest and relaxation, if he could fit it into his already pressing schedule.

'You need to be told you're full of shit,' raved the singer animatedly.

'After seven years living in a bubble, you end up spiritually, physically and emotionally spent. To write anything decent again, we needed to reacquaint ourselves with everyday human contact – taking the tube, going to the supermarket… it was as if the decision to take a break had already been made for us.'

Perhaps his hope of reaching normality had been successful. Two female fans recalled discovering him, to their delight, and notably in the Economy division, on a plane to Nice. Autograph requests attracted the attention of bemused fellow travellers, who gasped 'You must be really famous.' With uncharacteristic modesty, the singer replied 'Nah, I'm just in a band.'

He had certainly toned down his image and outlook on life. 'I've been this boy-girl for so long that I just thought it would be interesting and different to be a bloke again, wear jeans and a sweater and just wander around and be a regular Joe,' he admitted wryly. 'I wanted to be able to take the Tube and for people to go "Nah, can't be".'

Clearly his break and return to normal life with such activities as clubbing and taking the Tube – plus the occasional prank on gothic fans who were unconvinced as to his identity – had done him good.

The dichotomy was that Brian had an instinctive desire to be onstage, even in moments of relaxation, as this was when he felt he could truly shine. The band was scheduled to return to the studio in June, where work commitments would again intensify but this failed to stop the flurry of public appearances.

In June, Brian appeared at exclusive club Café de Paris in the heart of west London, where a private party took place for a friend's wedding. He took to the stage with Stefan, complete with a spiky punk inspired hair-do and an equally punky version of Billy Idol classic White Wedding. The song was a huge success, although the majority of the audience were not Placebo fans. Brian was seen spiritedly chatting to male friends at the bar and occasionally whispering words of affection to girlfriend Helena.

Earlier in the year, he had appeared at the same club for a public event, appearing alongside stars such as Cerys Matthews and Boy George. Brian collaborated with his friend Pam Hogg, a fashion designer of high repute. The song was 'Don't Go Breaking my Heart' by the marvellously camp Elton John and Kiki Dee – a perfect theme for a duet. Some would describe Brian's efforts as endearingly drunken renditions – although that was perfectly acceptable for somebody on a break.

Next Brian participated in the Trash Palace project, a sexual concept album appropriately titled Positions. The album, released first in France on October 15th 2002, features limitless imagination and fantasy and is more of a concept driven project than a musically accredited one. Nevertheless all 12 songs are magical and atmospheric, their sexy and frenetic bass lines conveying real passion and an insight into the artist's condition.

Trash Palace mastermind Dimitri Tikovoi, a Russian living in Paris, was a kindred spirit for Brian to work with. He shared not only the same birth date, in an astrological twist of fate guaranteeing their compatibility, but also a catalogue of work together. Dimitri would go on to produce the group's future album Meds, had an intuitive link with Brian and was delighted to secure his participation. Brian was featured on two songs, the first of which was the Metric System, a song on the theme of 'selling sperm to celebrity lesbians'. Brian's voice turned haunting and gravelly, inviting the listener into a world of sexual perversions, revelry and satisfaction.

Dimitri subsequently reported that Brian had written the words himself, unsurprisingly because he had always known he was a 'dirty boy.' Brian did nothing to refute these teasing rumours when a French radio station asked why he had participated. 'Well, you know me; I just like anything to do with sex, hahaha!' Airing the dirty laugh he is famous for, he confirmed his interest in the sexual theme and his respect for fellow artists.

He also performed a duet with Italian siren Asia Argento as part of the project, a gothic horror actress well-known for her appearance in her father's films, on a cover version of Serge Gainsbourg's Je T'aime Moi Non Plus.

The cover had the added twist of a gender role reversal with Asia supplying the male vocals and Brian supplying the female ones. The song was one that a cheeky Tikovoi had adapted after sampling pornographic sound-tracks and adding it to the Gainsbourg classic. Einsturzende Neubauten, one of Brian's favourite groups, had also penned a version, making it a hot choice for him to sample too.

Sadly the magnetic duo of Brian and Asia never met in person prior to the release of Positions, and vocals were recorded in separate studios. Whilst the sexual spark could not be ignited in person, Brian recalled the intelligence and intrigue that surrounded her in the pair's snatched telephone conversations. Brian hardly needed to make his passion for Asia clear. He'd already mischievously claimed in Kerrang magazine that she was 'gagging for a shagging,' probably little suspecting that one day he'd be working with her. Blushing Brian redeemed himself by stating that it was a staple question for the best male and female in the public eye. He had chuckled 'It's true that she does look like me, and I guess sexual attraction is quite narcissistic.'

It was inevitable that this project, comprising of numerous dynamic stars, would eventually become 'live.' Indeed, they became headliners at the Route du Rock festival in the remote coastal town of St Malo, France on August 13th 2002. Brian excelled even in a territory of Jean Louis Murat obsesses and although the audience were not typical Placebo fans, ensured attention was focused firmly on him.

Whilst French newspapers criticised his 'murder' of a Serge Gainsbourg classic, in which Brian sang the female vocals towards a giant video screen depicting Asia's face, many fans felt differently. The Metric System was met with confusion and intrigue, seeing Brian in a sexily aggressive stance as he yelled through a megaphone which was thrown to the side of the stage at the end.

He danced with fellow musician Alison Crane between some songs and cradled her in his lap during others. Some suspected that there could have been a burgeoning romance between the two waiting to ignite, whilst others believed it was a combination of tender friendship, onstage adrenaline and red wine. The affection was visible when Alison playfully pushed her hand into Brian's face as he danced towards her.

The two finally joined the entire group for a performance of Kylie Minogue's Can't Get You out of my Head, where the lyrics were changed to 'Boy, your dick is all I think about.' Not to be outdone by his counterparts, Brian then spectacularly jumped into the drum kit, nearly injuring a band member in the process.

The Trash Palace performance was a once-only event for Brian, although he made an incognito appearance at a short set in Paris. Donning dark sunglasses and a shiny PVC pinstripe suit, he performed the Metric System. However Brian was disgruntled with the musical format of the show, which included up and coming R & B artists such as Ms Dynamite. She was subject to his ridicule backstage as he imitated her latest single with mocking cries of 'Miss Dynamitee-hee,' and – unimpressed with the line-up generally – he left very early.

The artist Michael Sheehy took over Brian's role on the Metric System in subsequent shows. A show was announced at London pub the Water Rats although the identity of the singer was left to rumour. Brian appeared as a spectator that night, unshaven and almost unrecognisable in a green woollen hat which some fans felt needed investigation by the fashion police. He was notable for his loud and drunken commentary from the back of the room. Whilst his non-appearance as a singer had disappointed, he compensated by recording a video for the song.

In a continuation of the cheeky medical theme, Brian appeared in a surgeon's white coat. Surrounded by tubes that presumably contain sperm, he looked surprisingly masculine and if it weren't for the hospital environment could easily be mistaken for an Italian gangster in the French only release.

For someone who stated that it is difficult enough to be in one band, Brian was exceeding all expectation with his vast number of side projects. Recording commitments intensified following the August festival and the band continued to work on the album. The adventures of the studio were kept firmly under wraps, although as the new album underwent its final touches, there was a surprise announcement. Jeff Automatic of the Barfly had again invited Brian to be special guest at Club Sputnik on December 12th 2002.

Happy to accept, Brian satisfied feverish demand with a final one-night only event. Like his DJ session there 12 months earlier, the night was immensely popular and he had to be moved upstairs to create more room and a larger dance floor for the increased number of clubbers expected to descend on the venue. Some hardcore fans resented the loss of intimacy caused by the move, as Brian was now merely a distant face behind a glass window high above the floor. However a live camera view was projected into a large screen on the wall, enabling the audience to feel more involved. Brian used this opportunity to emphasise his new passion for electronic music, playing a selection of classics in the genre.

There were also more surprises in store as he tested out future single the Bitter End on his audience. The reaction of the public was interesting, with many not recognising Brian's distinctive vocals. Previously refusing to play Hole tracks at the author's request – 'It depends what mood I'm in!' this time he acquiesced whilst also playing the Sneaker Pimps' Solo – another electronic tune from the velvety voiced former female leader Kelli Ali. Whilst the Bitter End had an unmistakably rock feel, it was rumoured that the album was to feature abundant electronica and Brian's comments that rock was boring only served to reinforce those rumours.

Talking of his collaboration with the Alpinestars and with a hint to the experimental direction for the future, he revealed 'It sounds very different to Placebo – it's very upbeat and electronic even though there are guitars on it. At the moment electronic music is more original and exciting than rock music.'

With three separate collaborations, a small selection of live performances and a burgeoning new DJ career, Brian's time off had been exhausting, thrilling and unintentionally very creative. There was a burning energy that characterised their studio moments too, with session artist Bill Lloyd claiming 'Brian was on fire!' Despite this, the worst was not over and a rocky rollercoaster of highs and lows still lay ahead.

Brian had arranged a huge birthday party to mark his 30th, inviting 200 of his nearest and dearest to the event. The party took place in his central London flat and fortunately culminated without any significant damage. He had hired an orchestra to play classic songs like Nirvana's Smells Like Teen Spirit, an apt choice of song given that Brian was confronting his fears about turning 30. The guests at the bash included Heidi Slimane from Christian Dior, Neil Tennant of the Petshop Boys and French musician Etienne Daho. Noticing this unlikely combination of stars, doorman Brian found it very amusing. Some of the guests were more unusual than others however. 'Neil Tennant wasn't invited and I was really surprised to see him. I hadn't met him before!' Brian chuckled.

The comedown was not pretty. There had certainly been moments of joy although there were also intense downward slumps, exacerbated by the confusion of breaking free from a whirlwind tour and coming back down to earth. As with any sudden landings, Brian had a very sore head.

He had finally taken a break from public appearances to contemplate the decadent memories of the past. He had been forced to end the tour for the sake of his health yet to his cost he had lost the structured environment of a tour and its schedules and missed the VIP treatment. 'In the beginning I didn't know what to do,' he said. 'I just sat in my house where I had barely been before, waiting for someone to bring me my lunch.'

He continued 'I didn't have the constitution that I imagined I had, on either a physical or a spiritual level. I just couldn't go any further anymore and a lot of my pleasure-seeking was fuelled more by self-disgust than anything else. A lot of it was an attempt to block out the pain, block out the loneliness and the fact I didn't like myself very much. And because you're on that treadmill, you become too self-destructive. A lot of bands go in to that, but they don't come out the other side, but we have. We've been staring down the edge of the cliff for a while and now we're thinking, "Nah, it's too far down"'.

The constant collaborations and appearances had taken the focus off the real reason he had stopped work. Ultimately, sooner or later, he would need to recharge his batteries again.

'We were spent physically because we'd been on the road for so long, and emotionally, we were very messed up. We'd run out of realistic life experiences to write about. Nobody really cares about the colour of your tour bus, or how many notches on your bedpost you have at the end of the tour. We realised we needed a break for the first time in seven years. We needed to reacquaint ourselves with genuine everyday human contact and exchange.'

Part of this involved getting a new house to live in. He soon found an apartment that was suitable – a minimalist converted warehouse that was situated between Old Street and Angel, Islington. It satisfied his appetite for realism with a taste of the east central district, but more importantly it was close to his friends from the Goldsmiths days. 'I wasn't Brian Molko the rock-star anymore,' the singer had lamented with a touch of relief. 'I was just Brian Molko who needed to furnish his apartment.' However, Brian being Brian, even that didn't pass without event.

He was delighted and dumbstruck to come face to face with a personality who harked back to his Luxembourg days – the American singer Brix Smith-Start. 'In Luxembourg in the 1980s there was this legendary show called Snub TV, where a lot of people of my generation got introduced to alternative music. I liked [Brix's] song so much that I went out and bought the cassette. That was my first introduction to her, a kooky American lady on TV.'

Brian had taken his bid to be a normal person to heart, and he and a friend had been hauling his belongings up to the lift without aid when they were confronted by a shocking new neighbour. 'I ran into this American woman,' he recalled. 'I said "Hi, I'm Brian" and she said "Hi, I'm Brix." I couldn't believe it. I was moving in next door to the living legend who I'd been listening to for 10 years.'

Brix had a clothing store named Start, in Shoreditch, an arty district within walking distance of her own home. It was an area that Brian would describe as a 'universe of urban decay, dog shit and trust-fund hipness.' It made sense for him to make friends with the locals, a cunning strategy that had guaranteed him designer glamour wherever he went. When in Paris he had been treated to alleged truckloads of couture pieces from both eminent designer Agnes B and Heidi Slimane of Dior fame. However now that he was off tour and settled, he needed to find a shopping mecca with a rock-star discount – and he found that with Brix. 'I have fitted Brian in many a pair of jeans,' she reminisced.

After Brian's birthday, she was part of a New Year's Eve party that followed just a few weeks later. He started the fun by offering canapes to his guests and the party then moved from neighbour to neighbour – each offering some new cooking to the mix. Finally, it ended at Brix's house with champagne and dessert on the roof.

Despite having no shortage of understanding friends around him, Brian's personal problems continued. He looked back on his nomadic lifestyle on the road with extreme ambivalence, claiming 'It scared me how much I had become dependent on others and how hard it was for me to get through the day without a schedule.' Wistfully, he remembered 'When the battery of my cellphone was dead I didn't have a social life anymore.'

However he also acknowledged that he was jealous and restless when he wasn't living that life. 'Sometimes I felt lonely – I wasn't treated like a superstar anymore and missed the daily recognition of friends and people in the business.'

Therapy seemed like the best solution to a myriad of problems but it was something he was hugely ambivalent about trying. For a long time, he had avoided attending sessions that could have been vital in confronting his demons. 'I've considered it many times,' he told X-Ray magazine. 'I've been very close to going to see people and I've cancelled appointments on the day for many different reasons. But to be honest, I'm lucky to have the music, that's totally where I get it out. I'm quite happy with the amount of neuroses I've got now. They keep me ticking over. If I got rid of them all, who knows, I might become Sting for God's sake. And I can't imagine anything worse on this planet!'

Brian's desire for rest and responsibility-free partying had finally been satiated and his self-destructive tendencies curbed. Many lessons had been learnt. Now he was finally ready to face the world again, and to hit them with something new and profound.

'It's okay being me right now,' he confirmed. 'The demons don't shout as loud anymore.'

Chapter 7.

'I'm 30 now. I'm not worried though – I still feel completely immature!' – Brian Molko.

During his six-month break, alongside chaotic parties and an intensive work schedule, Brian had somehow found time to re-assess himself as a person. He had stepped off the treadmill and finally allowed himself an unbiased perspective on the life he had been leading for the past two years on tour. Sadly, the conclusion wasn't pretty.

It was this reflective atmosphere that had led to the birth of the band's fourth album. Brian had been facing fears about turning 30 and the new phase of adulthood it would bring. Previously gleefully irresponsible and not afraid to show it, the Jean Cocteau phrase 'A little too much is just enough for me' had been Brian's favourite philosophy. This was a man who was no stranger to the delights of excess and over-indulgence.

Whilst the days of downing a bottle of Jack Daniels each, just moments before the show, were now over, there were still issues with drugs and alcohol. Beginning to resent the caricature of himself that he witnessed in the media, Brian began to realise the problems that overshadowed his reputation as an artist were partially self-generated. He could no longer allow his personal problems to destroy his livelihood.

This realisation sparked a period of soul-searching and deep contemplation. Brian recalled the isolation he experienced at being the outsider in society, the boy who'd never fit in. Few of his fans could perceive him this way, or believe even for a few seconds that the rock-star with the mammoth ego and the voracious appetite for excess could be lonely, vulnerable or in self-doubt, let alone confused about his identity. Yet for Brian this was the harrowing reality. A man who had once cackled gleefully at not being recognised by his fans was now struggling to adapt to the sudden loss of attention. This was the crisis he faced at being uncomfortable in his own skin.

'I started looking around and seeing people in their expensive suits, running to the tube to be at their boring office job in time. I saw people I went to university with pushing a pram around, who already had babies. I started thinking how these people might look down on me, thinking 'That guy is trying to stay a teenager – how pathetic. I started doubting myself; maybe they were happier than me,' he confided.

It was clear that whilst the elation of thousands of fans screaming their appreciation on a daily basis had been indescribably addictive, it had also brought its fair share of problems. The comedown was one such issue.

Slightly older and wiser but, fans were assured, still very immature, the front-man reluctantly looked back at his younger self. Addressing the fact that he no longer appeared to be the trouble-maker of old, he revealed 'That was all down to far too much cocaine in social situations surrounded by the media. It provides you with this huge sense of false arrogance, this super-increased sense of self-importance. I was always off my head.'

He confided that he now made an effort to stay sober as much as possible to dodge the ensuing chaos. His detractors might presume that for Brian 'sober' entailed no more than three bottles of wine per night. Delightfully for his fans however, a lack of alcohol did not inhibit his trademark honesty.

Delivering a slice of the alarmingly honest front-man his fans knew and loved, Brian revisited his old persona. 'Certainly we were getting wasted – we fucked everything that moved,' he remembered. Fortunately for the faint-hearted among his fan base, this did not include the animal population. 'I've never indulged,' he once told Melody Maker. 'I've seen a few movies though. How filthy can you get?' Vomit fetishes were met with equal revulsion when further sexual extremes were suggested to them by Select. Despite endless lewd jokes, that was something which all three were revolted by.

'We did indulge in every drug under the sun,' Brian mused, 'but the simple fact that I'm getting older means that I can't party like its 1999 any more.' Indeed, his attitude had changed considerably since the early years. When questioned on their long-standing feud with the NME, Brian sighed, imparting the age-old adage 'If you argue with a fool you become one.'

Back in the studio, Jim Abbiss had been chosen as a producer for the new album. This was a man who traditionally straddled both the dance and popular music camps, so his involvement was a decision that surprised Placebo fans worldwide. Perhaps the choice echoed Brian's new found obsession with electronica. Abbiss, whose back catalogue included DJ

Shadow, Bjork and Madonna, promised the anxious trio he would provide a new direction for the group's ever-changing sound.

The result was slices of rock infused with contrastingly electronic beats. In characteristic Placebo style, the album was very different from any of its predecessors and featured a variety of rhythms and sounds – from dub reggae to rock to indefinably experimental, even featuring tubular bells. There was a distinctive nod to the happier and more melodic dance tracks that part-time fans would be astonished to learn that the band adored. In spite of this, it remained accessible to thousands of loyal supporters.

Jim Abbiss was an assertive producer, with specific and rigid ideas about the sound he sought. The band likewise were equally protective about maintaining their own identity. 'We weren't looking for a producer who would change our entire sound. We wanted someone who would look at us from a different perspective, not someone who'd change the sound just to guarantee us a hit single. We didn't want to make the same album all over again but we didn't want to go in a completely different direction either, a la Radiohead on Kid A,' Brian defended.

However, in spite of all reservations, the pair managed to forge a surprisingly successful working relationship. In fact, Placebo were just the beginning for Jim, who later went on to work with their counterparts Ladytron, Unkle and the Arctic Monkeys.

Brian sang his praises afterwards, offering impeccable references. 'We needed someone who was going to give us a kick up the ass, who was going to force us method-wise to do things we had never done before,' he enthused. 'He made us do things backwards, standing on our heads, and in zig-zags, which is what we needed.'

The group was engrossed in pushing the envelope of their sound, and so there were fewer guest participants this time around. However Simon Breed, an ex-band mate of Steve's was invited into the studio to play harmonica on one of the songs.

'It was quite funny,' Simon recalled. 'I think they always made out that it had to be me or nothing – and when I got there, Stefan was like "We tried everyone, we went through the whole list!" It was fun, Brian said he wanted one thing, Steve another, Stef another and the producer another!'

Regardless of the internal strife in the studio, if the relationship between musician and producer can be seen as an artistic love affair, the ensuing situation was nothing more than a series of passionate lovers' tiffs.

Simon added that whilst during the Without You I'm Nothing album there had been friction with the conflicting personalities, the atmosphere this time was one of happiness and joy. He laughed 'Brian asked me to do the song live with them at Brixton Academy, and I would have loved to, but I was going through a bit of a funny time emotionally at the time. Brian was cursing me – "Oh you made me have to brush up on my harmonica playing skills!"'

Protect Me From What I Want, the song in question, was helped immensely by Simon's input even if mental health problems prevented him from offering it in person, and it had its fair share of inspirations as well.

Deeply moved by the attention-grabbing art work of American slogan artist Jenny Holzer, whose work appeared on the walls of London train stations, Brian borrowed one of her most famous phrases.

He had experienced a turbulent break-up that year when his relationship with Benedicte had finally ended. When he saw the phrase 'Protect me from what I want' emblazoned across one of her posters, it seemed like the perfect phrase to embody his troubled emotions at that time. Was there anything else Brian needed to be protected from? 'From my urge to live excessively. I can hurt myself and my loved ones with it. But I have to say that I'm singing the song to myself more. I'm the one that has to protect me from me and luckily I'm getting quite good at it.' He also sourly joked 'I would ask for protection from the media – the only thing that is capable of destroying us.'

The recording continued with a series of tracks. Bulletproof Cupid was an energetic, dark and passionate heavy rock track with a sprinkling of a metal vibe. The only instrumental on the album, Brian had tried desperately to pen the lyrics although he recalled with a shudder that his efforts bore an 'unfortunate' resemblance to Napalm Death. Lyrics surfaced on the internet shortly afterwards, but it has never been confirmed whether these lyrics were Brian's own or whether they had been created by someone else. The recorded version remained wordless.

Brian teasingly told US magazine the Sentimentalist 'A minute into the song, [fans] are saying "Well, the lyrics have to start now" and they don't.'

The song was later incorporated into a film, the Edukators. Sharing a soundtrack with One Inch Punch, fronted by Justin Warfield, Depeche Mode and Franz Ferdinand, what similarities would the film have to its rocky backdrop? It begins as a young German girl becomes hopelessly indebted to a wealthy family after crashing into one of their expensive cars. Cursing her involvement with their precious Mercedes Benz and desperate to pay off the costs, she is forced either to leave her comfortable flat voluntarily or be evicted from it. Her solution is to move in with boyfriend Peter. In doing so, she learns of his secret night-time vocation – breaking into people's homes only to do little more than leave ambiguous messages. The unusual and subversive plot mirrored the Placebo vibe and this didn't go un-noticed by the director, who guaranteed their part in the movie.

The next track on the album meanwhile was an electronic offering that couldn't have been more different from its rocky predecessor. Brian confirmed 'English Summer Rain has absolutely nothing to do with Bulletproof Cupid. So even at the second song, the listener still doesn't know what the fuck this album is going to be about. Hopefully that creates a sense of intrigue as people are being pulled in.'

He continued 'They realise they are going to have to listen to at least the first half [of the album] to figure out what the fuck is going on. With Sum 41, you put on the first track and you know exactly what the rest of the album is going to sound like.'

Ever contrary, and constantly trying to break the mould, English Summer Rain became one of the most commercially friendly creations in Placebo history. With a nod to DJ Shadow, it also spelt the beginning of a long experiment: Brian on drums. He had set up a recording studio in his flat, complete with a drum kit and the latest digital technology, so that instrumental material could be sent between band members no matter where they were in the world. The group had recently bought a holiday home in Cannes, and wanted to ensure that artistic exchanges could be made cross-country.

In This Picture, the ashtray girl bears no resemblance to previous band name Ashtray Heart but was instead a nod to James Dean, providing a metaphor for the pain of self-destructive relationships. According to Brian, Dean had well-known masochistic tendencies. Rumour had it that the actor would ask his gay lovers to stub cigarettes out on his chest during coitus for the rush of pain and pleasure and the ensuing erotic thrill it provided.

Brian sought to recreate the endorphin rush musically, hissing in gravelly tones 'late at night, whilst on all fours, you used to watch me kiss the floor' as if reminiscing over an S & M relationship turned sour. The upbeat and catchy chorus then set in. Brian candidly admitted 'It recalls Dean's fetish although here the cigarettes are being stubbed out on my chest.'

Sleeping With Ghosts, the title track, had a far more serious side, with a far-away glimpse of hope and optimism. The phrase 'Soulmates Never Die', repeated throughout the chorus, was inspired by a psychologist of great repute who controversially reported his beliefs in reincarnation. Two of his patients were told they were soulmates who had spent numerous past lives together before being reincarnated in the present day. Psychologists are traditionally renowned for a scientific approach, so his views and the subsequent publication of his book caused a stir – one that Brian was happy to buy into.

The song also has another message. 'We live in a world that is filled with war mongering, religious hatred and I think we are facing an environmental Armageddon as well,' Brian stated. 'This is the setting around which the love story takes place.' Written for one special person in particular, the song insinuates confidence in the belief of all-enduring everlasting love – one so strong that it goes beyond death – because, ultimately, soulmates never die.

Something Rotten is an unusual song, delivered in a slur that mimics confusion or drug-induced hallucination. This approach to the delivery of the lyrics is reminiscent of Swallow, but the song itself couldn't be more different. The dub-reggae experiment was the band's challenge for producer Jim, who had been struggling with their proudly two-headed schizophrenic sound. Not a band to disappoint, the subject matter was equally controversial. It points to child abuse, a sinister tale of psycho-analysis where all is suggested but little is said. It mirrors a child's confusion over the motives of his perpetrator and there is morbidity about the song, a teasing possibility that the child has grown to enjoy the abuse because it is all that he has ever known.

Whilst Brian vehemently opposed violence, he had a personal vantage point from which to discuss it. 'I got knocked around as a kid and definitely felt scarred – to the point where it affected my idea of what masculinity was. It made my masculinity quite confusing because the role models I had for masculinity were quite violent and twisted.'

He also admitted that there were times when, after witnessing cruel treatment of a woman at the hands of a man, he had felt ashamed to be male. He had often struggled to quell the male instinct within himself for that very reason. Intriguingly, he also believed that it might account for his more feminine, gentle persona today. Never before had an album provided so many opportunities to come to terms with extreme emotions.

Plasticine is the one song that does not fit into the relationship theme of the album. The phrase 'Don't forget to be the way you are' encourages individuality on all levels. It explores the 'absurdity' of matters as personal as sexual attraction conforming to a fashion trend where people mindlessly follow each other's beliefs. Brian told fans that beauty was in the eye of the beholder, famously assuring his audience at the Astoria that year 'You don't have to be fucking Kate Moss to be beautiful – we think that's a load of fucking bullshit.'

He commented later 'We are bombarded continuously by the media with what ideals of beauty should be. I find it interesting how it's changed. All you have to do is look at paintings from the old masters, where these really portly women were the ideal of beauty,' he mused.

His comments came in the wake of a crisis for British body image. Over eight million women were said to suffer from eating disorders at the time – a figure which has since increased – and many impressionable girls were consumed by emulating the perfect figure of a Barbie doll. Yet Barbie's dimensions were so emaciated that, according to Time magazine, an adult woman who was proportionally similar would have room for just half a liver, be forced to walk on all fours, and finally die an untimely death from chronic malnutrition.

With the ideal in the UK being fashionably slim, it was an extremely topical debate and one that Placebo were just in time to join. As Brian had noticed, models such as Kate Moss might have proportions impossible to the average woman yet in the perfectionist climate of media advertising, they fitted in perfectly. It was a recipe for disaster.

Some might have seen Brian's assertions as hypocritical. He had previously gushed that Kate Moss's tomboyish look appealed, making him 'weak at the knees', before candidly telling Kerrang magazine 'I'm a fan of the waif.' In spite of his irrepressible tastes however, it seemed that Brian's heart was in the right place.

His words struck a chord with the many female fans struggling to find their place in the unforgiving, stringent aesthetic rules of society. Moreover, the sentiment remained the same – fans should have the confidence to be who they are. Merrily refusing to embody someone else's vision, Brian became the poster boy for embracing individuality.

Special Needs, featuring the refrain 'Six months off for bad behaviour' is a cheeky wink to the band's recent break whilst the song itself deals with a slightly more sinister message. It is the tale of a celebrity once the curtains have closed on him for the last time and fame is little more than a distant memory. The celebrity struggles to live in the shadow of his more confident and successful lover, fearing he will be forgotten.

The metaphor of stagnating in a wheelchair at the mercy of a sadistic partner – 'Remember me when I'm stuck in my chair that has four wheels' – bears a strong resemblance to the infamous Roman Polanski film Bitter Moon. The film features a cruel girlfriend's sadomasochistic relationship with a man bound to a wheelchair. She turns the tables on his previous infidelities and capitalises on his accident, poignantly caused when he leaves a nightclub with a beauty on each arm, so drunk he is unable to cross the road unaided.

She takes him back, revelling wickedly in the knowledge that he is now totally helpless. Enjoying his sudden dependence on her even more than she bargains for, she subjects him to a series of cruel taunts and sadistic pranks in a bid to gain revenge. It culminates in her openly having affairs while he sits pining, desperately aroused and unable to satisfy her, in the next room. Fittingly, a tragic ending, tinged with regret and arousal, follows moments later.

Despite the upbeat nature of the melody, Special Needs appears to be a guilty, anxiety infused song, predicting the loss of all that the author holds dear. Due to Brian's passion for film, and particularly the perverted variety, it would be little surprise if he had derived inspiration from the cult classic. On par with Blue American, it clearly stems from an immensely low point in the writer's life.

Paradoxically, I'll Be Yours turns the tables. It is another song about possessive relationships, but this time Brian is on the receiving end of someone's unrequited devotion. He is engulfed to the extent that his partner is emotionally suffocating him. 'It's about someone wanting to be your water, wanting to replace your bad habits with them, wanting to mother you and be your moral instructor. Sometimes people want to exist inside of you in a relationship and envelop you completely, to the point that you don't have an identity anymore.'

Clearly Brian had been on the receiving end of such an obsessive tryst and the song deals with the extreme co-dependency his lover is suffering. The thought of 'drowning in love' can be a positive or negative state but in this case it is the relationship's point of downfall.

Second Sight is a scathingly acidic song, caustically blasting a one night stand that has no self respect. It deals with the signs of someone unable to let go, who lingers clingingly in the morning to cook breakfast and becomes an unwanted presence in his life. The message is clear, according to Brian – 'Walk away for your own self-respect.' What remains unclear is whether the message is directed outwards, or whether it forms part of Brian's renowned self-disgust.

Indeed, he seems torn between his fears of losing a partner (Special Needs), and being totally submerged by one (Second Sight and I'll Be Yours.) Relationship issues inspire extreme ambivalence. Therefore it is fitting that Centrefolds should be a return to the theme of loss, where the schizophrenic dichotomy continues.

The song is a cautionary tale, an ode to a has-been celebrity whose career has seen better days. It is a paranoia-infused fantasy about the transitory nature of fame, and the cruelly short expiration date of celebrities.

Brian had already made his feelings known on the pitfalls of Pop Idol and the X Factor, claiming that reality TV show winners are exploited for capitalist interests. Sadly remonstrating on Rise TV, he recalled 'When brown envelopes start getting passed under tables, when people's whole lives are over by the age of 20 – that's when it starts to get a bit sick.' Whilst probably not the inspiration behind the song, it is a prime example of how short a pop star's career can be.

'Someone is telling a washed up celebrity "I'm the best you can get now so you'd better be mine,"' Brian revealed. With reference to all the centrefolds the celebrity can no longer afford, it is a bitter and cynical song where the subject is self-deprecating himself, questioning his status, and – despite his position of fame – suffering one of the worst crises of self-esteem.

Finally, the Bitter End is a punk-rock track reminiscent of Placebo's rockier roots yet completely opposite to anything that the rest of the album sounds like. It is a teasing taster of the diversity of Placebo's sound. If the aim was to invite listeners into their intriguing world, and to magnetise them into wishing to hear more, the group had certainly succeeded. This number is described as 'two people trying to come out of a relationship with the least scars' and is a confrontational track where the angry lovers continually try to gain the upper hand, scoring points off each other in the game to which their love has degenerated.

This was the first song to become a single from the diverse album that was Sleeping with Ghosts. Released on March 10th 2003, the video was shot on Jodrell Bank, the biggest communications satellite tower in Europe. Brian cheerfully announced his suspicions that it was the location where Americans spied on British telephone calls and emails. Rhyming slang for 'wank,' Jodrell Bank – which was also located just around the corner from Steve's mother's house in Manchester – was the perfect location to shoot the video. The singer used the opportunity to show off his fearless relationship with heights, strumming furiously on the guitar from the top.

The band endured a cold and windy atmosphere, evoking metaphorical images of a cold-blooded and tumultuous relationship. In such a partnership, the affection and all positive emotion has completely died.

Several other songs accompanied the Bitter End on the two CD release. On CD 1, Evalia was named after the brand of Brian's answering machine, which received an unexpected plug. The song featured drunken murmurs sent between Brian and a female caller on voice mail messages left for each other. The musical backdrop resembled some of Placebo's favourite inspirations, such as Aphex Twin and Boards of Canada. Drink You Pretty meanwhile chronicled Brian's struggle with the psychologically compelling effects of alcohol, and his desire to turn to the bottle when things got hard.

On CD 2 was a piano version of Teenage Angst and a cover of Boney M's Daddy Cool where Brian and Steve both provided vocals. The latter was intended as a birthday gift from Steve to his beloved daughter Emily, who longed to hear him sing.

Due to the unfortunate leaking of Sleeping With Ghosts onto the Internet shortly after the final recordings, the release date for the album was brought forward, formally arriving in stores just two weeks after the Bitter End on March 24th 2003. Brian summarised the album by saying: 'On a song writing level, I think we've gone back to what we do best which is writing twisted love stories. They have a certain darkness to them, an acid lullaby, which is important otherwise they become insipid and disposable.' That was one thing their sound could never have been accused of.

From that point onwards, Placebo were desperate to leave their furious detractors open-mouthed. They were ready for action. Several exclusive warm-up shows were duly performed to intimate audiences of just 400 people. The shows began in the small towns of Portsmouth and Southampton on March 8th and 9th. Similar small shows followed in Paris and Cologne, culminating with a concert at the romantic London Astoria on March 10th. This was a show that even the NME, who had a long-standing feud with Brian, could not fault, stating 'Follicly-challenged sex dwarf and cohorts return bigger and stronger.' Whilst it wasn't the glowing praise Brian might have hoped for, it remained an improvement.

It was at this show that Brian enjoyed the attentions of a pair of female fans who whipped off their shirts for the final song to reveal ample mammaries. 'Rock and roll!' he encouraged, with a flattered wink in their direction. In his own words, he was to find the abundance of 'pendulous breasts hanging over the barrier' very distracting, although it didn't detract from his live performance.

After the roaring success that this show provided, the band embarked on a month-long UK tour that spanned almost every major city. Starting in Cambridge on April 1st 2003 and ending in London a month later with a two-night extravaganza, it was also a success. Unfortunately two dates had to be pulled owing to a recurrence of tendonitis for bassist Stefan. Brian assured with a smirk that his injury was nothing to do with kinky sex with his accompanying boyfriend. He also jested 'We told him to stop wanking!' Stefan was quickly back on form, and gallantly appeared onstage for the final two dates sporting a giant bandage.

This gargantuan dedication didn't go un-noticed by the British press.

Previously reluctant to offer even the smallest words of praise, they were now raving about the tour. Brian told the Rolling Stone that the biggest misconception about Placebo was that he was going bald. If that was indeed the biggest misconception now, things had truly taken a turn for the better for the group.

Brian took the small club tour as an opportunity to reconnect with some of his fans. One amusing post-show conversation featured Brian's incredulous surprise when a teenage fan confessed he never watched films. Ever the drama student and film buff, Brian revealed his reluctance to go a week without watching at least one. Trying to unveil the mysteries of this elusive fan, Brian questioned him on his other hobbies. 'Swimming? Masturbation? Everyone likes to masturbate, don't they?' His fan was then thoughtfully provided with a link to the Suicide Girls website, but a refusal to elaborate on what he would find there. Further investigation would reveal a gothic-themed pay site for pornography and one with whom Brian has collaborated to provide interviews on a number of occasions. They surely appreciated the impromptu publicity shot.

Clearly, hormones were running high on the first leg of the tour. While Stefan was accused of excessive wanking, Brian made a telling comment about it being difficult to concentrate in the presence of the aforementioned female fans. Men do have two heads after all – it must be difficult to delegate.

Brian's other discussions both during the shows and afterwards encouraged fans to fight back against 'the evil empire of America.' The release of the album had coincided with one of the biggest security threats to Great Britain since World War Two. The band had taken part in an anti-war march in London that year and used the soapbox that the gigs provided to assert their position politically. Whilst the UK had shown support to America in fighting against Iraq if necessary, Brian vehemently opposed the move. At the end of each show he gave the clear message 'Stop the fucking war! Peace and keep the faith!'

If the political message was alive and kicking, the music was equally rousing. The live show took on a new ambience with a renewed set of visual projections onstage and Brian shared his enthusiasm for rap artists such as Public Enemy and Boogie Down Productions by calling their names in a spunky hip-hop intro to Teenage Angst.

There were some very special guests on this tour, including the twins who had appeared on the Without You I'm Nothing album cover, and who had become close acquaintances with the group. It was a calm tour in comparison to previous ones, with a record amount of sobriety. Nevertheless, a series of drug-fuelled arguments were alleged to be the cause of driver Malcom quitting the Placebo tour bus to join pastures new with Kelly Osbourne's band.

The press hesitantly praised the live show, with the website E-Festivals particularly enjoying the group's April 13th show in Nottingham. 'There was every type of person you could imagine in the audience – tall, short, thin, fat, rockers, goths, transvestites, lady boys. It was just like being on the streets of Amsterdam,' the reviewer claimed. 'Despite Brian's tantrums, Placebo is still one of the top live bands around, and they are looking in great form for their festival appearances.'

Indeed, the festival season proved to be a spectacular one for Placebo, with the group stepping in to take the reins and headline the Rock Am Ring, one of Germany's largest festivals, on June 7th 2003.

Linkin Park had been scheduled to headline but were forced to pull out due to illness and, to the organisers, there was no question who would take their place. It was an opportunity for Placebo to showcase their brand new album, and if the crowd were disappointed by the absence of the main attraction, it didn't make their applause for Placebo any less generous.

Some festivals were a little more difficult to stomach. Whilst Ultimate Guitar claimed that Muse was the 'love-child' of Placebo, with the two sharing similar sounds, there was no love lost between these bands. Following rumours that Brian's ex-girlfriend Benedicte was now dating Muse singer Matt Bellamy, the two groups were scheduled to appear together at European festivals. Whilst this passed without event, it was certain that Brian did not appreciate Muse's musical style either. He believed that Muse copied them, but shrugged it off, claiming 'Imitation is the best form of flattery.'

Highlights elsewhere in the world included a highly successful European tour. In Bulgaria, on September 13th 2003, Brian was presented with a bouquet of sunflowers. Blushingly, the singer made sure they were gratefully received with the impassioned words 'I love my job!' A spectator told the Sofia Echo teasingly 'I was extremely pleased with the concert. What impressed me though was how Molko bothered to pronounce 'Sofia' properly. Wonder if he knows how to spell it right...'

The group continued their journey on the road to success. Brian had raised glamorous actress Asia Argento's profile outside Italy and the USA with the Trash Palace concerts, and now it was time for her to return the favour. She agreed to perform in the video for Placebo's second single This Picture, released on July 15th 2003.

The video is an exotic combination of polaroids, high heels and fetish, centring around a young woman, the model Kimberley Johnson, who is struggling to find her face. The plot for the video could be a metaphor for the loss of identity some experience in intense sadomasochistic themed relationships. Indeed in this case Kimberley loses her identity in an all-consuming S & M tryst. She has drowned in twisted love to the extent that she rampages the streets in a quest to find her real self, culminating in a humiliating crawl on the bathroom floor. Hinting at control and power struggles, both consensual and otherwise, the video features a series of metaphorical images.

'What's wrong with this picture?' Brian observes from his seated position below an array of fetish models. The search is over when Johnson retrieves her face from a Polaroid – that of Asia Argento. This single was a huge success, reaching a top 40 position in the charts. The butterfly wings on the front cover of the CD provided inspiration for many fans' subsequent tattoos. The striking photography was courtesy of long time girlfriend Helena Berg.

Additionally Special Needs was released, on September 15th 2003, a video whose lead actress was cast according to Brian 'purely on the quality of her writhing.' The image on the front was of a lolita-like girl adorned with red lipstick which she smudges across her face with a demonic grin. The band was thrilled by the instant success of the single throughout Europe, which additionally achieved a number 27 spot in the UK singles chart.

Another notable moment in the band's career and one of their most famous to date was their 18,000 capacity show at the Paris Bercy, held on October 18th 2003. 'Put on your best frock,' Brian advised an excitable British fan channel-hopping just for the occasion, 'because it's going to be recorded.'

Indeed, the show was to form part of Placebo's first ever official DVD. Why Paris? From the literature, the movies and the music to the fans themselves and their unreserved genuine passion, Brian felt the pluses of this location were almost unparalleled. It was also the perfect place for a bit of glamour and sparkle, something with which Brian was by now very familiar. His cross-dressing adventures in old-style glamour had never been more expressive than in the French capital, where he always enjoyed raising the bar higher.

The front-man would be donning his best Dior for the show, and had made a mental note to avoid crowd-surfing. Last time he had tried, he had mourned the loss of his several thousand euro Dior leather jacket, ripped to shreds by an excitable crowd. That was not to mention the groping at his groin and frenzied removal of his pants. 'I'm gonna get arrested,' Brian had cackled later. 'I don't think it matters if you get it out, or if they get it out!'

His lust for sartorial splendour might not mix well with his crazy fan base, but he was looking forward to the show in Paris nonetheless. He had always adored the French public and his all consuming love affair with the country showed very little sign of ending. Fostered by growing up in a French speaking country, he was fluent in the language and often had a feeling of déjà vu on Parisian soil. Speaking of his special relationship with the city, he joked 'I've always suspected I was once a Parisian prostitute and that I've been on this earth before.'

Ultimately then, there was no question where such a momentous show, such a pioneering moment in the band's career, might take place.

Brian had never shouldered the pressure of headlining such a huge show before. Whilst there had been moments of elation playing in large stadiums, this had been as a mere support act for groups such as U2 and David Bowie. Now it was time to make it on their own – they were about to take on their largest solo show yet. It was of some consolation to Brian's shattered nerves that it was to take place in this city that loved them like no other.

Besides chronicling a very special 'first time' moment, there was another significant reason for capturing the event on tape. Frank Black of the Pixies, Brian's all-time hero, would be joining them onstage for a joint performance of the Pixies song 'Where is My Mind?' Brian had cheekily taken to ending each live show with the classic, so it was a song to which his fans were more than accustomed. Plus, for the older generation of fans, it was a collaboration from heaven with a rock artist that they remembered and revered from the first time round.

Visibly nervous as he took to the stage, yet elegantly manicured in peach nail varnish and war paint, Brian began the show with Bulletproof Cupid. The name of the song had set his mood – he wouldn't let the pressure of thousands of expectant fans frighten him. He would instead put on his armour and try to rise to the challenges provided.

He felt a mixture of trepidation and terrified elation that evening for a show that satisfied every fan. Not only did the show feature pure rock classics like Bionic, but it also saw a sprinkling of electronica in new crowd favourites English Summer Rain and Special Needs. For the gathered crowd that evening, the occasion was truly a special one.

The DVD Soulmates Never Die featured the complete show, plus an exclusive tour documentary with footage on the road. For those with a watchful eye, there was some hidden footage in store, including a five minute movie of Brian receiving B12 injections in his posterior. For Brian, the move was astonishing. 'I'm the vainest of the band, definitely,' he had assured Rocksound previously. 'I spend a lot of time in front of the mirror playing with my hair and worrying about my clothes. I have a lot of "Does my bum look big in this?" moments. I'm 100% guilty.'

However, much to the relief of those who harboured a Molko crush, he made the surprise decision to be filmed in the intimate procedure. 'I'm going to give you a little Placebo,' a grave-faced doctor told him. 'You wouldn't believe it, but that's the name of my band,' chuckled the singer before obligingly pulling down his trousers.

It was to be found in a secret section at the end, and only fans that cracked the DVD codes were able to access it. Ironically, the injections, described by the media as 'an accessory of megastar life', and which were taken by fellow stars Madonna and Justin Timberlake to name but a few, were said not to provide a genuine boost. The Sun scathingly remarked that rather than any real health benefit, it was likely to be down to – you guessed it – 'the Placebo effect.'

However the sight of Brian squirming face down and partially naked on a couch flashing his derriere for all to see provided a much needed boost to an over-enamoured female fan base across the globe. These fans believed that far from a fake, their own reactions at least were the real deal.

The world tour continued with the group making a huge impact wherever they went. In Mexico they experienced 'Beatlemania' with one tenacious fan running across Mexico City in pursuit of the band's car. Remarkably he caught up with them a breathless half hour later in a nearby bar to a tirade of camaraderie-laden laughter. One show saw the band play to a crowd of 40,000 in a football stadium, all screaming with the passion and unashamed devotion only a Latin audience could muster. Enjoying the feedback, Brian acknowledged that these were some of the best shows yet. 'You know they're here not because you're the trendy band or flavour of the month, they're here because they're your loyal, crazy fans,' Brian mused fondly.

Russia was equally dramatic in its reputation for mayhem and the adulation the band received in Moscow was unprecedented. The show was at Gorky Park, a stadium where political heroes Lenin and Stalin had once stood, gracing the same stage as a venue for their political speeches. The military doubled as security at this show, and Brian took the opportunity to flirt relentlessly with the stern-faced security guards. He raised a hint of a smile in one man, whose face had formerly been immovably neutral. Brian related the Russian tour and all its paradoxes to the heights of Mexico, stating 'Moscow was the most insane city we've ever played!'

'We were pickled in vodka,' he continued, 'and the security kept asking for our autographs and then selling them to the fans. It was completely surreal. Everywhere we had flocks of crazy Russians following us. It was like being in a Hard Day's Night.' A younger Brian, sitting motionless in his bedroom wishing for popularity as he strummed the guitar, could never have imagined that all his wildest dreams would come true.

But true they were, and the American tour was one of the most amusing yet. In the past, the group had achieved limited success in breaking the USA. Pure Morning had received phenomenal radio play, and Taste in Men had received nationwide exposure in a car advert that was televised across the country. However the band had remained a trend for the American people, little more than a passing interest, or a quirky novelty. Was 2003 to be the year that changed all of that?

A particularly memorable pre-concert moment took place at New York's Webster Hall on December 16th 2003. Brian had accidentally lost his backstage pass, and became extricated from the rest of the group. Passing around the block just moments before the show, he had hoped to slip inside by mere virtue of his fame, but was to be tragically mistaken. Many fans had already entered in anticipation of the support act or hoping to seize a place in the front row, but a large line of concert goers in their dozens still stretched around the block.

Brian panicked, fully aware of New York's notoriously no nonsense attitude to bending the rules. Alone in a city that for the most part barely recognised him, he was in trouble. Had this been Paris or Mexico City, a mere flutter of his eyelashes would have seen him ushered into the venue. Yet here as a virtual stranger in New York, he needed to think fast.

Whilst most of the hard-core fans were indeed now inside, fighting amongst themselves for a coveted place in front of his microphone, the queue was still growing. Casual clubbers failed to recognise him, and his attempts to gain backstage access were now in vain. 'I don't care who you are,' a strict female official told him. 'You're getting in line like everyone else.' His protests elicited no sympathy, so he reluctantly joined the growing queue. Tension amplified further when it was the red-faced singer's turn to enter the building.

'No-one's frisking me!' Brian squealed in indignation, wriggling free amid throes of confused locals to make an anxiety-fuelled rush for the doors.

Whatever the results of that scuffle, he made it to the show that night, taking delight in showcasing a selection of the group's new material. Support acts and fellow drinking partners Eagles of Death Metal – featuring Josh Homme on drums – provided the perfect atmosphere for camaraderie and his earlier indiscretions at the doors were soon forgotten.

Kneeling on the floor in ripped jeans, overtaken by passion for the song, Brian sang his heart out on English Summer Rain, demonstrating the classic Placebo style of abandonment to emotions. American fans loved the new electronic feel, which made the songs more accessible to the mainstream, and it was with a smile of satisfaction that Brian would end his night. Whether Brian had succeeded in inspiring larger audiences to pop a Placebo remained to be seen, but the tour ended on a high.

Did he have a grudge against the Big Apple for his frantic scuffle to get in that night? When German magazine IQ asked Brian if he was scared of America, he commented 'Oh yeah! They want to imprint their McDonalds lifestyle onto the rest of the world.' He added 'It makes a strong and united Europe all the more important.'

When asked by Bang magazine why he had not relinquished his dual-nationality passport, he had even less glowing praise in store. 'I don't think I've ever really felt proud to be American,' he claimed. 'I still travel on a US passport, but I considered giving it up after the appalling treatment of the internees at Guantanamo Bay, the travesty of justice there. Still, when I was weighing it up, I imagined what Bill Hicks would've said – you'd be giving up your right to scream about what's going on.'

Brian's hatred of America was also somewhat historical, after he let loose a shower of invective to Melody Maker in 2000 about George Bush. 'America has so much power that to have someone who believes he has God on his side when he executes somebody, it's kind of dangerous,' he frowned of the would-be president. 'He knows fuck all about foreign policy. He's kind of the runt of the Bush family and for him to become president is just a joke.' In a wry dig at the previous president Bill Clinton and his fling with Monica Lewinsky, he added 'I prefer a president who likes blowjobs!'

While he was politically unimpressed with the largest country in the West, and had once commented that it would be hard to get his music and image through some of the 'thick American skulls,' what he undeniably had a passion for was their live audience.

Throwing caution to the winds, the USA was the destination that saw Brian crowd-surf again. Riding the waves of his audience for the first time since the loss of his designer jacket, he was delighted with the response. He could also walk down the street almost free from recognition, feeling nothing like the fear he might in Mexico. Here, a blissful haven from the European hotspots where the public knew exactly who he was, he could enjoy a combination of electrifying praise at live shows, and complete anonymity and privacy everywhere else. Brian adored the small venues that they played in and had even dressed up as Marilyn Monroe in a striking blonde wig after some shows. This formed part of a game that was jokingly labelled 'Chicks with Dicks.'

Fun and frolics aside, when Brian returned to the UK he was to contribute to a very controversial debate. The album Sleeping with Ghosts had been re-released on September 22nd 2003 and was met with criticism by some cash-strapped fans due to the perception of this action as a heartless money-making tool. Whether a ruthless marketing ploy or not, Brian fought back against the allegations of exploitation, stating 'The music industry is in trouble.'

He told French regional magazine Jeunes a Paris 'People must realise that [with downloads] bands won't be able to make a living from music anymore. It's absurd to think rock-stars are content living in the gutter with a needle hanging from their arm whilst reciting poetry to the moon.' Presumably that would just be Pete Doherty then. The backdrop to this argument was a crisis for the British music industry. With the rise of websites such as Napster, which offered tracks available for free, the public were turning down traditional paid albums. 'We work very hard to give people joy,' Brian defended, 'and they'd like us to work for free!'

Whilst he acknowledged that the download crisis was partly the fault of the industry for its elevated CD prices – far higher than the actual printing costs – he also criticised those who made free downloads with no intention to purchase the album. The front-man added that his tolerance and ability to appreciate all perspectives of the debate was 'handicapping.'

As a reconciliation between both the financial needs of the industry and the musical needs of its fans, who feared prohibitively high prices, a two CD set was released. This included not just the old album, but a compilation of every cover version the band had ever performed – and more besides. Therefore those who already owned the album could have an extra surprise.

Quelling the rumours of exploitation, the band had added not one or two, but ten brand new tracks. Some were familiar to fans across the globe, including 'Where is My Mind' by the Pixies. Brian saw this as a way of presenting his influences and re-introducing an older group in a format where it would not be seen as old-fashioned. Brian grinned 'I'd love to see a teenager buying the Pixies' Surfer Rosa.'

In addition, there were some rarities such as the Ballad of Melody Nelson, a Serge Gainsbourg track. Brian's melodic tones, tinged with sadness and poignancy, whisper 'playing hurting games for fun,' reinventing Gainsbourg's classic in a moment.

Other previously unreleased tracks included Kate Bush's Running up that Hill – a cover recommended to them by Bush herself and soon to become a fan favourite due to its instalment in their live shows, as well as Sinead O Connor's Jackie.

So another year was over, a covers album and successful US tour just a small part of it. 2003 had provided solace in unexpected places. From the rapturous devotion of the Mexican audience to the more mellow yet intensely satisfying and refreshing small club vibe in the USA, the group had spread the Placebo message wherever they went.

Far from being over, the Sleeping With Ghosts tour had reached unprecedented heights. That left one burning question – what would the following year bring? One thing was for sure – the band couldn't wait to find out.

Chapter 8.

'Heterosexuality is not normal – it's just common!' – Brian Molko

Amid a crowd of adoring screams, an unrestrained mass of voices expressing their love, three very unusual men stand out against the sky. All good things are said to come in threes and this unique trio are no exception.

The bassist has 'Homo' emblazoned across his chest in siren red. The lead singer and guitarist is diminutive and eminently feminine, with a voice like the gathered crowd have never heard before. The Mancunian drummer meanwhile is an unlikely dose of masculinity among them – a welcome fixture in the diverse and dichotomous climate that is this group's live show. It is of course, lest you were unaware, the unmistakable Placebo. Welcome to one of the most unusual live events of the decade.

Outstretching his arms like a flag to rapturous applause, Stefan revelled in the perversity that was his adoration. The group was in Lebanon – a beautiful and privileged country, yet one which was steeped in warfare and homophobia. Placebo was a dangerous combination for them. Yet despite the iconic and hugely controversial slogan on his chest, leaving no stone unturned as to his proud homosexual identity, this country was accepting him. They were responsive and filled with the adoration he had longed for.

That adoration was more than reciprocated. 'My parents adored Lebanon,' Brian said softly in memory of his childhood years there. 'They said it was like the Paris of the Middle East.'

However, like much of the region, the country was renowned for strict disapproval and intolerance of homosexuality. Owing to Section 534 of Lebanese law, stating that homosexual acts are illegal and punishable by a prison sentence, two lesbian women who longed for matrimony were cruelly imprisoned for their love.

This was a country that had stifled, stoned and imprisoned its lesbian and gay community. Even back in England, the British Lebanese population had made their feelings clear, declaring an outcry against the use of gay characters in young children's story books. The complaints voiced disgust and disbelief at how homosexual behaviour could be discussed with children, and how it could ever have been paraded as 'normal.'

The year before, it was discovered that just 26% of AIDS sufferers in Lebanon were homosexual, whilst 52% were heterosexual. However, that made little difference to public loathing of this minority – gay sex was universally seen as deplorable. Whether in the eyes of the law, the religious book or the supposedly safe haven of family and friends, homosexuals could guarantee an unsympathetic audience.

Yet here performing to a mainstream audience on June 29th 2004, the roars of applause for Placebo were deafening. This said more about the secret diversity of Lebanon than their public face towards gays might admit. Stefan stormed out a powerful bass line to Plasticine, unashamed to write 'Homo' across his chest, as Brian delivered the all-important lyrics 'Don't forget to be the way you are.' The trio were offering an unmistakable message to this country and its extremist policies.

It echoed the words of Helem, Lebanon's first ever lesbian and gay organisation, who had implored that year 'What kind of country is it where it is normal for men to hold guns but not hands?'

Raising a middle finger to censorship, a politically charged Placebo dispensed with all pleasantries and prepared to deliver their hardest hitting live show yet. This was not just a victory of converting the uninitiated in yet another brand new territory, but also a victory against repression. What was even more astonishing was that a large mainstream crowd had loved it.

Brian addressed the audience in three different languages, making sure that no-one would misunderstand him. 'Shukran, merci and thank you,' he beamed. In spite of his 30 year absence, the situation was working better than he could ever have imagined. The band finally ended with Nancy Boy, as if to demonstrate to those who needed to question it that they would not change themselves for anyone. Inoffensive defiance was the flavour of the day and it was a time when the band never failed to shake things up.

It was not just an ordinary live show. Placebo had succeeded in providing strength and support to a community that was tortured, hidden and deeply misunderstood. They gave comfort to sexual minorities by their mere presence, and the effects were instant. Just one year later, Lebanon launched its first ever lesbian and gay magazine that was dedicated to forbidden love. Had Placebo played a part in their courage?

'I've lived in very cosmopolitan cities where sexuality isn't a big deal,' Brian recalled. 'But in some way globally, gay people still feel like strangers.' He gave a clear message to those who could not reconcile their sexuality with religion and convention. 'Knowing that you can't please everybody is a part of life. If you're not hurting people by it, you shouldn't be ashamed and you just have to let closed-minded people fuck off. If somebody doesn't like what we do, fuck them. It took me a long time to get this because I always thought of myself as a freak. You know what? There's something great about being successful for being a freak! I hope that inspires people.' He added 'Loving is loving. I'm sure you have an opinion of my sexuality right now and it doesn't bother me in the slightest – and that's what matters to me.'

With such strong feelings on the matter, it was little surprise that this was not the only move he made to eliminate homophobia. The group's acoustic show at the Paris Olympia on June 30th 2004 was another such demonstration of homosexual tolerance. The line up at the concert read like a list of gay musical icons – or at the very least, sexually and aesthetically experimental ones.

According to the organisers, that evening was a show 'dedicated to queer.' Performing with Etienne Daho, Mickey D and headline act the Cure, Placebo performed songs in an acoustic vibe, with Plasticine and This Picture being notable moments.

After winning tickets on a RTL2 radio show, the small gathering of fans consisted of only the most loyal, yet the broadcast the following night would reach households nationwide. It would be another middle finger to repression, even if the location was a much more liberated and light-hearted one. Despite the controversial and perhaps somewhat threatening image Placebo presented to ordinary people, they were in.

Moments like these, featuring performances from artists appreciable by not just outsiders but by mainstream culture, proved that good music could come from those who were considered 'freaks.'

The Daily Star had tellingly commented of the trio 'The once unfashionable glam and punk-rock act that stood out from the 1990s Brit pop craze like a drag queen in a plumber's convention is no longer the prerogative of angst-ridden teenagers. Eight years and four albums later… the band have resolutely claimed possession of its niche.'

Regardless of their controversial image, which was perhaps off-putting to more conventional members of society, Placebo hadn't failed in their ability to infiltrate the mainstream. Playing to a homophobic society in Lebanon and being met with nothing but adoration was a prime example of that. The law might condemn certain sexual practises, but the youth of

Lebanon had no such bigotry in mind. Could Placebo have broken the mould for a new generation who just needed a gentle shove towards a more tolerant future? That night in the more freedom granting, liberated Paris, their music had equal effect. With a little less repression in the house, but certainly no less passion, the fans were on a high, witnessing their band in a new and unusual setting.

Now recognised as a role model for fans struggling with their sexuality, Brian was called upon by the public of Germany for his advice. From a country who had previously announced their faith in his abilities as a politician, he was now taking on another guise – musician turned agony uncle. Echoing an age old adage and quote, Brian assured the population 'Heterosexuality is not normal, it's just common.'

Encouraging experimentation and a note of fearlessness in the pursuit of one's own sexual identity, Brian offered his support and understanding. Jokingly commenting on lesbian duo Tatu, he smirked 'Get two pretty girls, throw buckets of water all over them, get them to kiss and yeah, of course you're gonna have a hit. What do you expect?' His tone was incredulous but it also illuminated another interesting issue, the difference in the perception of male and female homosexuality – traditionally deviation in a female is considered erotic in western culture, whilst observation of male love is more commonly met with anger and violence. The latter had led Brian into trouble in the past, but according to the devout singer, his 'guardian angel' had always saved him.

With Brian's undeniable knack for provocation, the angel assigned to his case surely enjoyed very few days off. One such off day perhaps explained the event that culminated in a drunken reveller, fuelled by his bruised ego, picking up the diminutive singer and hurling him across the room. Nevertheless, those broken ribs surely taught him a lesson in diplomacy.

Brian believed that homophobia was one of the biggest social problems to blight worldwide culture. Psychoanalysts from Freud's day forward had proposed that disgust often arises through a subconscious identification with a feared and forbidden way of life. In other words, homophobic violence and bigotry could be a form of repressed gay urges, indicating how more conservative men feel about the despised wishes mounting and manifesting within themselves. The result of this confusion and internal pressure could lead to monumental anger and violence.

While he was taking on a large task, this was exactly what Brian had hoped to obliterate. He had turned uncharacteristically quiet when questioned on the sexual tastes of arch rival Limp Bizkit front-man Fred

Durst. Met with the suggestion that he might have more in common with Brian than he'd like to think, the response was a fascinated 'Interesting…'

Amid the rising tension faced by bisexual and gay counterparts, Placebo had played a huge part in asserting the right to express one's individuality and without the fear of reprisal. Prejudice, according to Placebo, was one of the seven deadly sins.

Placebo had learnt some tolerance lessons of their own when they returned to the dreaded Mama Kins in Boston earlier in the tour, the same venue they had previously dismissed as a 'culture shock.' The venue was part owned by Aerosmith lead singer Steven Tyler, but in spite of his endorsement, the city had no appetite for Placebo's brand of androgynous rock.

Was it that simple though? The event had gone unpublicised on the group's official website and, perhaps as a direct consequence, the front row was the only row.

The group still enjoyed a cult-like status in the USA, with a small number of followers possessing enough energy and devotion for a fan base twice their size. Many of the concert-goers would have been out of towners travelling for their band, although a lack of publicity outside of the local media had failed to alert them. The absence of a large crowd was sorely missed. Nevertheless the group played on as spiritedly as if it were the 40,000 capacity stadium they had graced merely months earlier, and with just as much humble sincerity. The grin on Brian's face suggested the adulation of 18,000 screaming Parisians at the Bercy was his backdrop – yet in reality no more than twenty people were anywhere other than the bar. 'From three thousand people to twenty, it was a bit much,' Brian cringed. 'We weren't really prepared for it at that point. We'd just done the biggest tour in our lives.'

On another occasion, a glitch with the ever-reliable international customs led to a show in Anaheim without the luxury of any equipment and with only a few hours to spare. Never a band to be defeated, an accapella show was devised in moments, seeing Brian cover Sinead O Connor's Jackie and NIN's Hurt.

However, the continual glitches did lead to exhaustion and chaos from time to time and emotions often ran high. 'When I look in the mirror, after having given hundreds of interviews, I hate myself,' Brian claimed. 'I am also too understanding. I understand the point of view of everyone – my record company, the journalists, the fans. Such a degree of tolerance is very handicapping.' In an attempt to escape the mounting pressure, he took a series of small breaks. 'You can't drive a car without gas – you need to fill up,' he sighed wearily. 'I'm having a break.'

True to his word, in February 2004 he visited India to 'rest, meditate and refresh myself' as well as doing some light work which saw the emergence of an old time friendship with Asia Argento. He had managed to find the time to record a song for her movie 'Ingannevole e il cuore sopra ogni cosa.' A telephone exchange project ensued. 'It was very hard work because I recorded my vocals in London and she did hers in Rome,' Brian sighed, clearly exasperated. 'We had to call each other by phone to re-listen to it all. It was like phone sex – frustrating.'

He was able to compensate for the irritation of their long distance chats by finally meeting up with her in person at the Cannes film festival on May 12th 2004. Brian was pictured smiling jubilantly with both her and other film industry acquaintances. As the two warmly embraced for the cameras, any irritation that Asia may have felt about Brian's 'gagging for a shagging' comment had been long forgotten. The two were now firm friends. She proved this for anyone in doubt by appearing at a private and very exclusive show he performed in the region.

To the surprise of his followers, he also found time to DJ again. Riverman management had business connections with the Metropolitan Hotel and Brian was offered a residency at their Bangkok branch. He DJed at the Met Bar – in the words of the Daily Mail, a shadowy, alluring Manhattan style don.' Every third Wednesday of the month, starting on April 7th 2004, he was to make an appearance on stage for the listening pleasure of upscale holiday-makers. It was a short-lived but successful journey that he had enjoyed very much.

On the globe-trotter's return, there was a multitude of new projects to stimulate his senses, including a collaboration with one very special woman. American songstress Kristeen Young was renowned for her 80s-style punky feminist rock anthems, and never more so than on her newest album X. Despite no initial evidence to the outsider that she and Brian would be compatible, underneath the surface lay dozens of similarities.

Brian was no stranger to possessive relationships – his autobiographical accounts of destructive trysts had adorned songs such as Protect Me From What I Want and I'll Be Yours. Kristeen's work complemented these themes by dealing with just that. Her concept album, based on the Ten Commandments, explored the similarities between religion and love. This was a theme to which Brian had frequently paid homage on numbers like Special K and Days before You Came. Brian lent his vocals to the track 'No Other God', which described an obsessive relationship. The singer wants to be the sole influence in her lover's life to the exclusion of all others. 'You'll have no other God but me,' the tune insists.

The insecurity, nagging jealousy and control issues that this song portrays can eventually lead to painful isolation. The song fitted Brian's interests exceedingly well and the recording was a success.

Following that collaboration was another – possibly one of Brian's biggest achievements to date – his participation in the solo album of Jane Birkin, due for release on April 29th 2004.

Since her discovery as an actress, Jane Birkin had been a singer, an award-winning figure on the silver screen and even a humanitiarian aid worker, teaming up with charities such as Amnesty International for worldwide welfare.

Jane was the first actress to show pubic hair in a movie, and that wasn't her only contribution to shaking up on-screen sexuality. Along with her husband Serge Gainsbourg, she released Je T'aime Moi Non Plus, a love song full of passionate moaning and breathy sighs. For modern-day Europe it might have been tame but at its time it was notoriously brave and raunchy.

Arguably one of the most controversial figures of her time in the permissive yet still largely conservative era of the 1970s, Birkin was in no mind to retire. In spite of her increasing age, and with few of her counterparts still around, Birkin's tenacity in the dog-eat-dog climate of the music industry never ceased. It matched Brian's, who was still going strong whilst the bands who had attended new talent festivals with Placebo years before had long since paled into insignificance.

Plus the two had more in common than they could ever have imagined. Brian had covered Jane and Serge Gainsbourg's 'Je T'aime Moi Non Plus', playing the part of Jane in a bizarre and gender-defying twist for the promiscuous, sexually ambigious Trash Palace project.

His first introduction to Gainsbourg had been watching a live TV show in which the star would make headlines. The singer had told Whitney Houston 'I want to fuck you' on the live screening. 'I thought that was great,' revealed Brian. 'I relate to him, especially his lack of confidence. We find a way to express ourselves in music – it offers the possibility of becoming someone else, of overcoming your ugliness.' Brian also appreciated the erotic elements of his work, shivering 'Gainsbourg's songs just give me the most incredible hard-on.' One of his favourite albums of all time was Histoire de Melody Nelson. 'It was one of the first concept albums ever made,' Brian enthused. 'It's about a French rock-star that falls in love with a 14-year old girl. In 27 minutes you get an entire lifetime of emotion. It's a work of sheer perverse genius.'

He was equally admiring of Jane's work too, and it was perhaps inevitable that the two would eventually get together on their own project. It was to no-one's surprise when Brian was invited to participate in the recording of Jane's brand new album Rendez Vous. As her first solo project, it was one that Brian was honoured and delighted to be a part of, and judging by French interview footage of the two, the feeling was unreservedly mutual.

The two shared deep appreciation and respect for each other's artistic endeavours, and both were keen to produce a collaboration of their own. Video clips had been televised demonstrating the writing process – Brian putting pen to paper for the lyrics as Jane looked on admiringly, and the two devising vocals side by side in the studio.

'Brian really knows his stuff,' Jane had commented. 'He's an intelligent guy. I thought only French song-writers paid such careful attention to words. I thought with English music, so long as people understood a song's title and could dance to it, they didn't bother much beyond that. But Brian wrote a really strong song for the album and a cheeky one at that. He's proved he's a good song-writer who has the ability to carry a word over onto the next line.'

Bursting with admiration for him, she added that even her mother had appreciated the vocal offering Smile. 'My mother absolutely loved the element of mischief and malice – it's not a respectful song at all.'

Indeed, knowing Jane's reputation for pushing the boundaries, Brian had dared to go a little further. The lyrics had berated a vicar who was 'too busy cruising your ass' and advised that 'frowning just makes you look ugly.'

Ultimately Jane loved the song. Back in the studio, Brian returned the sentiment, giving a proud thumbs up to the iconic and long-standing singer's vocal renditions.

Shortly after this appetiser, Smile was released for the public, leaving some fans very confused. The news of I Do, the first happy, strife-free Placebo love song, followed by such cheery sentiments as 'Smile and the whole world smiles with you'? Where was the darkness and gloom? Had Brian gone crazy? Evidently, and all the better for it, some might say.

Brian had once commented that every Placebo love song was perversely twisted and this number was no exception. Thanks to his vocal input, the lyrics proved to be as risqué and naughty as ever.

Following these collaborations, it was time for Brian to turn his attention to Placebo again. The next single was to be a French only release with a very unexpected flavour. Protect Me From What I Want became Protégé Moi.

The special French edition single needed an equally special visual accompaniment and that is where the band sought the talents of Mr Gaspar Noé.

Renowned for his series of violent and attention-grabbing films, the producer was most famously responsible for Irreversible. In the film, starlet Monica Belluci is subjected to a nine minute long brutal anal rape scene. Another frame sees an innocent man reduced to a pulp at the hands of a fire extinguisher.

The film had received mixed reviews, with some critics questioning how valid the film would be independent of the shock tactics it had employed. Others questioned whether the director intended to portray a harrowing message or whether it was simply sensationalism – marketing shock value for its own sake.

The Guardian claimed 'A similar tale to this became a sublime story of redemption in Ingmar Bergman's hands as The Virgin Spring, but as told by Noé it's just a squalid account of what can happen when macho men egg each other on to revenge under the influence of cocaine and alcohol.' Incidentally, the ending of his debut Seul Contre Tous was equally gory, featuring a 30-second countdown so that the squeamish at heart could leave the cinema and make a quick getaway.

A reviewer from the site Digital Retribution was even less forgiving, citing it 'one of the most worthless pieces of crap I've ever seen...an unengaging second rate gimmick… it comes across as a pompous take on an exploitation film, dressed up in gimmicks to placate those who won't admit to themselves they want to watch gratuitous sex and violence.' In fact, there were very few positive reviews of the director's work at all.

Was Noé's behaviour an attempt to gain attention without providing an adequate storyline once he had received it, or was he like Eminem before him, unapologetically holding a mirror up to the harsh side of the human condition? Despite mixed opinions about his authenticity as a director, he was the man chosen for the project of Protégé Moi.

Whatever anyone felt about Noé, one thing was for sure – with such a controversial director behind the project, it was guaranteed to attract attention. Thankfully for Placebo, Protégé Moi was no exception.

'Irreversible is a very moral and very important film,' Brian offered in Noe's defence, adding 'He was the ideal person to work with us on Protégé Moi.'

After the group had spent some time in the studio, a video with a difference emerged to satisfy all band members' expectations. 'It's basically a three and a half minute slice of hardcore pornography,' Brian announced cheerfully. So what was included in the plot?

The video featured amateur actors in a collection of clichéd pornographic poses. The two main actresses enter into a bisexual clinch, satisfying the predictable lesbian element in any soft-core film, whilst, even more predictably, a Placebo poster is glued to the wall above. They experiment with each other before joining a mild orgy stretching across a luxurious but lowly lit bedroom for the final frames. Neither sordid nor sophisticated, was this a no-man's land between light pornography and Noé's own attention seeking self indulgence? This would be a question for the media to answer.

Noe confided to Brian that he did not envy the actors in the clip due to fears of sexual inadequacy and performance anxiety. Brian agreed on the same grounds. Regrettably therefore the video became one of the few in which the band themselves did not appear.

Placebo and Noé needed one more talented collaborator to make the puzzle complete. The lady in question was Virginie Despentes – actress, film director and now translator. She had also been among the audience at the group's enormously successful Bercy show earlier in the tour. Immediately transfixed, Virginie, who counted the Libertines and Courtney Love among her influences wasted no time in becoming an additional team member for the project.

No stranger to twisted sexual themes, her last venture Baise Moi follows the violent killing spree of a debauched and fatally decadent group of ex-prostitutes seeking revenge on the male population. She was all too happy to provide a French translation of Placebo's equally dark lyrics and with collaborators of such repute, the video was guaranteed to attract attention.

However, releasing the single was a problem because of its content. CD stores such as FNAC, the French equivalent of HMV, refused to stock it, meaning that the band had to think quickly to find another method of presentation. Instead, a 64-page magazine was produced dedicated to Placebo, featuring interviews and news from the group's career, and the single was complimentary to those who bought it. The X-rated video and its accompanying magazine earned an 18+ warning tag and amusingly had to occupy the top shelf of most newsagents for legal reasons. On May 4th 2004, it hit the shops.

In spite of the obvious complications, Placebo was releasing a CD on their own terms and in their own way, regardless of potential financial loss. They had lost out on the under-18s side of the market but perfecting shop sales did not dissuade them from releasing a video in exactly the way that they wanted. Regardless of the outcome, their tenacity was a signature of true Placebo style.

The song took on a whole new meaning one night in Germany, when Brian toppled off the stage mid song. Shamefaced, he emerged with cries of 'That was a Spinal Tap moment!' and, never skipping a beat, altered the lyrics to 'Protect me when I fell off stage!'

The other single to have been released that year was English Summer Rain on February 23rd 2004, which peaked at a pleasing Number 23 in the UK chart. Innovatively, it was the result of a fan's animation submitted to the management all the way from South Africa. The band was delighted with the intricacy, using it as a final theme for the video. 'Can't breathe each time you're leaving' states the lipstick scrawled message across the chest of a man who adorns the front cover. These words echoed the lyrics of long time friend Simon Breed. 'I'd better be careful what I say here, but those are Breed lyrics,' chuckled Simon 'and I'd like to think I've been an inspiration.'

As the single was released, Brian began to incorporate added finishing touches to the live version. Mimicking Neil Young's infamous words, he sang 'You are like a hurricane, I wanna love you but I just get blown away.' To the fans, Brian's performance matched that of a hurricane in its fervour and intensity and the addition to what was previously just a blank guitar solo was greatly appreciated.

Having wowed audiences worldwide, the inevitable comedown was Placebo's perception back home. Returning from their transatlantic journeying, there was the small matter of the band's unhappy love affair with the UK. Their last memory of the UK media had been their stint at Brixton Academy on March 1st 2004, a little dampened by the ludicrous antics of some of their fans. A shower of rubber ducks had catapulted on to the stage, narrowly missing Brian himself, as the first chords rang out of Every You Every Me. Slightly bemused, Brian had blinked back surprise but managed to continue playing. This was a new trend which the Times summarised – 'Brian wished the audience love and respect. In return their fans at the front showered him with rubber ducks – the result of a radio interview in which Molko declared his enthusiasm for playing with such objects in the bath.' The singer later voiced his displeasure in an interview with the Mirror, wincing 'I'd like to personally ask that fans stop throwing rubber ducks on stage – it can be very off-putting.'

Disgruntled teenagers reluctantly closed the forums that they had created in memory of the incident and much to the relief of the band, things began to return to normal. Rubber ducks aside, the Brixton shows had been immensely successful sell-outs. 'Our shows are like the circus, where the freaks come out to play,' Brian had grinned. Indeed, the streets of Brixton hours before a show were a perfect example of that. Ordinarily a poverty stricken and gritty ghetto area of London, it was transformed into a paradise for the unconventional, a mass of pink hair, glittery eyeliner and leopard print tights. As always, the sell-out was a truly traffic-stopping occasion. People stopped to stare in disbelief at the patent five inch platform boots, seen more often on boys than girls.

Inside, fans had barely noticed their competent support acts in their desperation to see the main attraction. When the threesome eventually strode on stage, it was to rounds of hysterical applause. Amusement infiltrated their intense stage presence when, in a not so flattering advertisement for Motorola, Brian made a case for the polyphonic ring tones. 'Let's play a game of Name That Tune,' he announced before playing a tinny ring tone to the microphone. Most of the audience reacted blankly to a barely recognisable rendition of English Summer Rain. 'Go on,' he urged. 'Name that tune!'

The audience also heard the Bitter End, but were met with even more blank stares and a puzzled silence. Brian finally admitted defeat. A renowned technophobe, he had finally succumbed to pressure and joined the ranks of the mobile-phone owning community, something he felt obliged to show off to his followers. 'I wondered why he came on stage with a mobile phone in his pocket,' a more observant fan remembered.

After that show, a concert with a huge sense of community, some members of the media longed to break their influence. There was a feeling among the public that Brian was responsible for his cartoon-character perception and every last comic metaphor that dogged the band in their efforts to be taken more seriously. Yet few could deserve the sharp acidity of the media's tongue that Placebo seemed to have inspired.

'There's a feeling that everything Placebo do now is the last throw of the dice,' Kerrang commented theatrically of their Nimes show on July 15th 2004. 'So this is the perfect venue for them; a Roman gladiatorial arena – now used for bull-fighting – imbued with the orgiastic carnality and decadence of the empire. A place for Placebo to fight for their lives.'

Yet Brian felt he no longer needed to raise a middle finger to his detractors – for the music was speaking all by itself. And indeed, Kerrang were forced to concede of that concert 'They deliver with fire, energy, vigour and passion.' This is a sentiment that rang true for the fans whether in Nimes, Niederhehn or Nottingham.

However, this was never more the case than in France, a notoriously insular nation who were seen as patriotic in their approach to music. Brian's love of the French language and willingness to learn it had allowed him to bond with the nation. That had saved him from their disapproval and had made him one of the gang. In fact, France was the first country to tease some information out of Brian on the rumours that he would release his own material on a solo album. However, in typical Brian style, his response was laced with sarcasm. Living up to his reputation as a merciless tease, he immediately deflected the question, giggling that he might release collaborations with Jay Z and P Diddy. The mischievous remark sent a wave of terror through indignant French minds and 'self respecting alternative music fans' as he broadcast the news to Europe 2.

However, after time spent in Russia, Iceland and France, the band once again returned to the UK to greet the media onslaught in person. The purpose of their attendance? To promote new album Once More with Feeling, released on October 25th 2004. A collection of the group's most memorable singles on one disc, plus two new offerings and an exclusive documentary, the CD was to present an important opportunity for the band in matters of publicity. Reminding the uninitiated of just how many singles the past nine years had held, Once More with Feeling was a challenge to the disbelievers who doubted the power of Placebo.

Presenting a much stronger unit than in previous years, the band had been increasing in cohesiveness since Steve's arrival. In fact, the union had become like one of matrimony. 'It's like a marriage,' Brian laughed, 'but unfortunately without sex.' Questioned on the sadness of this fact, he cheekily countered 'I'd say it's normal – like most marriages!' This was something that surely stopped prejudice driven homophobes in their tracks.

Brian recalled with resigned incredulity the narrow minded fans he had encountered. 'They say, "So when you get on your bus, do you guys fuck each other up the ass all night?"' Contrary to rumour, the eight-year marriage had remained entirely unconsummated. Since the day Steve had supplemented Robert, there had been an atmosphere of unity and what better way to document the band's frequently misunderstood relationship than singles collection Once More with Feeling?

Two new songs appeared on the album to maintain fans' attention. Like the Gingerbread house, the walls of Placebo's world comprised of colourful candy, each slab a new musical mystery. What then did new track I Do have to offer alongside the illicit and criminally sugary treats of the band's past?

Leaving fans on the edge of their seats, a move which was no doubt completely intentional, I Do was an ode to the sanctity of marriage and the possibility of ever-lasting love. Brian merrily chirps about his desire to emulate his female partner in all that she does, name-checking her extensive collection of MAC, Chanel and Maybelline cosmetics. 'I wanna be a girl like you,' he sings with touching sincerity, his verse culminating in the unquestionably clear statement of intent 'I wanna say I do.'

It might have been a classic love song, but in Placebo's terms it was about as atypical as it could get. Free from a powerful, gripping and ultimately twisted storyline, and from the connotations of despair faced in Without You I'm Nothing, an album devoted to the 'impossibility of love', this is one love story remarkably devoid of trademark drama and pain. Occasionally it can be like that for the tragic group.

'It's our first unashamed happy love song,' Brian confirmed. 'It's got no guitar on it, which we're really happy about. It's a song that sounds like it's under Prozac. It's like "Medication time, boys!" It's so deliriously happy that it can't be natural.'

The band had been daring each other for years to create this type of song, and it had finally been delivered, to the uproar of fans across the world. Brian's primary aim had been to confuse and to push the boundaries of what a Placebo song should sound like. 'Confusion is sexy,' he grinned in an ode to Sonic Youth. What was more, it was not the first time he'd done so – he had shaken up not only societal expectations but had caused a stirring within his own fan base too.

'I hate rap,' wailed one indignant forum member on discovering Brian's love of Boogie Down Productions in one live show with a difference. 'I don't understand why he likes it.' Fans seemed disproportionately wounded and let down by his 'disloyalty' to the rock camp and it seemed as though tolerance lessons could be learnt closer to home as well.

'I could have cried when he says he listens to it,' stated another forum member with alarming severity. However Brian was convinced that the band sounded the way they did because of its vast range of influences. He claimed that unlike some rock albums, where the first track is a reliable precedent of the exact direction of the next hour's 'listening pleasure', every Placebo song is a distinct surprise.

Yet the best example of Placebo's contrary nature was at M'era Luna a year earlier, a gothic heavy rock festival in Germany that they were chosen to headline on August 10th 2003. Wasting no time in his quest for candour, Brian had immediately told an interviewer that he had no idea what they were doing there. 'We don't really belong here,' he reasoned. 'We're quite confused that we're headlining, but if people want to see us, we're there.' In a statement of stubborn diversity, the group deliberately stood out amongst the sea of black eyes and lips and the mass of metal artists by choosing to dress entirely in white! Arriving on stage in fluorescently bright hues of the colour, no-one could miss them. Wherever Placebo went, there was bound to be an element of surprise.

Whilst new song I Do was just as surprising, 20 Years contrasted it with a return to the melancholic rock for which the group was usually known.

Devised with Paul Campion, it had been intended as an AC Acoustics song originally, before Brian claimed it for Placebo.

Offering reassurance of the band's future presence and a promise of longevity, the track can be seen as a look forwards. It had been a thrilling past for Brian, but one which promised an even better future.

Now nearing the end of a world tour, the band set about finding an extra-special way to make their temporary goodbye to fans one that they would remember. Brixton Academy had already seen four sell-out shows on this leg of the tour but, unfazed by fatigue, the band set about creating their biggest live show yet – at London's Wembley Arena. Taking place on November 5th 2004, it was to be the last time Placebo would step out on stage until 2006.

When show day arrived, the 10,000 capacity arena was packed out. It was to be the biggest show in the UK so far, something to silence the perpetually antsy British media. Placebo had decided upon a collaboration to make the night extra-special – one as equally famed as last year's triumphant duet with Frank Black. In lieu of this, a face from the past re-emerged to share the stage with them. That certain someone was a singer Brian had previously interviewed for French lifestyle and entertainment magazine Les Inrockuptibles, and one who had been responsible for Steve's eccentric teenage hairstyles – 'Everyone called me Spider!' If the tantalising tips offer no clues, fast forward to November 2004, and the show day of the ultimate concert of the tour.

Brian shared vocals with none other than Robert Smith of the Cure, gracing the same stage as him for Without You I'm Nothing as well for The Cure's Boys Don't Cry. Fans from across Europe were gathered together on the night, with the group spotting familiar faces from Poland, Germany and a wide array of European cities.

'Journalists everywhere are really pissed off right now!' Zane Lowe had commented and this throwaway comment wasn't far from the truth. Achieving a sell-out show at the same arena as world-famous artist Beyonce, were Placebo becoming a group who rivalled her in needing no introduction? Whatever the case, it was an accomplishment indeed. For despite their status as outsiders, Placebo had joined the ranks of mainstream artists.

'With his jet black hair teased into a futuristic mullet and his eyelids plastered with kohl, Molko had an otherworldly androgynous pitched somewhere between goth and glam,' the Times reported. Delighting at the duet between Brian and Robert, it confirmed 'The jubilance of the occasion did not dispel the menace and sleazy romance which are at the heart of

Placebo's songs. His high voice rang out with a lascivious urgency as he sang his tales of pleasure, pain and deviant sex.'

Whilst the reviews arguably entered the realm of the cliché, the media were finally warming a little to Placebo. As the lights faded on the final show of the year, Brian's proud smiles left no-one in doubt that they had made a great decision indeed.

If this wasn't the ultimate way to end the immensely successful two year world tour, the collaboration went one step further, with Brian appearing on Canal Plus with Smith to perform the legendary Cure song 'If Only Tonight We Could Sleep.' Steve performed extra percussion at the side of the stage. The grins between himself and Brian spoke a million words, representing a heart warming sign of a band that, for now, still got on excellently, were in their prime and knew it. The band evidently viewed this as a resounding success, and proudly chose it as one of the few tracks to appear in a subsequent bonus DVD with their next album.

And so the Sleeping With Ghosts tour was over. So many treasured moments and special memories, yet as always it was a fatigued as well as fulfilled group that turned their back on the bright lights of the stage this time around. They were ready to enter the world of rest and recreation once more, and, in the words of the singer, only a hard-hearted soul could accuse them of being lazy. The break was to be a long one.

Chapter 9.

'I guess the line between being paranoid and being a rock-star is smaller than one would expect' – Brian Molko

Before disappearing completely from the media's beady eye, Brian could not turn down the invitation to attend the prestigious European Music Awards ceremony on November 6th 2004. Along with the Evanescence singer Amy Lee, Brian was due to present the gong for best male group amongst a selection of renowned nominees. Whilst Franz Ferdinand was a firm favourite to win, Brian was equally respectful of the eventual winner of the title, Muse.

At his pre-show interview, he voiced a guilty confession – an appreciation of Usher. He mentioned how much he was looking forward to the singer's solo performance, gushing 'He's got moves!'

Whether this partially ironic comment gained him any credibility in the rock world, it was difficult to say. However it was clear that, following a gruelling 18-month tour, Brian was becoming tired. Since his cancelled performance at V99, he had suffered recurring bouts of tonsillitis and he had endeavoured to wrap up warmly ever since. 'Having pus dragged from your tonsils with six-inch needles is an eye-opener,' the singer had shuddered time and again in memory of the pain. His trademark woollen hats had certainly kept him warm but had become a standing joke amongst his more fashion-conscious fans.

However, Brian had now lost his voice again in one of his rare relapses into illness. On arrival at the ceremony, he appeared intoxicated, prompting critics to chastise his lack of sobriety. Fans indignantly argued that he was on a much-needed break and that there was no live performance in sight, but it failed to silence his detractors.

Explaining in husky tones and at great length that he was experiencing problems with his voice, and that journalists should bear with him, Brian joined a star-studded press conference.

After his lengthy explanation, he appeared surprised and somewhat indignant that he received just one question. 'What – does no-one else have any questions?' Brian asked incredulously. There was a ghostly silence as the TV host visibly cringed and a row of journalists stood entirely still.

'You have seven questions for Linkin Park and you only have one for me?' he continued. 'OK – enjoy Sting and Phil Collins and Simply Red.'

Whilst the European Music Awards catered predominantly for mainstream artists, the snub had come as a surprise to the front-man. He had a calmer stance at the main event, dressed in a suit jacket printed with the words 'Those who fear death do not enjoy life.' True to the slogan, he had managed to enjoy himself to excess by the time he took to the stage. Strutting several paces ahead of Amy Lee, who tried in vain to catch up, he presented the award for Best Male Act to his arch rivals Muse. Despite the perceived tension, he embraced the band members warmly, showing no visible sign of a feud.

Moments later, away from the bright lights and the confrontation, Brian was interviewed again by the energetic Australian presenter Zane Lowe. Due to his exhaustion, he begged that the interview be conducted on the floor. Cross-legged, he began to talk about his plans for his forthcoming break.

Discussing his coveted desire to spend six months in India, he confided 'I want to go to a different planet – as far away from the music business as possible.' Surrounded by thousands of fans all demanding attention and acknowledgement, Brian was in desperate need of an escape. Alienated by Western culture, he sought a place where he could go unrecognised again and could rediscover himself, free from the harsh glare of the media spotlight.

It had been a tumultuous time for Brian. He had recently discovered that his girlfriend Helena was pregnant, which was an unplanned, terrifying yet appealing concept for the singer, and he was also mourning the death of one of his closest friends. These life and death issues confirmed it was time to step away from the rock and roll circuit. It was time to reflect on past misadventures, to grieve for his losses and to digest the intense emotions he had barely had time to process on the tour.

His career had been hugely successful – Sleeping With Ghosts had reached the top 20 in the UK and had sold over 700,000 copies in France alone, earning it the status of 3x Platinum. The Bitter End had attained the number one spot in Portugal, and the album had made the top two in the previously unresponsive nation of Germany. Brian had once cited this country as the reason for excessive alcohol abuse, due to the punters' lack of enthusiasm, so things were clearly looking up. Millions of concert tickets sold, hundreds of elation-filled shows further on, he had surpassed his greatest goals and set new ones. However he was slowly learning that all of this did not need to come at the cost of his personal life or his sanity.

Despite the adulation and the enormity of his success, underneath it all he was deeply unhappy. He was unable to reconcile the adoration of his followers with the self-hatred he felt inside. 'Ever felt like you were in a goldfish bowl?' he snapped at journalists and fans alike as the pressure began to build. He had reached a point where even his most ardent fans had begun to find fault with him, yet tragically no-one was more critical of him than Brian himself.

He confessed during a low moment 'My weakness, my selfishness, my emotional cruelty, how egocentric I can be – these are all things I don't like about myself. I think it was Socrates who said "Know thyself and do no evil" – and that's what I'm trying to do. It's a continual search within me because I'm not someone who often feels comfortable in his own skin or someone who likes himself very much.' In a final parting shot to those who despised his arrogance, he countered 'People see me as self-assured and very confident, but I'm often falling apart – I'm very fragile.'

Of course he had enjoyed his lifestyle of non-stop touring but he inevitably found that even that had its difficulties. 'It's so much better than having a real job,' he had conceded. 'I get to see so many different places, enjoy different cultures and meet new people who enrich my life. I'm very blessed.' While Brian was certainly not ungrateful for these experiences, deep down he realised it was time to step off the roller-coaster for a while.

He began to plan a much-anticipated journey that would begin in Thailand and follow to the heavenly beach destination of India's Goa. He would enjoy exploration of these two places and everywhere in between. As a person of extremes, he needed an experience that would suit his adventurous spirit, one that would be a means of relaxation but also a challenge. Fans might have been surprised to learn of his plans to go incognito and become a backpacker. 'I'm going to slum it for a while – somewhere between backpacking and a three and a half star.' He explained his unusual choice simply – 'I've had too much champagne!'

Indeed, he had spent his time on tour in the lap of luxury, with deluxe penthouse suites, pink champagne and a wardrobe crammed full of Dior and Y3. Now all this was about to change and he would embark on the culture shock of his life.

While Brian was away in India, bandmate Steve was embarking on a very different event – the reunion concert of his former group, Breed. Steve was due to play drums, bringing the band together again for the first time in almost ten years. Whilst Brian was not there to support him, session bassist Bill Lloyd and technician Morgan, who had inspired Introvenus, were proudly waiting in the wings. It was an unforgettable experience for the drummer and one which had attracted Breed fans and Placebo fans alike. Lead singer Simon recognised the latter type of fan as those who 'were drooping their heads on the stage – my fans don't normally do that!' Nonetheless, this was a rare opportunity to witness Steve's skill in much closer proximity, so Placebo fans had attended in their droves.

Simon recalled his bittersweet memories of the days of excess when Steve was a fully fledged member, laughing 'Drugs don't take over your personality – they make you more like the prick you were in the first place!' In reference to the Placebo fans, he took their perceived disinterest in good humour, revealing 'What was so funny was that they were all just adoring Steve and the fact that they were about a yard away from him, whereas if they'd been at Wembley Arena…!'

He added 'Initially people were there for Steve, but I like to think I had a little to do with it as well. He was doing his orgasm face all the way through, with his teeth showing,' he laughed, 'and I kept looking at him to make sure he got all the cues. We were a little bit rusty after all those years, but we just played two rehearsals together and that was it – we remembered it all. I thoroughly fucking enjoyed it.'

He continued 'One of the lovely things about the gig is that Steve's mum came down, I was really pleased that she was there and she loved it! Afterwards she grabbed me by the ears and went "Fantastic!"'

However, his elation was short-lived. After a communal screaming session, the other members of the group partied long into the night, whilst Simon dutifully retreated into a back room to 'do the accounts.' He had been right behind the concert from day one, tenaciously standing out in the rain to distribute leaflets in Camden High Street. The suspicious fans looked at him in disbelief but were eventually persuaded that the project was for real. For Simon, it had been a long outstanding project indeed. Plans had emerged to do the show as early as 1998 but in early talks their emotions had got the better of them. 'Within 20 minutes, Andrew and Steve were fighting and I was getting shouted down again – just like the old days!' he beamed.

Finally, the trio had managed to make it happen. However, Steve wasn't the only Placebo member to enjoy an extra glimpse of fame during their break. Stefan had also been busy, adding the final touches to the new electro project, Hotel Persona. Together with his two Spanish bandmates David Amen and Javier Solo, he had been devising 'cold, Ladytron style beats.' He had felt that the sound mimicked the anonymity and isolation of a guest in a large chain hotel and had named the project accordingly. It was also Stefan's chance for a little anonymity himself, as his first low-key project away from Placebo since the group had started.

In celebration, DJ nights debuted in Madrid, Barcelona, Paris, Rio de Janeiro and London, all with Stefan's supportive Spanish boyfriend in tow. Brian had donated his vocals to one of their tracks, Modern Kids, and singer Samantha Fox had also lent her voice. The debut album In The Clouds was painstakingly created over three different cities – London, Madrid and New York, before finally reaching fruition. The trio also offered their talents to Queens of the Stone Age and She Wants Revenge, creating remixes of tracks for them. The Myspace page, offering music and tour dates, was spartan and – in Stefan's classically Nordic style – silent, allowing the music to speak for itself.

Notably, Steve was now the only Placebo member never to have hosted a DJ night. When asked the reason why, he reportedly giggled 'I'm not a prima donna!' Indeed, despite being endowed with many talents, he was not naturally flamboyant, preferring to take a back seat whilst his exhibitionistic band mates took the lead.

Meanwhile Brian stepped out of the shadows again when he was invited to France to become a judge at the Deauville Film festival, in March 2005. A culture addict and renowned film buff, he happily accepted the challenge. With a panel of four other judges, he was asked to decide the winner of Best Film from the theme Asia Action. The category showcased a large variety of silver screen talent from the region and it was immensely difficult for him to choose.

The ultimate winner was Lost in Translation. The story is about a touching and increasingly addictive friendship between two Americans in Tokyo. . It shared thematic similarities with Michael Jackson's lonely pathos-packed song 'Stranger in Moscow.' Brian related to the experience of being lost in another country and another culture, finding that it mimicked the way that he felt on tour. It was an ideal way to express the frustrations of the nomadic life he had been leading, and there was no argument as the other four judges agreed with him it was the best contender of 2005.

That year was an important one as it also marked the year that Hassan, the first gay and lesbian magazine to exist in the Arab world, was first published in Lebanon. Homosexuality remains a crime in the region, and reports would suggest that gay rape perpetrators in the region are rarely reprimanded. There is said to be a widespread belief that victims have invited assault upon themselves. Nevertheless, despite deep-seated prejudices and the enormous opposition, legal loopholes allowed the magazine to find its way to the news-stands that year. It left the burning question of whether the group was in any way responsible because of their candid performance the previous year. Stefan's courageous depiction of the word 'Homo' across his chest could have seen him arrested for indecency, and was overlooked only because he fronted a pop group from abroad. In a country of fierce censorship, where free speech has legal and familial repercussions, could it have been Placebo's outside influence that provided the gentle nudge activists needed to pioneer change? They had certainly shell-shocked a nation.

Whilst campaigns for freedom were taking shape in the Muslim world, what was Brian doing? He was embarking on yet another tour with Placebo – that of South America to promote the singles collection Once More with Feeling.

Tearing himself away from his idyllic beach existence in Goa, he rediscovered a burning desire to return to the stage. After a mere four month break, he was more than ready to wow audiences with their hardest hitting performances yet. In memory of the holiday, Brian recalled 'I was in need of anonymity so I rented a small house on the beach. After that, I wasn't Brian Molko anymore, just Brian. The naïve and desperate Brian that I still am. But of course after three months I started to itch. I had to go back onstage.'

And back on stage he went. The tour began in Porto Alegre, Brazil, on March 19th 2005. Demonstrating his desire to remain 'one haircut ahead of the fans', he sported a totally shaven head. Brian's haircuts have been – ironically for a band that was once chronically unfashionable – responsible for waves of custom in the hairdressing economy. However, from his spiky Black Market Music crop to his much imitated Louise Brooks style bob, this was one style that the majority of his fans would not be emulating.

The speculation had begun in 2000, when Brian – by now well-known for his charitable acts – was rumoured to be shaving his head in aid of Children In Need. Whilst this turned out to be a mere rumour without foundation, he was now, five years later, doing exactly that. However the live performances were reported to be so breathtaking that the astonishingly masculine cut was the last thing on fans' lips or minds.

The live set was intense and the month long tour diverse, covering a range of countries including Argentina, Chile and Brazil. I Do received a mixed reception due to its allegedly cheesy lyrics and sugar-coated melody.

Some critics took offence to its cheery nature – a fact that probably caused some mirth within the group. Yet despite inspiring a collective groan from the more gothic members of the fan base, it was ultimately met with more passion than venom.

36 Degrees was the classic highlight of many live shows, with a slower and more heart-felt acoustic style reflecting the band's current state of mind. The remake ensured that they were able to update songs that they no longer felt a connection with in order to relate to them in a modern context. 'We couldn't deny fans their favourites,' smiled Brian by way of explanation. 'But some songs we just didn't feel a personal connection to anymore. We didn't want to be dishonest, so we did a remake.' It had some of their more emotional fans in tears whilst South American followers caught a glimpse of something very special – the group's fascinating evolution.

The group also made new friends during the tour, one of whom indicated that Timo Maas wasn't the only person to recognise Brian's distinctive Dr Jekyll and Mr Hyde persona. Carol Woljta, a Brazilian DJ and pin-up model with unconventional sex appeal, became close to the singer following a chance meeting on the Brazilian leg of the tour. The DJ, who was photographed sunbathing with the singer and attending his after-show parties, claimed 'He's a sensitive guy, gentle and loving. But as he said himself in Blackeyed, he's "borderline bipolar, forever biting on your nuts." He goes from one extreme to the other in seconds – he's like a Dr Jekyll and Mr Hyde and the Hyde part terrifies me.'

She compared him to Evita Peron, a feminist activist who married Juan Peron, the ex-president of Argentina, claiming that – like her – Brian had his 'diva moments.' For instance, when Evita heard that George VI would not be able to personally meet her at a time of her choosing during a state visit to the UK, she allegedly cancelled in indignation, citing an official reason of exhaustion. 'Like any rock-star, he has his Evita Peron moments,' Carol smiled. 'You need great patience to withstand them.'

However, she reported that the singer remained focused on his job for the most part. She recalled that he was 'obsessed with work' and would take it 'super-seriously.' His work paid off as her strongest recollection in Brazil was of an audience 'shouting Brian's name as if he was the saviour Jesus Christ.'

Meanwhile back home, Placebo received a nomination at the British Video Awards. The DVD Soulmates Never Die was shortlisted in the 'Best British DVD' category, alongside such contemporaries as Little Britain. Whilst the group was not victorious this time around, the nomination and the notoriety of their competitors made it a prestigious accolade nonetheless.

Despite wooing thousands of angst-ridden South Americans on the fringes of society who represented the mainstream's polar opposite, at the same time they had conquered the mainstream, entering the world's most renowned award ceremonies and playing star-studded venues such as Wembley Arena.

Following the South American tour, the band was invited to participate in Live 8 on July 2nd 2005. Organised by Bob Geldof, the event was a charity concert crammed full of big name artists, all with one common aim –eradicating poverty and injustice in Africa. 20 years previously, Geldof had held concerts in London and Philadelphia to fight back against famine in the region, raising more than $100 million for the cause.

Now he intended to repeat the mission, but this time on a much larger scale. The world would have to make way for one of the biggest charitable events of all time. Geldof organised shows in London's Hyde Park, Paris's Chateau de Versailles, Moscow's Red Square, Rome's Circus Maximus and Philadelphia's Museum of Art to name but a few. The shows were intended as a message to the leaders of the world's eight most powerful countries, urging them to use their influence to drop the debt in poverty-stricken nations and to increase much needed aid to save a continent in chaos.

Placebo immediately agreed to participate, and they were far from the only artists to be seduced by a good cause. Madonna, The Cure, Dido, Muse, The Killers, Robbie Williams, Stereophonics and U2 were also among the line-up. Unfortunately for Brian, the band he loathed with a passion – Coldplay – had been dispatched to the London event, although Placebo were scheduled to perform in Paris, creating some distance between the two.

The event had led some to hail Geldof a hero, including Brian himself, but his critics were less than impressed by his 'do-gooder' reputation. Many thought it was perverse that the shows were for the most part absent of ethnic music. Meanwhile the ethnic artists that did attend were denied main stage positions and high visibility in favour of more prominent and popular artists such as Dido.

Damon Albarn of Gorillaz and Blur fame hit out, claiming 'Black culture is an integral part of society – so why is the bill so darn Anglo Saxon?' Whilst he later retracted his comments, some of the black population wholeheartedly agreed with him. Sengalese musician Baaba Maal claimed 'I do feel it's very patronising as an African artist that more of us aren't involved.' Some felt ridiculed by their exclusion, and others were disappointed to think that the show would not achieve its potential of celebrating African culture and music. How else could outsiders gain an understanding of Africa and the real people and real emotions behind the tragic stereotypes attached to the region?

TV presenter Andy Kershaw concurred 'Geldof appears not to be interested in Africa's strengths – only in an Africa on its knees.' Meanwhile Peter Gabriel, host of one of the events, backed Geldof, explaining 'Bob's sole criteria is … to keep millions of eyes around the world glued to the television and he felt that if it was an unknown artist… people might switch off.'

However, responding to criticism, Geldof quickly added more ethnic names to the bill. These included Ms Dynamite, Snoop Dogg, and the Sengalese performer Youssou N'Dour, who was to perform a passionate rendition of the song Seven Seconds with Neneh Cherry. Geldof also organised an event called Africa Calling at the Eden Project in Cornwall, which comprised entirely of British artists.

However some were still dissatisfied. There was a consensus among critics that the shows had largely been created to boost Geldof's own ego. He was belittled in the press and christened a 'flagging, aging rock-star.'

He had claimed that Live 8 would be a free event, which aimed to raise awareness instead of profit, but again critics argued that this was a shameful waste of a revenue-generating opportunity. Geldof had also not bargained for the tenacious greed of unscrupulous Brits who sold their free tickets on the auction website eBay. The site promised to donate a percentage of their profits to Live 8 but, faced with enormous indignation and outrage, eventually backed down and removed the auctions from sale altogether.

Whilst the event itself was free, artists allegedly received gift bags packed full of designer goodies at some venues. These gifts, valued at around $3000 per person, included Hugo Boss suits and Gibson guitars. Whilst this could lead to bulging bank accounts for the stars, the opportunity to send money back to Africa was woefully wasted. Was the decision to reward artists for their participation appropriate?

Finally, critics argued that not only was the event a publicity stunt for Geldof, but that the timing was heinously inadequate. In the wake of a crippling tsunami that had devastated the world, priority and resources were being directed towards the immediate crisis, rendering the timing of Live 8 very insensitive.

In spite of the overwhelmingly hostile reception for Geldof, Brian was delighted to participate and had had no such qualms. 'For me, fame has no cultural value, except if you use it to save the world like Bono or Angelina

Jolie,' he claimed. Getting a good table in a restaurant doesn't make you a better person.'

Brian and Geldof had faced similar criticism for being 'champagne socialists' due to their elite background. However, Brian was undeterred by negative press, and concentrated on wholeheartedly dedicating himself to what he believed was a pure cause. 'Geldof has pure passion and blind faith – these are qualities that I think are beyond admirable,' he gushed. Some of us are born with them in huge amounts, and he is one of them. Geldof is beyond a saint – I want him to be president of Europe, if not the world!'

Placebo's appearance was extremely significant, as 20 Years was on the bill. This poignant song marked the occasion as it had been exactly 20 years since the last Live Aid concert. Most importantly, the song had positive undertones, suggesting that there were another 20 years to go and that the rescue mission was far from over. 'Who will hold the rope?' demanded Brian, delivering not just a lyric but an important message to the eight world leaders about the bondage Africa were suffering.

Whatever complaints people may have had about Geldof himself, his concerts had certainly had the desired effect. Five days later, the G8 leaders met at a Gleneagles Ho summit, to discuss their hope for change in the world's poorest countries.

The meeting was a fruitful one. They promised to increase aid by $50 billion per year by 2010. They also pledged to cancel debt for 38 African countries, and to make education and AIDS medication available to all. They assured that they would help with vaccinations against life threatening polio, and offer mosquito nets for beds and better health care to treat malaria. 'If these promises are kept, they could save over four million lives a year by 2010. You personally helped to make that happen,' Live8 wrote on its website, with a note of jubilance.

There was certainly no doubt in Brian's mind that the charity show had been hugely successful, and he was soon inspired to start some charitable activism of his own.

While he had been enjoying anonymity away from the media for months, his endeavours in the charity world were just beginning to take shape. In February 2005, he had formed the Playing Alive foundation as a collaboration with Pete Tong. Teaming up with record producers and industry moguls, a registered charity was created that aimed to make a difference. Inspired by shows that raised phenomenal amounts of aid and assistance for victims of the tsunami, as well as Geldof's own efforts months later, this foundation made waves for the war torn region of Darfur.

Unlike at Geldof's shows, Brian helped to organise a predominantly ethnic money-raiser called Tribal Gathering. Billed as an event to help victims of natural and man-made disaster, it promised to provide a psychedelic atmosphere and an abundance of ethnic music.

'This is officially the most important rave of your life,' boasted the website, perhaps truthfully. 'This time we're not just dancing for ourselves, but we are dancing for these people suffering thousands of miles away. You've never met them, and chances are you never will, but… by simply coming out dancing… you have the power to change the lives of not just people who are alive today, but generations to come.'

Financial strife or political impotence was no longer an excuse for standing still – this event enabled everyone to help no matter what their background – and even while engaged in their favourite pastimes.

Brian also helped to organise Jazz Aid, a brave move for someone totally uninitiated in the jazz world. 'Our next album will be free jazz,' Brian had jokingly sneered to tease interviewers time and time again, little realising that one day he would be organising a very atypical event such as this one.

'We wholeheartedly support the great fund-raising efforts of Playing Alive in response to the humanitarian disasters in Darfur and elsewhere in Sudan,' Brian had announced in a press statement. Whilst his desire to help charity had once been a closely guarded secret, he was now defying critics who labelled him 'uncool' by very publicly demonstrating what he felt and urging others to do the same. 'You have a responsibility to use the fame that you have for a good cause,' he stated.

After a burst of fruitful activism, he returned to anonymity for the remainder of the summer. However, shrouded from the media once more, he refused to stand still and instead got to work collaborating with two divergent and very different artists.

Firstly he recorded three songs with German dance DJ Timo Maas for the album Pictures, to be released on June 20th 2005. Despite their apparent musical differences, each had an unusual background and an unconventional way of working, so perhaps it would come as no surprise that the two found harmony.

Like Brian, Timo had possessed a rebellious spirit as a teenager, and a desire to do things differently had led to his removal from numerous DJ clubs who were unimpressed with the way he worked. 'I got kicked out for playing techno,' he confessed, without a hint of an apology. Both groups had a love for the unusual and an interest in fusion between diverse genres of music, plus a loyalty to their passions no matter how unfashionable. The meeting was destiny for them both.

'I've never met a person with a face as interesting as Brian's,' Timo enthused, mimicking the thoughts of the Alpinestars when they had realised he was the ideal face for the Carbon Kid. While they saw him as an angel, Timo recalled his own unique perception. 'Sometimes he looks like a little boy laughing, then at other times, he looks completely mad, like Dr Jekyll and Mr Hyde. It's sort of disturbing but in a really magical way.' These lopsided endearments were more than reciprocated by Brian's equal passion for the DJ. 'Timo is just a bundle of cuddly, German loveliness!' he laughed.

The first collaboration between them was Pictures, a sinister but sexy tune featuring a pounding bass line and gravelly vocals. 'Take off your clothes,' Brian commands in it with surprising authority. 'I wanna take pictures of you.' Secretive and full of spontaneous surprises, Brian had written the song a while previously and had been waiting for the right opportunity to release it. Similar to This Picture in its theme and sound, its sinister S & M vibe was reluctantly received by Timo.

The first time Brian had presented it to him, he had dismissed it and requested a re-recording. However he slowly persuaded the doubtful DJ of the song's potential and it was merely minor changes that needed to be made before the song's ultimate release.

Brian also appeared on the album's first major single 'First Day' along with a female accompaniment. The harmonies were closely matched, rendering it difficult to separate the pair's voices at all. The track had an upbeat dance vibe that would not have been out of place in an Ibiza nightclub. Brian's willingness to embrace this type of music saw him praised by fans for his diversity, traits which would stand him in good stead for imaginative song-writing.

Brian's appearance in DJ magazine was a cross-cultural experiment in itself, with the confused monthly describing him as a 'skinny version of Robert Smith.' As this was a project to combine elements of rock and dance and promote understanding between the two camps, what better person to do so than one who had flirted with both sides – and successfully?

The product of a feverish imagination, final song Like Siamese served up intensity and melancholia in abundance. Inspired by his Indian odyssey, its sound had a distinctly Asian flavour. Theme-wise, it spoke of desperate loss and pining to be reunited with your loved one, mirroring the desperation and senselessness of love portrayed in Taste in Men, but in a very different package.

The song was also said to be an after-effect of over exposure to CNN and BBC World during the Sleeping With Ghosts tour. 'That became a song about dragging your dead loved one through a warzone,' Brian offered. 'It's about half-praying and half believing your loved one isn't dead.' It was also influenced by memories of his emotions on a specific war – the tsunami. A bemused Brian had received a flurry of hysterical phone calls and text messages from concerned friends while abroad. Fortunately for him, despite being in the Asian subcontinent at the time, he remained far from the disaster zone. Due to his fragility and sensitive temperament however, it remained in his mind and he experienced delayed post-traumatic shock, realising the full impact of the atrocities only on his return to the UK.

Perhaps serene and remote holiday locations were an impetus for powerful song-writing, because Brian produced yet another song during his absence from the rock world – this time on a return journey to Thailand. Afraid to smoke in the presence of his heavily pregnant girlfriend, Brian claimed to have had the inspiration for the track Pink Water during his numerous trips to the toilet for nicotine fixes.

Brian has confessed before to writing lyrics and composing music whilst 'taking a shit' and was no stranger to 'verbal diarrhoea.' His Freudian creativity methods were not in vain, as that day's time in the toilet would see the birth of Pink Water.

Despite the bizarre nature of the song's conception, it was intended as a gift for friends Indochine. His friendship with lead singer Nicholas has been heavily documented, with the French front-man mischievously singing the praises of Molko's backside. Whether parodying his song lyrics or speaking in genuine passion, Nicholas always remembered Brian for his less musical assets – 'his beautiful ass.' However it was far from just his aesthetic that appealed to Nicholas and the feeling of honour was mutual.

Brian was just nine when L'Aventurier was released, but he recalled it fondly. 'Just being friends with Nicholas is amazing, but to get involved with him musically, with the guy who represented something huge when I was a kid, that was really incredible. The simple fact that he asked me to write something with him.. I felt very honoured.' Valued not just for his ass, but also for his competent song-writing, Brian had entered a new league of writing with his idols. Whilst the song lacked mainstream commercial viability, it was appreciated by fans of Indochine and Placebo alike.

Since his first meeting with Nicholas in 1999 at the Zenith in Paris, the chemistry had been instant. Three years later he had DJed as an opening act for Indochine, a surprising display of modesty on his part and – finding that they shared musical ground – a new opportunity had been borne. The two had intended to work together for some time, but hectic schedules had conspired to prevent it. Finally during his break, it became a natural progression to compose a song together. 'Nicholas contacted me and said "I'm trying to write a track in English." Brian had sweetly volunteered his help, suggesting "For years people have wanted us to work together, so let's pretend that we're not, but let's write this song for the both of us."'

Pink Water was duly created, and took pride of place on Indochine's cult album Alice and June. Both an English and a French version were made available to an eager public on December 19th 2005.

This time, Brian's six months off had not been for bad behaviour but for charitable action against humanitarian crisis, alongside deep contemplation. As with every album, Brian was changing. Gone was the brash candour associated with his former self – at least for now – replaced by an inner calm and tranquillity. What did the future hold next for this front-man who, although much reformed, was still trying a little harder than usual to shake off the sadness?

Chapter 10.

'Napster is one big ass – and we're gonna fuck it without lube!' – Brian Molko

6am at Club Koko, Camden Town. Throngs of black eyeliner adorned female fans queue outside, undeterred by a freezing cold January morning. Some have been stationed here since midnight, shivering violently but refusing to move a muscle. All are united by one common desire – to see their favourite group for the first time in over a year.

The scene is the video shoot for the new single Because I Want You from Placebo's hugely anticipated forthcoming fifth album, Meds. The shoot, which was advertised on local London radio and fan websites, was intended to be an exclusive gathering of just 400 people. However, word spread quickly and chaos had descended on the capital as thousands of fans arrived, desperate to see the show.

Around ten hours later, a small number were rewarded for their patience by entry into the venue, whilst the group's gift of Domino's Pizza was a consolation prize to those who didn't make it. An act of kindness to the starving crowds outside, the warm meal was devoured by hangers-on, who huddled together to share their disappointment.

Meanwhile, it was heating up inside Koko, as the more dedicated queuers received a direct insight into how a music video is produced. The fortunate few were introduced to Brian's makeup artists, who preserved his ever feminine image by redoing his eyeliner between takes.

During the show, Brian attempted a stage dive, warning sombrely 'Be respectful of my nether regions! And be careful of the jacket – it's very expensive.' Sadly the group of hungry Placebo fans were rather tempted to ignore this warning, although this time his Christian Dior jacket remained relatively unscathed.

The crowd were unable to hold the weight of the slight singer successfully and he toppled, descending chaotically into a sea of groping hands, much to the dismay of security guards present. They had longed for order, but with Placebo around that was very unlikely, if not impossible. Non-plussed by the animalistic tendencies of their followers, the group continued.

Because I Want You, a short, sharp and passionate rock track dedicated to tenacious love, was a mere taster of things to come, and the audience were treated to a seven song appetiser in advance of the album. However, first would follow dozens of takes of the single.

Brian apologised emphatically as the group replicated the song. 'I know you've heard it 70 times already!' he blushed by way of apology. His rolled eyes and remorseful demeanour failed to silence an impassioned audience, whose roars of approval could plausibly be heard for miles around.

Autographs and conversation galore followed the short set, with Brian jibing that once signing had begun, he 'couldn't really get away.' Hopefully the show of stamina was a promise of things to come.

However, personal tragedy had marred the band's triumphant return. Just a week prior to the show at Koko, on January 17th 2006, an unscrupulous record company employee leaked the entire album onto the Internet, making it available for free. 'Some bloke in Brazil leaked it, and get this – he worked for Virgin!' said Steve, before retorting 'We were ready to break his legs.'

In a matter of a few short months, 26,000 illegal downloads were made. 'It's hard when something like that happens, because we put a lot of effort into the record and then you hand your baby over to management who look at it as a product,' Steve agonised, verbalising what the entire band had been thinking. 'The CD wasn't even finished. We were gutted but it's the nature of the beast these days.' Repressing frustration, Brian grimaced 'I got really upset that day – you are minded to get very vengeful but you have to move on.'

In fact, the group had first hand experience of that. At their very first show that year, the Bangkok Rock Festival on February 19th 2006, they made a journey into an illegal bootleg emporium nearby. It revealed a multitude of badly produced bogus CDs, their sleeves littered with a tirany of inaccuracies and spelling errors. To add insult to injury, the price was just 100 Baht – approximately £1.50 – and could have been ten times less than the legitimate sale price back in the UK.

Mentally waving goodbye to any hope of good sales figures from the Thai market, Brian and friends simply had to grin and bear it. However their confrontation of the store owner made for some entertainment when he remained confused as to their identity.

Amusingly, it wasn't the first time the group had been plagued by illegal copies of merchandise. One seller had openly promoted his wares outside a London venue where they were playing. Steve had enquired whether he could have one of the CDs and was met with an amused 'Why should you get one for free?' 'Because I'm in the fucking band!' Steve had retorted, an incredulous grin spreading across his face.

Whilst the band responded to such situations with a mixture of humour and embitterment, the reality was a bleak one. Whilst Brian understood the desire to own the new material at the earliest opportunity, he suspected that not all fans were just looking for a sneak preview. Album theft was becoming the greatest threat to musicians' livelihoods, and Placebo was no exception. However, in a taste of revenge, Meds became the fastest-selling album of the group's career.

Talking to the Times about the growing problem, Brian commented 'If you don't buy your favourite band's music, they won't be able to house themselves, put food on the table and put their kids through school. If you love your favourite band, you have to support them.' That aside, Placebo's experience of the Bangkok Rock Festival had been a good one. Brian silenced his fury at illegal bootleg stallholders and instead put his energy into an amazing show.

MTV Asia was full of praise, recalling 'Flying all the way to another country for a concert may seem a little extravagant to some, but judging by the number of foreigners I saw at the concert, the Bangkok Rock Festival was an event worth being extravagant for.' Reportedly the biggest rock music festival in South East Asia, it certainly had its fair share of out of towners as well as ecstatic locals who added their cries of pleasure to the mix. All were 'treated to a thrilling rock festival that came tantalisingly close to being the real deal.' Placebo fought off competition from rivals such as Oasis to become the undisputed stars of the show.

'Brian Molko cut a handsome figure on stage as shouts of "I Love You, Brian" affirmed his appeal,' continued MTV Asia. 'But nothing could cut a figure as striking as bassist-guitarist Stefan Olsdal, who stood tall and formidable. Their performance was nothing short of sterling… the fans moshed, water flew everywhere drenching the audience, a man bodysurfed and landed on the ground with a few possibly broken bones, a few girls get hurt by the elbows of adjacent overly vigorous males… it was mayhem out there, but it sure was an incredible experience.'

Brian agreed. 'It was like putting on a suit to see if it still fits, or like having sex after a long beak. You don't forget how to and you remember the great sensation, but you're also concentrating on doing it well.' If the crowd's screams were anything to go by, he had performed brilliantly.

As damage limitation, the single Because I Want You was released on March 8th 2006, with the album following less than a week later. The huge number of illegal downloads rendered any further delay to the album's release impossible. Earlier than planned but prepared impeccably, Placebo emerged victorious from the attempted exploitation. They gained revenge on freeloaders and their perpetrators when Meds became the fastest selling album of their career.

Whilst media interest had died down somewhat, Because I Want You was one of their best selling singles to date, achieving the number 13 spot in the UK. What had the backdrop been to such overwhelming success?

Partly penned in India, creating it had helped Brian through some tough times. He had been recovering from the death of a close friend yet the walls were closing in on him for more reasons than one. A feeling of intense self-loathing and inescapable despair followed him from the bright lights of the stage all the way to rural India. Clearly the one person he'd never be able to escape was himself.

Even free of the western world and all of its trappings – champagne, groupies, superficial hangers-on and other temptresses of the modern age – Brian simply couldn't find a way to be happy. 'I was in a vicious circle,' he admitted. 'I felt only sadness and permanent dissatisfaction.' His misdemeanours had continued to haunt him and he was harsh and self-critical about them to the end.

'Can you imagine anything worse than your best friend shouting at you "You are one of God's mistakes, you crying tragic waste of skin" at you? Well, I need to tell myself that,' he sighed.

Fortunately, he had the catharsis of his song-writing to get him through. 'I managed to exorcise a few personal demons,' Brian confessed. 'Song writing does allow me to lead a more balanced existence than I would without it. I feel blessed to have that outlet, to be able to express yourself to the world, to use your art as a form of catharsis or therapy. I think without it I'd be much, much more messed up than I am.'

Not falling prey to the ego-inflating rock-star lifestyle and its false sense of arrogance and self importance, Brian was now striving to change his bad habits of the past and this was a theme that permeated the entire album. As someone who had famously been the queen of bravado, his willingness to be self-deprecating might come as a surprise. Behind his unfaltering attitude on the exterior, and beneath the murky world of showbiz and the heavy screen of narcotics, lay a man with huge insecurities to rival most of the population.

The making of Meds reflected the devastation he had experienced at the dramatic transformation from a rock-star to a nobody, a move he both adored and despised at the same time. Following his close yet ill fated relationships with love and addiction, the album depicted a confused and isolated man, drowning in disorientation. Yet whilst he had been to the very edge of the cliff numerous times, his survival instinct had always seemed to free him from the perpetual cycle of debauchery that had become his life.

'I don't want to follow the path of Jim Morrison, Janis Joplin, Jimi Hendrix, Kurt Cobain or even worse, Pete Doherty,' he had shuddered with thinly disguised contempt.

Doherty, the singer in the now defunct group Babyshambles, is well renowned for lifestyle over music and excess over balance, and is more famous for his tumultuous relationship with supermodel Kate Moss than for his musical talents. The singer has struggled with heroin addiction, has been known to vomit and defecate on stage and has continuously let down the fans who depended upon him by cancelling shows. His substance abuse is rumoured to have ultimately been more important.

'I've always had a problem with the glorification of rock-stars,' Brian mused. 'A junkie in the gutter is a junkie in the gutter. But I can't deny it – I had also taken that dead end road. The world doesn't need another dead rock-star.'

This was the turning point for Brian. The most debauched and addicted stars have often been associated with a hint of glamour and excitement, and often to their detriment. A journalist quizzing Brian the previous year had begun with the controversial question 'Don't you think the best thing you could do for your career is die?' Brian passed this off by snorting that it was a 'charming' way to start an interview, but it was illuminating of the romanticism in Western culture of tragic endings, and a lifestyle that is dangerous, gluttonous and ultimately deadly.

Instead of falling prey to these toxic ways of life, the front-man exorcised them through song. Trash Palace producer Dimitri Tikovoi was an ideal candidate to help him do that, and agreed to produce his album. 'The obvious thing to do with an album is to get a big name producer, so we went in the opposite direction and tried somebody that's less well known and hungry to achieve something,' stated Steve.

Dimitri was passionate, fanciful and hugely imaginative. He aimed for a raw sound rather than the polished sound a more experienced producer might churn out. He had proved his worth to Placebo with Trash Palace and had been around the group for much of their ten year career, so was able to mix raw talent and expertise with familiarity and understanding.

Even better, he was a firm friend of the group. 'He came in and forced us to try new things,' Steve recalled. 'Most of the songs we recorded live in the studio without post production, with less layering and less studio trickery.'

Brian still bore a grudge at the over-produced sound of Without You I'm Nothing, and claimed that artificial effects had been added that he 'didn't even know where they had come from.' Dimitri's style was the opposite of that, and of the computerised electronic vibe of Sleeping With Ghosts. Its live feel transported the threesome back to the days of Black Market Music.

Brian took up the story. 'Under the guidance of Dimitri, he rightly felt that it was important for us to make an album as if it was our first record, as if our lives depended on it. He felt that technology was a bit of a comfort zone for us and that it would take us out of that zone, create more risk taking and put us back in touch with the soul and essence of the band. We recorded almost as live as possible. It's something you can only really do if you feel you have the songs to back it up.'

Brian reconciled subjects such as love and addiction by combining them in ballads such as Blind. Focusing on a relationship turned sour, it is a plea of desperation to a lover who threatens to leave his life forever. It offers an insight into the decapacitating grief of a co-dependent relationship. Longing and senseless craving is portrayed in the heart-rending plea of 'Please don't drive me blind.'

An inability to see clearly without one's significant other is a metaphor delivered with remarkable and outstanding sincerity. Anyone who had experienced the devastation and loss of self of a toxic breakup would sorely feel Blind resonating within them, a tune to reach their broken hearts.

To enhance the sonic value of the CD, Brian invited an unusual and unlikely contender to participate in the vocals for Meds. Alison Mosshart, lead singer of the Kills, had been introduced to Brian by her fellow band mate Jamie Hince whom he had known since his days at Goldsmiths College. Hince would later go on to date the catwalk supermodel Kate Moss.

'I've known him for almost 17 years – we went to university together,' recalled Brian. 'I've watched him create and tear apart several bands, until he found Alison and started the Kills. Once Alison was present, the fusion was complete.'

To prove that he thought so, Brian had invited the Kills to be a support act for Placebo in the past. He added 'When we were thinking of female vocalists, we thought of Courtney Love. Then we figured she would be a pain,' Brian revealed wryly. 'Dimitri suggested Alison, and Meds just screams her.'

Excitedly, Brian dragged her to the studio to record some vocals. 'She's incredibly shy,' he remembered, 'so we recorded the song in the dark.' Her tough exterior evidently could not portray the nerves she felt inside, but to her relief, Brian felt that she had transformed the song from a skeleton version to a competent and professional one.

Backing Brian's vocals, she breathes 'Did you forget to take your meds?' adding a female influence to dichotomise the gravelly and intense male vocal. Brian has always appreciated breathy, sexy female voices in rock. In fact, Special K had featured the backing vocals of ex-girlfriend Caroline Finch from the group Linoleum. Alison was another such target and Brian recalled that no man in the studio could resist getting an erection when she took to the microphone.

When it seemed that the band's ambition for collaboration had to be complete, fans were rewarded with another exciting duo – Brian and Michael Stipe on the duet Broken Promise. This was a song about adultery, anger and betrayal. Despite searches, no female vocalist could be found who met the band's exacting standards and so, in a modern-day twist, Brian decided to defy expectations by playing out the wounded love scene between two men.

Since 1998, when Stipe had been the executive producer of Velvet Goldmine, Brian had established a close relationship with him and he became the perfect answer to the problem in the studio. Placebo would never write an ordinary love song, and this was no exception.

'We wanted to take this potentially cliche song and give it extra gravitas and more edge,' Brian smiled. 'It became more than just a duet about adultery, because it occurred to us that there were thousands of songs about adultery, but are there any songs by two men? I still haven't found one.'

This homosexual love song quickly became a firm favourite of fans intrigued by the way their voices harmonised. It was yet another victory for the recognition of gay partnerships.

Follow the Cops Back Home dealt with a different sort of issue – that of a social nature.

Brian had been touring in Iceland when he penned the song, a country so small that 3% of its population attended his show. Whilst there, he formed a friendship with the native band Sigur Ros and recalled his alarm at meeting the group, Icelandic nationals who already had seven year old children by the age of 25.

Unable to conceal his horror, he spoke out on the isolation in a city filled with silence. 'We wondered what teenagers get up to in Iceland, because there are no police and barely any crime. Everyone is busy making babies because there's nothing else to do.'

Brian had always been sensitive to the plight of social isolation owing to his ill-fated earlier days in Luxembourg and driving through a country filled with little more than volcanoes and geysers had brought back cruel memories and an inner sense of his own loneliness and past. Pouring out his heart in the song, he confessed that it had a special resonance for him unparalleled for the other members of the group.

Following the motto, 'The devil finds destruction for idle hands', Brian depicted an imaginary scenario where alcohol fuelled with boredom sparks devastating consequences. 'You get wasted in a bar, you bump into another drunk guy, you decide he is your new best friend and you go and fuck around. The most stupid thing you can do is to follow the cops back home to rob their houses. If someone tells themselves it's a cool idea, he deserves to go to jail.' A slightly unlikely reaction to the sights of Iceland, yet this nevertheless was the product of Brian's fevered and perhaps similarly alcohol-fuelled imagination. The result was Follow the Cops Back Home, a song that inspired pride later when thousands of fans were singing the lyrics back in unison.

Cold Light of Morning and One of a Kind also depict isolation and, like Pure Morning before them, deal with detachment from the outside world. The former, heavily inspired by Leonard Cohen, depicts the inevitable comedown of a reveller walking home early one morning watching the rest of the world get up and go to work. His fate meanwhile is a morning cradled in the sanctuary of sleep.

One of a Kind also depicts 'feeling completely dislocated from the rest of the world,' a state with which Brian was very familiar. It mirrors Brian's previous agony at realising he was not part of society. Whilst droves of his classmates attained respectable jobs, had long-term career plans, a fashionable car and 2.4 children, Brian remained an outsider and a perpetual child. He was unwilling and unable to join the ranks of those who were satisfied with a 9-5 job. In his only ever real employment, a paper-shredding task proved so monotonous that he would frequently excuse himself for fevered masturbation sessions in the staff toilet.

While Brian knew stardom had been the right choice for him – after all, it had been his key to liberation – he still faced self-doubt and uncertainty. The more people that adored him, the more confused Brian felt about his right to be adored. Underneath his perceived lifestyle of glitz and glamour was the same little boy who had been condemned as a freak, a loser, an outsider and a nobody.

One of a Kind thus addresses Brian's ongoing battle with self-doubt, but ultimately delivers a positive message – that being individual and the odd one out can be a blessing. 'You are unique,' Brian declared. 'You realise that there is only one you.'

One line – 'Out of the womb and into the void' – is an ode to Brian's young son, Cody.

Born a Virgo in September 2005, the little boy was instantly Brian's pride and joy, someone who he hoped would 'have the courage to follow his dreams' just as Brian himself had done. He described the birth as the most awe-inspiring experience he'd ever encountered and how he hoped to protect his new-born from the pitfalls of life.

The phrase 'into the void' also describes Brian's own troubled childhood as much as Cody's birth, a time that was characterised by depression, fear and loneliness. Aside from the loving mentions of his child, Brian reassured the public 'I don't think I'll be writing songs about my child's first tooth.'

Post Blue is another track featuring unhealthy addiction – 'It's about how one person can be your reason for living. They become your escape and the answer to all of your questions.' Whilst allowing an upbeat tempo, the influence behind the track is much more sinister. Optimism was present, but truthfulness and realism also prevailed. Post Blue was ultimately a fearless confrontation of the self destructive side of relationships.

Heartbreak became a more interesting avenue sonically for Brian to explore than the rather predictable conclusion of 'happy ever after' and fans appreciated the sentiment, seeing it as much more true to life. 'We don't write songs that go 'Oh I love you baby,' Stefan had said, 'because life's not like that. It's not all about loving your baby.'

For those who seek a distraction, an escape from the pain of reality, or an anaesthetic to take their mind off their suffering and sorrow, a mainstream pop group will do the trick. However Placebo's fans felt that they needed something meatier. They saw pain, loss and heartbreak as convertible to a beautiful, relatable work of art, and they found solace through the song.

Pierrot the Clown is another take on dangerous relationships. 'The target of the violence is a vulnerable man trapped in a violent and destructive relationship,' Brian recalled. The man is experiencing physical abuse from his volatile lover and the song explores the fascinating process of becoming accustomed to abuse, enjoying it and even becoming sexually aroused by it. There is an intriguing hint that the volatility of the union may have been what drew the man into it in the first place. Brian told an interviewer 'It's about seeing someone you once had a relationship with and remembering why you were attracted to them,' compounding that theory. Whilst it is a politically incorrect and most unorthodox statement, the perversity of its truth is far more compelling than any traditional love story.

There are also references to Pierrot, a fictional clown in the circus who stood out from the crowd due to his unusual sadness. The paradox of a sad clown is one that Brian compared to the imagery in Bowie's music video Ashes to Ashes. 'It's a strong image for me, how you can feel so alone in a couple – very cheerful, isn't it?'

Although the title might conjur up images of Brian in fishnets and suspenders, Drag is instead a song about an obsessive relationship. 'I had just fallen in love and I wanted to write something dealing with feeling inferior to someone,' Brian confessed. 'You see the other person above yourself – "I'll always be in your shadow." You find the person you love perfect and feel like the piece of shit on their shoe.'

This was perhaps not a surprising statement from someone who famously stated in Kerrang that he could never envisage entering a lifelong courtship with someone who was not both aesthetically and intellectually superior. Some of his most devoted fans might be perplexed by his low self-esteem but beauty is in the eye of the beholder.

Infrared refers to the perils of alcohol consumption. Whether Brian's subject of resentment is a bootlegger, a deranged stalker or a contemptuous ex lover, when under the influence of alcohol, revenge comes into play with full force.

'Someone call the ambulance,' Brian chides menacingly. 'There's gonna be an accident!' He interpreted the meaning behind the rockiest and perhaps most tumultuous track on the album with the following words – 'When you get very drunk and you've got a bee in your bonnet about something, this vengeful quality emerges. You start thinking about people who've done you wrong and wanting to set the record straight. If you don't have access to the person who's wronged you in some way, anyone will do.'

Brian had been experimenting with the writing process, writing his lyrics backwards for the first time ever. He was practising an instinctual approach rather than a calculated one, where the subject matter of the song would gradually reveal itself. The singer compared this to 'free association,' a form of psychoanalytic treatment where patients speak random words to uncover their subconscious thoughts for therapeutic causes.

Space Monkey also implements Brian's interest in 'talking in tongues,' a mass of gobbledegook initially pioneered in the Bitter End. Yet another instinctive process, slurred words replaced legibility with ever intensified passion. Talking of 'dominoes in drag' and 'the carnival of me,' the song reaches a fever pitch of both sensuality and disorientation. However, complaining of strain on his voice, Brian often cut this song from the set list when performing live.

Finally, Song to Say Goodbye deals dramatically with Brian's hatred and self-loathing. In the past, Brian's loved ones have dragged him away from the cliff edge, from Steve to Morgan, but this time the voice of reason comes from Brian himself, who is well aware that he has gone too far. 'I'm not a fan of the rock and roll cliché. The cliché of the troubled song writer who wakes up in the morning, kicks the groupies out of his bed, shoots heroin into his eye and starts screaming poetry to the moon. We've been signed since 1996 so we've done our fair share of all that nonsense,' Brian exclaimed disdainfully. 'That lifestyle is real hard work and it's just not worth it…the consequences are not worth it at all.'

The consequences for Brian, whose recent transition into fatherhood had urged him to consider quitting the debauchery, had resulted in him seeing himself as 'a tragic waste of skin.' This song, along with Because I Want You, became one of the most acclaimed offerings on the album.

Its release on April 4th 2006 had included a documentary entitled The Death of Nancy Boy. The song had inspired mixed emotion within the band, with Brian repeatedly apologising for how ludicrous the lyrical content had been. Despite being a huge influence in catapulting them to fame, and offering them the highest chart position in Placebo history, Brian knew it was time to grow up. 'I don't think I was trying to be provocative,' he explained. 'I just think I wasn't as good a song writer as I am now.'

He remained as embarrassed as an adult confronted with his lovelorn teenage poetry, referring to his creation with a grimace as 'the song about bodily fluids.' The album sleeve depicted a drag queen in a state of decomposure, a metaphor for both the death of Nancy Boy and a new stage of Placebo.

'I think there are a lot more important things to talk about. I recently lost a friend and saw how the partner full of sorrow was the complete opposite to being in love. The cycle of life and death is very interesting indeed. I also have a new light in my life,' he beamed.

He was, of course, referring to his baby son. Nancy Boy was a song written by a young man with raging hormones and a taste for sleaze. Now, five albums on and with parenthood calling, Brian no longer felt it represented his best efforts. With that, the death of Nancy Boy was made official.

Armed with their brand new album and an attitude to match, the group began the tour with an Asian flavour, venturing first into Singapore.

Brian's notorious potty mouth had already come into play there, seeing that mischievous journalists got their full come-uppance. A cheeky 'Don't rock-stars drink vodka for breakfast?' was delivered on noticing an early morning mineral water for the singer. However, Brian met that with the snappy retort 'Don't journalists talk shit for breakfast?' This was a man who refused with defiance to be pigeon-holed.

Indeed, throughout his career, Brian has never been shy in speaking his mind and – as broken ribs and lost contracts have demonstrated – has been utterly fearless of the consequences.

Another journalist who dared to question the credibility of the band's material at the same press conference was promptly ejected from the room at Brian's request. His bare-bones honesty was highly entertaining to listeners, although perhaps less so for the humiliated journalist.

He followed his mischievous remarks by playing a show for MTV Singapore on March 23rd 2006, as part of the Fashionably Loud festival. Combining fashion modelling with modern music, the show was pioneered in Ngee Am City and was immensely popular with young, hip fashionistas.

While rows of scantily clad and stunningly beautiful models strutted the catwalk, for Brian it became a pleasant yet distracting feature of the scenery. The Designerama festival in Germany a few years previously had rendered similar results, causing Brian to cry 'It's always nice being surrounded by top models!' The show also gave him a rare opportunity to be part of a unique blend of art and fashion.

An on-trend Molko, clad in Dior and YSL, was quick to counter the comments that his references to sex and drugs 'now seem calculating rather than risqué.' In his eyes, the music, a multitude of differing sounds, disputed these claims all by itself. In fact, this album appeared their least deliberately shocking to date. In the preceding one, Brian had revealed 'I'm really proud of the fact that there are no drug references in this one.' Whatever people might say, Brian was growing up fast. The only thing he had never learned to curb was his tongue.

Whilst taking oral sadism to its limits was a favourite pastime of Brian's, he also put his relentless ability for criticism to good use when he participated in a heart-felt campaign against the evils of the arms trade. Figures estimated that by 2020, the number of deaths and injuries as a result of war and violence would overtake the number of deaths and injuries caused by disease. This was a carefully chosen statistic, and one that was open to criticism as the number of deaths from suicide each year is the greatest tally of all three.

However, Brian's strong feelings on this situation drove him to action. A petition worldwide had reached its target of a million signatures, but Brian offered a celebrity component to raise awareness for the campaign. The aim was for an International Arms Trade treaty, one which remains ongoing.

The band produced several music videos to publicise Meds. A Song to Say Goodbye was released on the same date as Because I Want You to create extra media attention. The video for it, based on the film Sam I Am, features a child who in a curious twist of fate becomes responsible for parenting his own parents. The visuals correspond with the song's message not to lose one's abilities due to a lack of self control.

The band also released Infrared on June 19th 2006, featuring a sinister plot to overthrow the government and finally Meds on October 4th 2006 where Brian stumbles around a hotel room in a state of hallucination, an advertisement for the perils of drug misuse. This song quickly earned a place in the top 50 most played alternative songs of 2006.

Due to phenomenal popularity, the band had also begun to play a cover version of Kate Bush's Running Up That Hill at each live set. Meeting Kate herself at a party, their cover met with her own personal seal of approval and – encouraged by her enthusiasm – they began to make plans for a single. Instead of producing their own plot this time around, Placebo invited fans to send in video clips of themselves singing along to the track. A selection of the best ones were chosen, then mixed and matched to create a very personal video dedicated to the fans. This appeared on the second release of the Meds album in 2007.

Meanwhile, other artistic endeavours included Brian's pursuit of modelling. To some he had impish good looks that were breathtakingly gorgeous and but to others they were a very acquired taste. Brian was not deterred by the mixed reactions, chuckling 'I love it that I'm either seen as incredibly gorgeous or fucking ugly.' That was Placebo – never inspiring indifference. He had previously modelled in UK magazine Scene and French Elle. However his Gucci photo shoot, where he attempted to do a gender role reversal with designer skirts, had ended in disaster. 'I think they just humoured me and then put in the can,' Brian recalled ruefully.

A project of considerably more acclaim was his appearance in Jean Baptiste Mondino's book Guitar Eros. It featured a series of artistic digital photographs related to musicianship. He posed lying down, straddling a guitar seductively, with a totally bare leg revealed – it became the front cover. A review stated 'This instrument stands for the mesmerising combination of music, erotica and modernism.' The photograph showed a modern and sensual side to a musician's relationship with his most treasured tool.

Alongside his modelling, the tour continued, seeing the group conquer previously little-known territories including Beijing in China and the Romanian capital of Bucharest. The Meds revolution also wowed audiences from Australia to Slovenia.

The band always enjoyed time spent in Australia, despite their initial bad impressions. 'It's the only place where the girls can drink us under the table,' Brian remarked candidly. It had also been the location for mayhem – Steve had once pushed an Australian fan into a fountain for his persistence in seeking an autograph. The fan was immediately admonished by stern security who told him 'Oi! There's no swimming in there, mate!' There were no hilarious anecdotes on the scale of the Black Market Music tour this time around, but both personally and professionally it remained one of the band's countries of choice – whether for a relaxed sunny beach holiday or an equally easygoing concert tour.

Then of course there was the small matter of Placebo's troubled love affair with the USA. Brian famously declared to French magazine Elegy, 'To be honest, if I don't go back, I'll be the happiest man alive.' Reeling from his controversial and arguably unsubstantiated comments about the country, fans also heard 'I don't want to go to a fucking country that takes our fingerprints to let us come in. Fuck off United States! They are responsible for everything. They financed Saddam Hussein, armed Osama Bin Laden...' These revelations, whilst of no concern to the French public, were to fall less kindly on American ears.

However, the group did return. The album was released in the USA almost a year subsequent to its release in the rest of the world, on January 23rd 2007, featuring special bonus tracks Running Up That Hill and Uneedmemorethanineedu. It lacked one song common to other countries – Cold Light of Morning, due to resistance from the record company. Previously signed to Astralwerks, they were given a contract with Virgin under certain conditions and this was where Brian's rebellious spirit clashed with American policy.

Given the chance to bleep out the so-called offensive words, or abstain from releasing the song completely, Brian defiantly chose the latter.

'I refused to let them bleep out the words cock and dildo,' ranted Brian. 'Virgin picked up the album and said "You've got to remove all the naked ladies from inside your album." It was like, "Fine, you can release it in a piece of fucking tin foil if you want, but do not start fucking with the material." I insisted that they remove the song.'

Censorship was a theme that had blighted the band's attempts for self-expression throughout their career. It had affected Special K, the Nancy Boy video, Protege Moi and now Cold Light of Morning.

However, American fans need not have been despondent. His claim that he wished never to come back echoed a statement made in Perth, Australia, years earlier, which all three band members now adore. He told gothic porn website Suicide Girls 'We've got a cult following in the US. It's cool... you can get kind of complacent about success and [America] helps keep our hunger alive.'

Brian and band mates went on to complete two American tours in the name of Meds, picking up some devoted followers in the process. Several had travelled across the West coast on both occasions, and Placebo rewarded these fans' spontaneity with a special acoustic set at LA's Virgin Megastore on October 22nd 2006. It included the Jackie rendition from the covers album, and these slow, tender and impassioned ballads went down a storm with California.

The band had made a courageous attempt to break America, but perhaps one of the most notable moments of the entire tour was their performance in Vilnius, Lithuania. The 'fateful day' was May 31st 2007. Striding on stage with unfaltering confidence that night, Brian and Stefan shared a lingering kiss to the appreciative screams of a large devoted audience. Their public display of homosexual choice was not the first – another had been witnessed the previous year at Rock and Coke, a festival in Istanbul. However today's demonstration held a special message. Stefan was locking lips with his precocious band mate in the name of gay rights.

In the early 1990s, homosexuality was illegal and Lithuania was recorded as having the lowest acceptance rate of gays in the whole of Europe. Under Soviet law, gay sex was then punishable by a prison sentence of up to five years. Finally, the country's Ministry of Justice claimed that the word 'gay' did not exist in Lithuanian, meaning that a gay association was forbidden to exist. This was a country determined to repress its people from following a homosexual lifestyle. The Ministry of Health even published a feature in its official magazine condemning gays as 'perverse' and 'disgusting.' The life of a gay man in Lithuania would be a very miserable one indeed.

The band had heard the mayor of Lithuania's plans to ban an anti-discrimination bus from entering the capital, citing potential riots as the reason. However, his previous actions in favour of stamping out tolerance of gay minorities suggested otherwise. Stefan and his band mates were determined to put a stop to the bigotry and widespread hatred. He calmly said of the kiss at the Upa Arena, 'Every year the EU sends a bus around Europe to promote anti-discrimination rallies. This year the mayor of Vilnius banned it from entering… he said it would cause riots and unrest. He has supported actions in the past that have put a stop to pro-tolerance of sexual minorities in the workplace too.'

While touring Eastern Europe it had come to the band's attention that discrimination was not the exception in the region, but the rule. 'A lot of hard work is needed for discrimination to disappear,' Stefan continued. 'In our way, we did our bit that night.'

Indeed, Brian and Stefan's 20-second long kiss was a defiant protest against small minded people, and one that formed their introduction that night to the stage. With their characteristic individuality, the words 'We are Placebo' were scarcely necessary.

The mayor might have stamped out gay rights but that did not mean Lithuania shared his views. In fact, the true people of Vilnius cheered ecstatically at the proud, warm kiss of defiance. If there was ever an occasion for celebration of gay rights, this was it. It was a jubilant night and one fans would never forget.

Shortly afterwards, the band received an offer they could not refuse – to participate in the touring festival Projekt Revolution, which began on July 25th 2007 and ended with a final show on September 3rd 2007. Headlined by Linkin Park, the six month festival toured various states in America to provide a showcase of popular rock music. Taking their show out on the road was Linkin Park, who personally invited Placebo, remembering their kindness about lead singer Chester's illness when they guest headlined for them at Rock am Ring.

After an exhausting 18-month tour, Placebo confessed that being met with thousands of adoring fans was a pleasurable experience reminiscent of 'preaching to the choir,' – however in the case of Projekt Revolution, the group was in for a shock. 'We swaggered out there with our bravado, which was immediately crushed by a few thousand disinterested Linkin Park fans.'

They were transported to an era circa 1996 where they needed to fight for the audience's attention. They no longer enjoyed headline status and, puzzlingly to Brian's ego, were no longer the main attraction. This cruel and harsh reality was initially disheartening but it proved not to be an issue for long.

'It took us three or four gigs ... and set changes to realise that Linkin Park and My Chemical Romance fans at 5 o' clock in the afternoon did not want to be wooed by our particular brand of European melancholia. They want to be slapped across the face.'

And slap across the face they did. Rising to that challenge, they pulled out a selection of the punkiest and hardest hitting rock tracks in their back catalogue. Once the audience were treated to a vibe specific to their tastes, they began to warm to Placebo. 'You have to be adaptable and have a Darwinian attitude towards things,' chuckled Brian, entirely undiscouraged.

Projekt Revolution marked the end of an eventful tour and all the adventures it had provided. It came as a surprise to everyone, given the notable camaraderie and laughter amongst the band to learn just a month later that Steve Hewitt had left the group.

Legendary Placebo drummer for the past 11 years, he would be sorely missed. His speedy departure was the result of irreconcilable differences dating back to as early as 2005. An interview with Placebo's deadliest media enemy to date, the NME, revealed that they could no longer live under the same musical roof. Brian said: 'Being in a band is very much like being in a marriage, and in couples – in this case a triple – people can grow apart over the years. To say that you don't love your partner anymore is inaccurate, considering all that you've been through and achieved together. There simply comes a point when you realize that you want different things from your relationship and that you can no longer live under the same roof, so to speak.'

Like Stefan, Steve had begun work on his own side project, Ancient B, and had always favoured a hip-hop style with a more ethnic identity, in stark contrast with Brian's predominantly rock and roll roots. However the two shared a passion for Public Enemy, the Roots, Boogie Down Productions, and even Prince. In the early days, their differences were described as refreshing, and Brian was delighted that Steve had been 'bringing back the funk' to Placebo. He joked 'The beat just flows out from his big black cock...he's a black man in a white man's body.' However, the differences had become too wide and too numbered. Rumour also had it that Steve's partying lifestyle no longer suited Brian's shift in priorities due to becoming a father.

In the last few months of the tour, the band had been partying separately, breaking a long-standing Placebo tradition, and Steve had famously made some disparaging comments to his fan base in Moscow at having spent 'ten fucking years in Placebo.' His exasperation was barely concealable. Unfortunately, the fondest relationships and most profound connections, regardless of the love and professional respect between them, are sometimes prone to eventual break down. Whatever the reasons for his departure, fans wished him well, knowing that the dynamic of Placebo would be irrevocably changed forever.

Whilst feverish rumours circulated and speculation increased as to the new drummer's identity, the question of who would replace Steve in the group remained unanswered. Thankfully, however, any dispute about whether Placebo would return in full force for a sixth album was less ambiguous – the group had plans, with or without a drummer, to return to the studio in 2008.

Their final work following the tour was for the new Mexican film Amor, dolo y vice versa (Love, pain and vice versa). Producers were seeking a perfect auditory accompaniment and who better to emulate the dark mood of this suspenseful thriller than Placebo? Knowing of the band's rapturous reception amongst Mexican audiences, this appeared to be the perfect project for them to participate in.

The requested song was a Placebo classic, I Know, which had made a regular appearance in the band's 2007 live set. The group also contributed Without You I'm Nothing recorded with David Bowie. Striving for perfection, they re-recorded I Know specifically for the film. Sadly there was a notable absence of Steve on percussion – he was replaced by the drummer of fellow Riverman-signed band the Officers.

Set to return to the recording world later that year at ICP studios in Brussels, where they would join Indochine for a dual recording of both albums, the future for Placebo was looking bright and offered the tantalising prospect of collaboration. The loss of their drummer was something they would have to take in their stride if they were to succeed. In Stefan's words, it was 'not a case of killing Placebo, but just a case of finding the remedy.'

Chapter 11

'It was never a case of killing Placebo, but of finding the remedy' – Stefan Olsdal.

With a rummage in the medicine cabinet, the two remaining band members did just that. As the final chords signalling the end of the tour rang out across a stadium buoyant with applause, Brian should have been deliriously happy. Instead he was wracked with self-doubt and insecurity – this show represented the end of Placebo as he'd known it. Could his friendship with Stefan survive the mayhem? More importantly, could he find a new drummer with whom he shared an enduring chemistry?

The problems had begun during the recording of Meds, but Brian had soldiered on. The trio had put on a show of unity while the finishing touches were added to the album, but even before the tour began, the cracks were beginning to show. Exhausted, heartbroken and world weary, Brian had already begun to give up the fight. A world tour was the last thing he was ready to contemplate.

However, he soon found himself on a stage that had become a battlefield. 'We marched on to the front line as if nothing had happened. I hoped it would heal the wounds, but it bruised them. For two years, I felt really alone, but I had no choice but to continue. I knew nothing else.'

As young men, Brian and Steve had shared an unconventional dream for the future – both were passionate about making it in rock music on their own terms, and both had endured the indignity of not belonging. The pair were both square pegs in round holes. 'I felt totally divorced from society,' Brian recalled of the early years. 'I knew I couldn't find my place in it.' His goal, like Steve's, was to escape the daily grind for something more satisfying. In doing so, Brian and Steve had felt on top of the world.

He noted 'The whole reason you start a band is to create an alternative reality, where you don't feel like you're going to work.' Yet suddenly being in Placebo had become torturous and agonising – no longer the dizzying rollercoaster of a fun fair but something as monotonous and soul destroying as the dead-end office jobs he'd always despised. Suddenly, the camaraderie of a trio united by music vanished until they were little more than strangers.

'When Steve joined the band, we were united by substance abuse,' Brian recalled, perhaps a little bitterly. 'But when myself and Stefan began to calm down, it became apparent that we no longer had a great deal in common and that our priorities were really different.'

What Brian had once readily indulged in, he now viewed sneeringly. He was contemptuous of the drug shopping lists that had once adorned both his lyrics and his life. Having recently found fatherhood, he found himself a changed man.

He had a reason to stay clean and was desperate to be a dedicated parent who respected the world he lived in – the one he would pass onto his son. 'When you have someone in your life that you care about more than yourself, it's a massive shift of perspective in the way you view the world,' Brian confirmed. 'It makes you less selfish...you realise how vulnerable little human beings can be and when they're your own, you want to protect them.'

Steve was also a father, to a gorgeous daughter named Emily. Yet the two no longer shared common ground – instead of parenting being something they could share, it seemed only to have divided them. 'Even on stage we were pretending,' Brian revealed with both candour and resignation. 'It wasn't us against the rest of the world any more.'

In his heart Brian knew something had to change. It was the end of the road for the current lineup and failure to take action would mean the end of the group altogether. Talking of the final shows of Projekt Revolution, Brian revealed just how much the group had degenerated. 'We hadn't said a word to each other in months. It was very difficult to feel a sense of unity at that point. We were just like "We can't continue this way" with the frustration, the disappointment, the lack of camaraderie. It was quite painful, but we had commitments to fulfil so we weren't going to shirk away from that...the Projekt Revolution tour was the death knell for what we call Placebo Mark II.'

With barely concealed exasperation, Brian continued 'The idea of brotherhood wasn't really there any more. It gets to the point where you look at the person you've been in a band with all these years and go "Who the fuck is this stranger?"... Can you imagine the disappointment to wake up one day and find yourself in a band with a total stranger and that total stranger used to be your brother?'

His optimism and self-esteem had taken a battering that even anti-depressants could not numb – yet in spite of all of this, Brian could not bring himself to walk out on Placebo. He had spent the past 13 years as front-man of the troubled group and, in his eyes, walking away was simply not an option.

After a series of crisis talks with Stefan, Brian decided to break the news to Steve that the three could no longer function in a group together, and that 'for the sake of his health and happiness', Steve was out. Brian claimed he feared his drummer so much that he couldn't bear to talk to him in person, claiming he was frightening and unpredictable. He had even feared physical violence from the man he had once loved dearly. 'I was scared of his reaction emotionally and even physically,' he said.

However, it was clear that he could no longer go on avoiding the problem.

The snap decision he'd made felt like a divorce to Brian. 'There is no difference between marriage and being in a band. In the beginning the sex is awesome,' Brian chuckled. 'Our gigs were fantastic at first, but in the end it wasn't like that anymore – they were even really bad.'

Unable to deal with the heartbreaking reality, Brian shrouded himself in the anonymity of technology, tapping out an email to his beloved ex-brother. A formal announcement from the group's management followed confirming that Steve had been officially ousted from Placebo.

If anyone had anticipated fireworks, they were to be dramatically proved wrong – Steve maintained a dignified silence, walking away without a word.

It had been with a tinge of sadness that Brian had pressed send, knowing that with one small click of a button, there would be no going back. He recalled sadly his hopes that he and Steve would be making music together in years to come, and then growing old together gracefully, reminiscing in their 60s about the good old days. 'So far my predictions have been correct,' he announced a few years earlier. In spite of the aching loss of his hopes, he knew he would be making the right decision.

The remaining two bandmates rallied together to prevent a domino effect destroying everything they had worked so hard to build. Stefan knew that while they might have fallen on hard times, it was far from the end. For the second time that year, he told the press 'It was never a case of killing Placebo. It was just a case of finding the remedy.' He and Brian began to communicate again, healing their bruised egos with the power of song. Defiantly, they insisted to the media that they were 'in no hurry' to find a new drummer. However, a new drummer ended up finding them.

Enter 21 year old Steve Forrest, a passionate young percussionist from California, and a huge fan of Placebo. Steve, who had supported Placebo live on two occasions with his previous band Evaline, could not remember a time when he had not been blown away by music. Employed in a series of dead end jobs just to scrape together enough money to buy new equipment, a younger Steve had shunned university to pursue his musical dreams. 'I never went to college and barely even went to high school. I would just basically lock myself away in my room for as long as possible and just play. I was constantly studying music in any way that I could.'

Steve had struck up a firm friendship with Placebo, but just a couple of months after his last tour with them, in a bizarre twist of fate, Steve too had parted company with his band. A keen tattoist, he threw himself into designing and inking them for a living in a small parlour in his native California. His entire chest was covered with tattoo work and he'd already earned Brian's admiration with the word 'Open-minded' tattooed across his knuckles, letter by letter. Clearly this was someone who understood the Placebo ethos entirely.

He still hankered after music, an addiction that tattooing could not replace, and on hearing that there was a vacancy for a drummer, he instantly sought out Brian. He approached his management for contact details before sending a five-minute video resume. His persistence paid off – Brian was delighted to catch sight of an old friend and seduced by familiarity, gave him a call. 'How would you like to come to London for a couple of weeks to hang out and jam with us?' Brian asked, wasting no time in extending an invitation to his long lost tour buddy. 'See how it feels and if it works out, we'll go from there.'

Steve accepted instantly and left California with barely a backward glance. He was supported by a meagre advance yet an all-enduring passion for success would be his driving force. This was exactly what Placebo needed. 'We didn't want another guy in the band who had been in seven bands and were just as cynical as we were,' Brian explained. While he had become jaded by the passage of time, Steve was tirelessly optimistic – according to Brian, irritatingly so. 'We could live a little vicariously through his childlike wonder at everything happening to Steve for the first time – that was what was so attractive about him.'

Another thing that instantly appealed was his age. 'We searched deliberately for the age difference, for the generation gap,' Brian confessed, 'because we really wanted fresh young blood in the band.'

Brian had been so intently focused on playing music that he often forgot to tune into what was new and popular on the streets – leading to albums that, on release, were already 'hideously unfashionable.' Steve was his passport to youth, keeping him in touch with that scene. What was more, the drummer was bursting with barely containable enthusiasm. A gruelling schedule and lack of support from the media might be difficult, but with Steve's bright optimism, how could they stay disheartened for long?

Steve's energy, vigour and hunger transformed the viewpoint of Placebo from hardened professionals in their mid 30s to the 'kids in a candy shop' they had been during the making of their first album. With the pain of the last few years, Brian had all but forgotten the joys of achievement, but Steve was more than capable of reminding him. 'I've experienced things with him I haven't experienced in 15 years. I've been next to him the first time he's heard himself on the radio, I've been next to him the first time he's seen himself on TV. Those are amazing things, which I'd forgotten about – that absolute rush of adrenalin, that feeling of 'My God, I'm finally getting somewhere with my life.' It's wonderful to experience it once more.' Prophetically, Brian envisaged travelling the world with his new companion, taking on his contagious enthusiasm with pleasure. 'He's the kind of person you want to travel with for two years, 10 years, 15 years...' the singer beamed, already caught up in Steve's contagious excitement.

Of course the age gap did encourage some playful teasing and good-natured ribbing. 'I'm the same age as his mother,' Brian giggled 'and I lost my virginity in the same year that he was born, which is funny... but I'm not his father!'

Steve shook off the teasing and began a new era with the group. He'd always felt an affinity with London so he was delighted to be moving there. At the beginning, he had claimed to be friendless and isolated in a new city but even that did not deter his unbreakable positivity – and of course his new companions Brian and Stefan were about to change all that. They were only too happy to take him out on the town.

What better way to bond than through a mutual love of rock and roll music? The three began to paint the town red at London's top nightspots, to the backdrop of great music. Their partying had no boundaries, with just one exception – Steve had been banned from enjoying the forbidden fruits that were Class A drugs. 'I've been there,' Brian grimaced, making it clear that no further words were needed.

One of the first groups the new trio saw together was Explosions in the Sky. Symbolically the band was, in Stefan's words, 'dying a death' and perhaps this marked the end of a phase and the beginning of a promising new one. Steve brought punk influences to the group again, favouring the feisty sounds of Green Day and Jimmie Eat World. In turn, Brian introduced him to experimental, electronic partnerships such as TV on the Radio and Bjork.

He was determined that music should spark friendship with a celebration of what had first brought them together – and his plan was working.

'The future seems a lot brighter now than it used to,' Stefan smiled. 'I don't wake up in a panic anymore. I wake up quite happy to come to work and see my boys.'

Steve was equally happy. 'To crawl my way up to this point, it's the best feeling in the world... I don't ever want it to end.' The day Brian shook his hand and said 'Welcome to the family,' it seemed like all his dreams had come true at once. He had hoped it would continue.

However, more serious issues were hampering the start of the threesome's creative future together. Thematically in Placebo's world, tragedy and treasure had always gone hand in hand and this time there was no exception. They'd overcome huge obstacles that year but they were about to face their biggest obstacle yet, one that would make the loss of one of their much loved drummers seem positively inconsequential in comparison.

Their record deal with EMI, formerly known as Virgin, had expired, leaving the group with some important decisions to make. Placebo no longer wanted to be under the thumb of a large corporate company – they strived instead for full control. After all they had been through, why shouldn't they choose their own route and destiny?

Brian thought they had struck gold when Virgin had first signed them – following the success of the Spice Girls, the band had been able to reap the financial benefits. However, as time went on, he couldn't escape the nagging impression that to them, his pride and joy had become little more than a mere product. 'These people have no passion, they're just calculating,' he mused. Realising the danger of getting caught in the 'filthy lucre' of the marketing world, he was in no hurry to negotiate a new contract, Having come this far, he was expecting complete dominion over the material.

'Total artistic control, even on how to present ourselves to the world is a fundamental thing for us – this is something that we've pursued over the last five years but for various reasons we were unable to obtain... but a contract is a contract and we had signed it,' he said.

Brian's ambitions had been completely at odds with the marketing department – for example, his desire to release an entire collection of singles on vinyl had gone down like a lead balloon. In fact EMI were terrified to learn of Brian's self-confessed 'absolute fetish' for the long forgotten listening format, which was just not commercially friendly. EMI might have felt Placebo had already reached the peak of their success, but they felt differently. The solution was obvious – to take matters into their own hands.

The group decided to self-fund their own CD and take an active role in every aspect of production. 'It felt good without the marketing manager on our back,' Brian chuckled. 'The pressure was off and the fun in the studio began. We would walk into the rehearsal room and there would be no tension.' However before they could embrace the power of the studio, a new live opportunity was offered that the group could simply not resist – a show in Cambodia.

To the trio's delight and their stage was the unlikely 12th century temple of Angkor Wat. The beauitful UNESCO heritage site might be best known for its appearance on the action film Tomb Raider, but behind the glitz and glamour of a Hollywood movie was a terrifying backdrop.

For the vulnerable Cambodians on these very streets, their lives were far from the American dream. In fact, just yards from this majestic temple of worship with all its history, their peace and faith in humanity had been shattered by the cruel profession of human trafficking. Their lives were being silently destroyed by slave labour and forced prostitution.

But wait – hadn't Placebo already played the ultimate show of the year at Projekt Revolution? Maybe so, but this was no ordinary occasion and this very real plight was worth breaking the rules for.

Placebo knew first hand what it was like to suffer, but they could never have imagined in their wildest nightmares the heart-rending pain of trafficked people. It was with a heart full of compassion that they entered the line up of one extra special charity concert. The group was one of several Western artists chosen to appear alongside local talent in aiding the fight against this immoral profession.

The ruins had been left untouched by musical fervour since 2002 when renowned tenor Jose Carreras had graced the stage for a charity gala dinner. Now MTV would play a part in organising the temple's first ever rock show.

'Placebo is to headline, putting years of catering to their fans' teenage angst behind them to speak out against human trafficking,' announced ABC News.The concert, to take place on December 7th 2008, was not for profit and a low ticket price guaranteed awareness amongst not just wealthy expatriates but the poverty-stricken locals who were in need of a warning of the plight the most.

'At any point in time, there are around 2.5 million people being trafficked against their will,' Brian agonised following his research. 'They're kidnapped, beaten into submission and sold like livestock.'

Cambodia has had a reputation for some of the world's worst people trafficking for decades. Whilst the government acted by banning marriages between foreigners and locals in early 2008, in a bid to stop the exploitation, the plight was far from over. Speculation mounted that police chief Hok Lundy was using his position of authority to traffic prostitutes himself, leading the USA to refuse him a visa altogether in indignation. It echoed a similar stunt in Bosnia the previous year where the United Nations had used child prostitutes they had been employed to rescue, and financially bribed them to keep quiet. Corruption at the highest levels and in the most unexpected places ensured that human trafficking remained a very real problem.

'I cannot believe that in a supposedly civilised world this heinous form of human slavery still exists,' Brian said, echoing the beliefs of many passionate campaigners. 'When we first heard about human trafficking and that slavery is still going on, in a world where young women are forced to be prostitutes, or that people are being abused and exploited to produce the goods we buy, this resonated deeply. The evil that is present in some human beings, how people could do that to each other – it is shocking.'

Brian believed that very few teenagers and young adults were aware of the plight – neither in the Western world nor in the poverty-stricken locals most likely to encounter it – and he applauded any attempt to highlight and eradicate it. 'The majority of people who are trafficked into sexual slavery or indentured servitude or into sweatshops are teenagers and young adults, which is exactly the audience that MTV has,' Brian claimed. It was for that reason that he was delighted to participate despite the concert's lowly financial rewards. For him, using his position to make a difference was what counted and far more important than any monetary gain.

'It's not about presenting your most accessible work to an audience that doesn't know you very well,' the big hearted singer asserted. 'That smacks a bit of commercialism and that is not really the issue here.' Stefan concurred 'We're not here for self-promotion.'

There was another reason for excitement – it was the first time Steve would ever take to the stage live with the group. It was new to him for more than one reason. 'I didn't even know where Cambodia was,' he said, showing a flash of the youthful naivety his band mates had grown to love about him. It would be a truly special show – one of new beginnings both for the group and for the endlessly exploited locals.

The site of crumbling ruins was not the most conventional location for a rock concert, and the group immediately worked together on a strategy to preserve their hard hitting rock sound. Brian locked himself into the studio for an intensive three week rework of the setlist. Determined to produce a sound as unique as the event it was playing for, he came to some unexpected conclusions.

'We love noise... massive walls of sound, three guitars going absolutely crazy,' Brian enthused. 'But we didn't think that was going to be appropriate for this setting, so we were forced to look inside ourselves... and create new arrangements that we thought would fit inside this incredible setting.'

The first decision was to recruit violinist Fiona Brice, a blonde bombshell who had successfully collaborated with Kanye West, Sugababes, Kate Nash and Brian's most hated band, Simply Red.

An extra long instrumental solo of 20 Years was just one of the surprises Fiona would bring to the group's sound. 'We were forced to deconstruct our songs... tear them to pieces and put them back together in novel and unusual ways,' Brian recalled. The back to basics location was excellent for atmosphere but much less so for electronic success, so Placebo relied on their innate passion to carry them through. They also had to find appropriate songs that expressed sensitivity to the cause, and this involved re-evaluating their entire musical past.

'We had a very tortured relationship with our back catalogue, so we had to find new ways of interpreting the songs to make them interesting to us, which is basically what we spent three weeks doing. Because the whole event is so unique for us, we wanted the performance itself to be unique and so we created a new sound for us specifically for this performance,' he claimed with audible excitement. 'It may not be repeated. It's a little bit gentler than what we are famous for, but equally as valid.' It was with this pursuit in mind that Placebo set off the concert.

Whilst the group's UK fans were battling a bitterly cold winter, shivering against a backdrop of a pure white blanket of snow, Placebo were enjoying tropical temperatures in the remote jungle setting of Cambodia. Whilst Britain might have thought that with their sub-zero temperatures that they had it hard, their suffering paled in comparison to the bleak torture of Cambodian slaves, those whose lives had been assigned a cold hard cash price – and that was exactly the point Placebo tried to get across when they joined 1200 natives on December 7th 2008, with a fight in mind.

The group slowed down the pace as promised, and performed a semi-acoustic set that was fitting for the occasion. Instead of the gleeful stampeding and moshing of an ordinary show, local fans were glued to the spot and, according to Brian, 'really listening.'

The new sound did not escape the media's attention either. 'Blind and Drag resonated off the temple walls with Molko's evocative vocals creating a trance-like power,' gushed one ardent reporter, before adding 'Teenage Angst stripped bare was black yet soft as velvet.'

Indeed, its haunting vocals served up a slice of pain as devastating as the real life teenagers here who had fallen prey to needless suffering. Their enforced suffering might have been meaningless to their callous captors, and may have escaped the eyes of the music fans, whilst cruelly overlooked by corrupt officials, but Brian made sure these youths had not, and never would be, forgotten.

He had attended the 'breathtaking' temple ruins already three years previously – it had been a welcome diversion from real life during his time off – but nothing could compare to the rush of actually performing there. He had been expecting 'a lot of confused faces' but in fact nothing could have been further from the truth. His new found fans wholeheartedly endorsed both the cause and his frame of mind. 'I truly believe we can all do something to stop this,' Brian told his audience of the seemingly endless suffering. 'It all starts with caring and compassion.'

Demonstrating astonishing modesty and humbleness, the so-called diva called upon others to join him, claiming 'It might seem that what we're doing here is a drop in the ocean, but every drop helps.' He added 'There may be people who wish to get more involved in trying to change things. That's all we can do as a rock band. We are not politicians and we are not heads of police.'

Brian had two hopes – firstly that he would raise awareness and inspire change by stimulating debate amongst his fan base, and secondly that he could simply put on a show that led the audience to leave with a smile on their faces. Such heart-felt sincerity could barely be misunderstood, and it was with an equal passion that the audience responded. Just as he'd hoped, they took to it immediately.

The singer had visited women's' shelters in the area to familiarise himself with their plight before playing and had experienced first hand the pain of victims of human trafficking. This meant the band's rescue mission could be borne out of true compassion.

As the last bars rang out on the dramatic climax that had been 20 Years, it was with a sigh of satisfaction that Brian had laid his microphone down. He had achieved something unique – 'a performance that we haven't done in the past that we may not repeat in the future.' He concluded 'We wanted to take a stand, to be included. Being able to do that by using our music is an amazing privilege.'

The singer also proudly mentioned how much he hoped that his son Cody, named after the explorer Buffalo Bill, would have the same courage that he had shown.

This wasn't the only mission Placebo had been on. Brian had also been invited to pay tribute to his idol, the late Serge Gainsbourg, as part of a French television show. Brian saw himself in the fearless, straight-talking and sexually charged star, beaming 'This is someone who has followed his thoughts and beliefs without censorship – that's why I admire him enormously. He was a fascinating figure, and a troubled figure – one with demons. I guess I see a little bit of myself in him.'

Brian also thought of the singer as a troublemaker – a trait which many of his idols shared. He had once chuckled 'I'd like to go for a drink with John McEnroe' purely on the basis that he had huge temper tantrums without reservation. The tennis player had once thrown his racket across the court, while squealing irately 'You cannot be serious!' at the long-suffering referee. Like McEnroe, Gainsbourg was outspoken and notoriously feisty. One incident had led to him burning money live on television and another had been the well-documented TV scandal with Whitney Houston, where he had told her 'I want to fuck you' live on air. However, unlike McEnroe, Brian believed 'He has never been a troublemaker without reason – there was always something political behind it.'

There was one thing Brian had in common with all the troublemakers he had witnessed and that was a desire to do things his own way. It was this trait of stubbornness that had prevailed during the tribute show.

As his side-projects drew to a close, the small man with a big heart finally devoted himself to the cause that his fans would say needed him the most – Placebo. This spelt the future for the group's comeback, and failure was not a risk the feisty front-man was willing to take.

He locked himself in the studio consumed with the desire to produce a perfect sixth album. He certainly had high hopes for it, boldly declaring 'Meds was claustrophobic, hopeless, full of debauchery. I was dreaming of an album more positive, more colourful – in Technicolour rather than black and white coarse grained.'

To achieve this, Brian turned to famed producer Dave Bottrill. He chose him to fulfil the group's desires for an 'epic, authentic record' and they were not to be disappointed. When they had recorded Meds, the atmosphere had been laced with grit, and not solely due to Steve's influence. 'On the first day of recording, Dimitri – who is also my best friend – stopped treating me like a best friend so I threw a diva fit and walked out,' Brian smiled.

'Dave Bottrill isn't like that...he's one of those people who does have a lot of people skills. Working with him is the best experience we've ever had in a studio.'

Stefan took things a step further, confessing that Placebo had never got on well with a producer before that day. 'We came out of [the last] five recording sessions pretty fucking traumatised. We have always had a dysfunctional relationship with our producers – all the recording processes have been quite painful.' David played the role of counsellor and mentor too, boosting their bruised and fragile egos, and willing them to succeed. 'He always made us feel like what we were doing was worthwhile,' Stefan claimed. 'He was very good at communicating with us and bringing out the best in us.' Indeed, the group raced through the songs at record-breaking speed with 18 tracks completed in just two months.

Alan Moulder helped with additional mixing. As someone who had worked with Smashing Pumpkins and Depeche Mode successfully, the band knew they were in safe hands. Finally the missing pieces of the puzzle were falling into place. In a tribute to their struggle, the album was christened Battle for the Sun.

In a bid to remove the temptations of London's drug-fuelled club scene and put their indulgent past behind them once and for all, the group had departed for neutral territory for the recording – Canada. Their destination was Toronto, a barren area with few of the delights one might come to expect of a big city. This of course was exactly what the former party animals had intended.

However it didn't keep them out of mischief in their manager's eyes. 'Even our manager didn't know what we were doing,' Brian revealed gleefully. 'She was receiving invoices for brass and string recordings and was worried about what was going on!'

During the recording of Meds, the group had joked that they felt as though they were sharing a studio with Darth Vader. This time around, it wasn't just the producer that they had gelled with, but each other.

Enjoying their new found liberation, the group set to work in an atmosphere of overwhelming positivity. Amid a backdrop of negative rock songs such as Them Crooked Vultures' 'No-one Loves Me and Neither Do I' and Nirvana's 'I Hate Myself and I Want To Die', Placebo simply stepped up the optimism and bravery and of course battling for the sun. It could be said that the music had begun to reflect their new found peace. New sounds were the theme of the album – flute, horns, jazz orchestras and even a piccolo trumpet. This was intertwined with the unmistakable Placebo theme of toy instruments.

Above all, the album was representative of the group's work in its commitment to revealing raw, honest emotion. 'We don't write vacuous pop music and insipid music that is just about complete escapism,' Brian said. 'What we want to do is communicate emotions that people have by holding up a mirror to the human condition.' The album would celebrate freedom, success and triumph over tragedy. It symbolised hope and optimism, although - as Stefan had joked – 'It is really hard to get any darker and bleaker than Meds.'

Battle for the Sun was to continue the band's tumultuous journey by exploring the dark side of humanity turned light. The title track breathes frustration and the determination to break the ties that bind pours out of Brian's voice. It is the soundtrack to a gritty tenacity to conquer his demons. As someone who had battled loneliness, depression and overwhelming sadness since his teenage years and who had been on medication for clinical depression at the tender age of 23, finding the sun was always going to be an incredible battle. Yet it was one Brian never dared to believe he wouldn't win.

'Dream brother, my killer, my lover,' breathes Brian in a fever of dichotomy. The refrain, now sung by millions of fans across the world, hints at a reference to Steve Hewitt – a much loved partner in crime who ultimately spelt the destruction of all that he held dear. Even the infuriatingly optimistic Steve Forrest understood the concept.

'To me, "I will battle for the sun" means that I will fight for what I want in this life, for what I love and for what I need to live,' he said. 'The lyrics "I have stared down the barrel of a gun" mean that you've faced death or the possibility of death in the face, in the sense that you saw that your path was going to lead to certain destruction and decided it's best to change your routine.'

Fatherhood had undeniably been the turning point in Brian's life, prompting him to turn his back on his old ways and it had been the point when he painfully realised he and their former drummer no longer had anything in common. Steve's definition of the song offered a tantalising snapshot into why the rock world's most perfect threesome had disintegrated.

The album starts with Kitty Litter, an erotically charged song about uncontrollable desire. The oldest track to appear on the CD, it first took shape in 1994 when Brian and Stefan were playing alongside 99 others for a composition called '101 Guitars.' The two were appearing as part of Rhys Chatham's orchestra. The composer was a pioneer of the Sonic Youth style alternative tunings that Brian loved so much, and it inspired him to create the perfect tune backstage. 'Chatham asked us to tune all the guitars' strings at the same level,' revealed Brian, 'and this is how we composed a lot of riffs for Placebo, including Kitty Litter.'

Thankfully bearing absolutely no resemblance to a cat's litter tray lining, the song instead channels an obsessive pining for a lover and the need to get close. It portrays the electric chemistry between two people in sonic terms and the teasing aspect of their distance making them all the more irresistible. It relives the pleasurable paralysis of the muscles familiar to anyone in lust. A heavy, throbbing bass line completes the picture. 'Your surreptitious glancing, the way you crack a smile, you really start a fire,' Brian sings.

Stefan laughed 'It's strange how some songs take five minutes to write and others take fourteen years!' For fans, taking a little time had merely led to perfection.

Ashtray Heart, named after a Captain Beefheart song and an early incarnation of Placebo featuring a drunken Steve Hewitt on bongoes, is a firm favourite amongst their fan base.

Brian had written the song during a holiday in the central American destination of Nicaragua. A perpetual chain smoker, Brian's Spanish vocabulary had to be quickly updated to include the word 'ashtray.' In every coffee shop or restaurant he visited, Brian took to pleading 'a cenicero cenicero' for a smoking table. The words 'cenicero cenicero mi corazon' translated as Ashtray Heart and seemed to be the perfect completion to the demo. It was the first Placebo song on which Brian had not collaborated with Stefan, his career long musical partner.

For What It's Worth is the result of Brian's compulsive desire to push the boundaries of the group's sound. The chorus features two 'soul divas' on backing vocals, neither of whom seem instantly compatible with a Placebo song. One was a session artist for Jamiroquai whilst the other was a member of the alternative jazz group Galliano. The unusual set up added layering and a unique texture to the group's sound. Brian harmonised with the female voice, adding an element of raw, heart-felt passion to an otherwise polished and slightly clinical sound.

Brian has been renowned among his followers for balancing perfection and passion – providing both performance based method acting and unguarded genuine emotion. This dichotomy symbolises exactly what the song is about – someone desperately isolated without friends or a lover, but who is determined to be a success nonetheless, and find joy in a world of darkness. Like You Don't Care About Us, the tune itself radiates positivity despite its gloomy content – a craftily designed paradox of its own.

'It's about time Placebo did a track that got people shaking their booty on the dance floor!' Brian had huckled, brimming with enthusiasm at the memory. 'It's a song I started writing on a tour bus between New York and Boston, borne out of boredom and the need to do something creative. Its lustful and celebratory – infused with a kind of lust for life.'

Brian has always been an unlikely supporter of booty-shaking pop music – from his DJ nights swaying to Destiny's Child's Bootylicious and trying to rival Beyonce's moves on the dance floor to his guilty nights in bopping to Abba in the kitchen. As much as it might have disappointed the goths, it was clearly only a matter of time before his penchant for ass-shaking made its way into his own CD. This desire for musical variation, coupled with two 'really experienced and fantastic backing singers' completed one of the most memorable Placebo tunes in history. Although shamelessly pop, it doesn't disappoint in also paying tribute to the band's rock roots. Even with their first venture into the pop world, Placebo had been anything but predictable.

Devil in the Details is a darker song, brimming with anger and resignation. 'He's a fucking pal of mine,' Brian spits with barely concealed frustration, 'that devil in the details.' Whilst every cloud might have a silver lining, for Brian – someone who lyrically describes himself as 'born to lose' – the same can be true in reverse. The song captures a look at the defeated, chronically depressed and desperately pained Brian beneath the surface, the one beneath the stage makeup who – away from the spotlight of the stage – desperately craves reassurance. The one the world was yet to discover.

Despite the elation of pop music and the satisfaction of life on the stage, for chronic depressives like Brian, the devil and the dark side are bound to come back. The song is suggestive of his fight with mental illness and his every day up hill struggle just to survive.

'I don't really believe in God,' Brian claimed, 'but I believe in the existence of the devil. There's no doubt – it's a force that must be faced. The conflict is sometimes surmountable, sometimes not.'

Whilst the album contains lots of religious imagery, Brian has been at pains to point out that none of it is Christian. 'I would be more attracted to Buddhism, where the figure of God is less represented,' Brian claimed. He had plenty of opportunities to familiarise himself with the ancient teachings on tour in the Far East and what he learnt was an inspiration for the Neverending Why, where alternative forms of religion are used to question the meaning of life. Deeply philosophical and spiritually enlightening, it's an unlikely fit for the average rock musician, but Brian prided himself on not falling prey to redundant stereotypes. Confessing the song's Eastern philosophy, Brian summed it up as simply being about the questions that can never be answered. 'Anyone who has an interest in the meaning of life will come up against a brick wall, but you must accept the fact that there will be no answers and get the best out of now.'

Formerly a born-again Christian, Brian had come to despise religion and everything it represented, using the slogan 'He who fears death does not enjoy life' to sum up his feelings. He lost his belief in reincarnation and, dismissing his fears of punishment in the after life, decided to be true to himself and simply live for today. His religious struggle is chronicled in the moody, contemplative verses of the Neverending Why.

Speak in Tongues meanwhile is a return to the classic sound of Placebo, harking back to the tender warmth of Passive Aggressive. Both Brian and Steve Forrest cite this as their all time favourite Placebo song. It hints at Biblical imagery of someone who is possessed by the Holy Ghost, talking in tongues of different languages.

Far from the angry young man involved in politics, this song shows a gentler and more spiritual side to Brian. However, as Steve assured the French press, 'What Brian means in this song is French kissing.' He added 'To me it conjures up the image of a flickering light and at the end you need a seatbelt to get through the explosion.'

Brian's recollections were even more vivid. 'It starts off sounding like cocktail hour at the mental hospital and halfway through it becomes this really big stadium anthem. The hook of that song is the phrase that goes "We can build a better tomorrow today" and I think that kind of embodies the attitude behind the song,' he told OK Australia.

With the colourful imagery that the first-time band mates shared of the rhyme, it became clear that they would adore performing it together. Another of the group's favourites was the anthemic Bright Lights – raging optimism with an anxious hint of sadness. Despite the depressive cloud the group might have been under, the bright lights symbolised that there were ever-present glimmers of hope.

Like Devil in the Detail, it explains the damaging desires that can lead Brian into trouble – 'It's all about the demon in me and writing songs to make it disappear.' Cathartic for Brian and downright climactic for his fans, it is the first time that there were no characters, no acting and no pretense – the narrative voice was Brian's alone. 'On former records, I used to invent characters through which I could talk about my feelings and fears... I used them as self protection to express myself,' he recalled. 'This time I didn't do that – the voice of the story teller is my own.'

Expressing delight at creating a more honest and personal CD through his brave disclosures, Brian continued 'I have to be good to myself. I have to stop pushing the self-destruct button constantly...to carry love in myself... I have to finally meet my life instead of running away from it.'

If Bright Lights was intensely confessional, Julien was more of a mystery. If anything though, it simply added to the atmosphere. It begins with a long electronic opening before crashing into a totally unexpected rock riff. The mystery character, Julien, is the subject of a postponed suicide.

Happy You're Gone was penned by Brian whilst living on a tranquil riverboat in Paris. 'I've always wanted to do that... it's a very romantic and kind of bohemian existence,' he enthused. 'I've never slept so well in my life, so I recommend that experience for all insomniacs.' The experience was setting him back £10,000 per month but it was the starting point for some tunes that were truly priceless.

He was inspired by the romantic imagery to start writing an ode to a departed lover or friend. It features the lyric 'Now I can't even look you in the eye.' This closely resembles Brian's assertion about Steve's departure that 'at the end of the tour we couldn't even look each other in the eye.' Could this song be fuelled by the tangled emotions of losing Steve, his closest ally and partner in crime?

Brian put paid to that rumour quickly, claiming 'There's not one song about him in the album... forgive me for being unnecessarily brutal, but it's a little bit pathetic if you start writing songs about ex-drummers.'

Despite his dismissive retort, evidence points to it being at least partly related to Steve. Whilst on the boat, recovering from the fast-paced and emotionally wounding atmosphere of the Meds tour, Brian also penned Kings of Medicine. The dark imagery is at times grotesque, a matter of fact depiction of 'picking up pieces of you' and finding a mystery man in a body bag 'before the day is over.' Confusingly, the media were quick to attribute these lyrics to Steve's departure too. One thing was for certain, Brian hardly had murderous intentions.

'I was contacted by an advertising company who asked me to write a song for a drink-driving campaign in the UK and the song I wrote was Kings of Medicine.' Bringing sense to the macabre imagery, he added 'I tried to bring clues and references to driving and drinking... Eventually the anti drink driving campaign didn't happen and I was kind of left with this song.'

Far from a spare part, it was to comprise a valuable part of the sixth album. Its imagery is completely opposed to the elation of the tune. Horns, flute, trombones and a piccolo trumpet coupled with a fanfare make for an eclectic theme that demonstrated Brian's desire to emulate the Beatles track 'All You Need Is love.'

It might come as a surprise to Placebo's hard rock fanbase but Brian had been a fan of the Liverpool foursome for many a year.

'My favourite Beatles album has always been the White Album,' he revealed. 'I discovered Yer Blues which blew my mind because it's such a brutal slice of nihilism and depression. It was quite a shocking departure from that pastoral sound they had become famous for.'

Their ability to push the boundaries inspired Brian to try something different, creating dramatic horn-led fanfares and an upbeat tune combined with a message of contrasting bleakness. '[The Beatles] gave me a lot of hope that you don't need to be tied down to one specific identity as an artist... it's important to us to try and push the limits of what our perceived identity is and surprise ourselves. We wanted to showcase our Beatles' obsession on Battle for the Sun.' Finally he confessed, 'If you're going to learn, you may as well learn from the greats.'

Brian wanted not just to change his style and replicate one of music's greatest success stories, but also to keep his hardcore fanbase on their toes. 'Brian's motto is 'Let's freak the goths out,' chuckled Stefan affectionately, before revealing that it had been his very aim in creating Kings of Medicine. 'We have always been seen as the purveyors of melancholy... I think on this record we had a bit more fun.'

Away from the tension of a blighted trio, the new Placebo was beginning to reconnect in musical terms, with a sixth album that was gloriously multicultural.

What's more, Brian wasn't alone in his appreciation of the Beatles – some of his firm favourites such as Cornershop, Sonic Youth, Ash and Gary Numan were also huge fans. Even Ash, who had toured with Placebo as a support in the early days, counted the Beatles among their greatest inspirations. The Liverpudlian foursome clearly had a lot to answer for.

In spite of the obsession, the remaining two songs on the album were as different from the Beatles as anyone could imagine. Come Undone is a crashing ballad rivalling Lady of the Flowers or Leni. It speaks of a musician filled with arrogance and fearlessness, who cares not for the damage his bravado-fuelled behaviour is causing. This song speaks of the comedown, the self-destruction and the ill-advised candour – the plight of 'coming undone.' However, in musical terms, fans would never accuse the singer of saying too much –for them, he had barely said enough.

More struggling is in store in Breathe Underwater. One of the faster and rockier tracks, with the edginess of Bruise Pristine, it is another survival story. Brian sings poignantly 'It's hard to reconcile what I've become with the wounded child that lies deep inside,' speaking of the disparity between his success and the secret suffering harboured beneath the surface. In an instant, it transports listeners to the unenviable darkness of his past.

Transforming from loser and outsider to rock heart-throb and success story in a few short years had left Brian with scars. The imagery of breathing underwater and coming up for air reveals the battle between past and present, darkness and light. From a shy childhood to the present day, he had come full circle in his quest to battle for the sun.

Brian was also keen to believe his emotional development had been arrested at the tender age of 22, leaving him little more than a teenager in the wake of success. He told of an article about Michael Jackson he had read in the press, claiming that development in emotional areas would cease the moment a child became famous.

'In the case of Michael Jackson, his emotional development would have been arrested at around 10-12 years old. It could be why he is a confused adult. For me it would be around 22 or 23 years old. That's why I'm still somewhat a teenager. But it's the whole story of rock and roll – the quest for eternal adolescence.'

The recording of Battle for the Sun represented a turning point in Placebo's career, so it was fitting that the album should express a theme – telling the story of the group's journey from beginning to end.

Kitty Litter starts play, featuring the raw, passionate sexuality coursing through Brian's veins in the early days, as he composed sexually charged classics like Bionic as a frustrated teenager in his bedroom.

Next, Ashtray Heart symbolises the very first incarnation of Placebo, with a drunken Steve Hewitt playing on bongoes – an apt place for the band's life story to begin. The group had pledged at the start to call themselves Ashtray Heart.

Battle for the Sun could refer to the onset of Brian's depressive illness in his early 20s, an ongoing battle that still is a challenge for him today. It also symbolises the beginnings of success and paradoxically the havoc that it wreaked on their relationships, mental health and sanity. It speaks of a group who was professionally polished but personally was on the brink of destruction.

The journey continues through to the final song, Kings of Medicine. According to popular belief, this song released pent up emotions about Steve's departure, although Brian has denied that emphatically, insisting that none of the songs were about the ex-drummer. Whatever the case might be, the album seems to reflect the journey of Placebo, in chronological order, ending with a hint of optimism.

As for what the future might hold for the trio that had survived the madness and emerged smiling, the group could only imagine – but they were about to find out.

Adding the finishing touches to the album, the band delegated the cover art to an American graphic design company who had been responsible for CDs by TV on the Radio and Queens of the Stone Age. He left them with just one instruction – to make it unique. A striking image of an eclipse of the sun made it as the front cover – the result of giving creative control to an unknown quantity.

Whilst Brian claimed that it was not an original idea, he was delighted by the concept nonetheless. 'It speaks of a certain pleasure gleaned in the depths of darkness,' he said. 'Above all, it's completely timeless. Like The Dark Side of the Moon by Pink Floyd, it's intellectually accessible to anyone.'

Album complete, the group was about to step out of the shadows. On March 17th 2009, an exclusive concert was performed by invitation only in a shadowy West London bar. Industry moguls and journalists alike joined the band for a showcase of the new album, followed by an unexpected treat – a cover version of Nik Kershaw's Wouldn't It Be Good. Unusually Brian claimed he had 'never been a fan' of Kershaw but had chosen the track merely because he felt it suited his voice. Impatient fans were disappointed by their exclusion from the concert, but Placebo compensated by releasing a sneak preview of the title track on XFM Radio the same day.

A video was produced to accompany the track and Howard Greenhalgh was the man to make their dream vision a reality. He'd been responsible for Special K, Nancy Boy and the Bitter End before it. This video lacked the attention-seeking visuals of Nancy Boy's provocative cum shots, the high budget perfection and limitless imagination of Special K and the unmissable publicity stunt of performance atop a satellite dish. In spite of this, Placebo was not worried in the least. They were amongst friends – unusual in the cut throat music biz world – and knew they were dealing with a likeminded 'pervert' who understood the Placebo ethos perfectly and better still, how to embody it. 'He knows our twisted sense of humour and the perverse side of what we do,' Brian explained. 'Plus he has quite a healthy connection to the dark side.'

Despite their continuing relationship with perversity, journalists had begun a backlash, suggesting that the latest work was 'less sexually charged.' Brian hit back defiantly, and as always with a wicked sense of humour, claiming 'Perhaps the sexuality is more subtle – it's not coming at you in terms of a transvestite on crystal meth.'

Indeed, Brian intended to make good his promise of laying the Nancy Boy vibe to rest, but affirmed that he had wanted Battle for the Sun to be 'libidinous' and 'a celebration of sexuality.'

Determined to translate their passion into a live context, Placebo arranged three live shows in Sheffield, Bournemouth and London on May 8th 10th, 12th respectively – intimate affairs to introduce the fans to the new material.

'Exhibitionism is as necessary for me as eating and drinking,' Brian mused. 'Without the stage I could not be happy.' With these shows, both band and fans alike were feeding their desires and healing their wounds and it was with humble sincerity that Brian assured his audience 'It's good to be back.'

Shows in a variety of countries followed. In Romania on June 21st 2009, the onstage chemistry between Brian and Stefan had returned in full force. The flirtatious front-man affectionately dubbed Stefan 'the queen of Sweden' and the bassist responded that Brian was his 'drama queen.' None of the tension that had pervaded the pair's last moments with Steve Hewitt was present. Brian also made a playful joke about the English laws prohibiting smoking in public places. 'I envy you,' he addressed the crowd before lighting up, thanks to their relaxed stance on nicotine. 'In England they are taking away our liberties little by little. Let's fill our lungs together.'

An exclusive invitation-only show at London's Roundhouse also piqued the attention of fans. Performing as part of the I Tunes Festival, the band extended an invitation to lucky winners on Facebook who were awarded complimentary tickets. Londoners clamoured to gain access, and the occasion was every bit as special to Brian himself.

'We always want to shine [in London]. Sometimes it's harder because your average music fan is exposed to more high quality music than, say, the Czech Republic,' he said. The competitive front-man continued 'Sometimes, in my fantasy world, I'd like to bring fire eaters and maybe a circus troupe, but that could detract from the music.'

Brian was speaking from experience – his elaborate burlesque fantasies were no different from his penchant for eyeliner and black nail varnish in the early days – attention grabbing for all the wrong reasons. Returning his attention to the music, he pondered the addition of a horn or string section for sonic effect. 'We don't get too much support from the media, but our fanbase has been steadily growing,' he added. 'We want to reward the faithful.'

Following the show at the Roundhouse on July 14th, which passed without intervention from the circus, the tour moved onto previously unchartered territory. A journey to Asia included a show in Seoul, the capital of South Korea on August 7th 2009. This time there was a sprinkling of white throughout the audience thanks to Stefan's gentle reminder 'We urge all fans to wear white!

There is too much black in our audiences.' An obedient Korean crowd didn't disappoint.

However tragedy struck on August 9th when the tour moved to Japan. During an intensive show at the Summer Sonic rock festival in Japan's Osaka, Brian began to feel the pressure. To the horror of his fans, he keeled over mid-performance and fainted. There was a stunned silence as security rushed onstage to carry the singer to safety, limbs splayed out and hanging limply from their arms.

A statement was released to dampen speculation, claiming 'We have undertaken a gruelling and intensive schedule over the last few months and the last couple of weeks alone played five countries in three days,' it said. 'Brian picked up a virus which, coupled with jet lag and exhaustion, caused his collapse on stage. Thanks to prompt and professional care, Brian is recovering well.'

His accident followed the fate of Mic Cester, singer in the rock group Jet. The singer continued his tour despite medical advice prohibiting him from playing live, but – to his credit – Brian was more cautious, thinking of the long-term effect over exertion would spell for his fans.

Courageously, he had been ignoring his ill health to avoid disappointing them, but this was a long over due wake up call. He promptly cancelled the USA tour, scheduled for the following month. Rumours circulated suggesting that the mystery virus was swine flu. The infection had begun in Mexico earlier that year, before spreading and fatally hitting several dozen UK citizens – mainly those with underlying health problems.

There was another shock in store for Brian too. Less than a year after his ejection from Placebo, Steve Hewitt was planning a triumphant return. The former percussionist had formed a Facebook page to talk about his new project, Love Amongst Ruin. Fans had initially met this news with scorn, thinking he was a mere impersonator. In response to their cynicism, Steve posted a picture of himself holding a newspaper – that day's edition of the Telegraph.

He told astonished viewers 'Obviously all of you know, or maybe you don't know, that I have left Placebo. It was not my decision to leave, but I was given no choice... eleven years of being in Placebo isn't easy to kiss off into the sky, but instead of going down the route of debauchery, abuse, self pity and confusion, I decided to use my emotions towards a creative urge. I miss you, the fans, dearly and thanks for all of your support while I was with Placebo.' Not wanting to be defeated, he continued 'For every action there is a reaction! My reaction to this situation was to write, record and produce a new album.'

With a nod to his dear friend Simon Breed in his choice of words, he apologised that he had not been online to the public for a number of years. 'I was faithless, broken and powerless,' he said.

Indeed, his time in Placebo had been longer than many marriages and it was not proving easy to readjust. Finally, however, he had dusted himself off and started again. Grabbing two friends – bassist Jon Thorne from the alternative rock group Lamb and beloved brother Nick Hewitt – 'a very accomplished guitarist', he booked a recording studio and began to jam like he had never jammed before.

This occasion was full of memories for Steve – the studio in Bath had been the location for the recording of Without You I'm Nothing and the producer was Paul Corkett, who had worked with Placebo on Black Market Music. Steve was undeterred by the bittersweet memories.

'This became a very creative time for me,' he blogged. 'It kept my faith in music and helped me move on in a new direction...We began to use a number of different instruments on the recordings that I have never worked with before.'

He stayed connected with his fans by regularly blogging on Facebook and Twitter, taking the time to reply to messages and tributes personally. He even posted a photograph of a pair of stuffed moles, the studio's mascots. In addition, he experimented with a double bass and a three hundred year old cello previously played by Beth Porter on his voyage of musical discovery. Steve, whose previous singing experience had been limited to the Boney M cover of Daddy Cool, had decided to come out from behind the drum kit and front the band vocally.

Onalle from Roni Size Reprazent provided backing vocals along with a more unusual choice – Steve's prepubescent daughter Emily Reid also joined the team. Finally an album was complete, and it was mastered in LA by the notorious Brian Gardner, responsible for work by the Foo Fighters and Jane's Addiction.

It was imperative for Steve to find a competent management before he could take the next step on his journey. He achieved this and then found a band for himself – his original line up was unavailable due to prior commitments and was well on the way to success. In the meanwhile, he described Love Amongst Ruin as a 'multi-faceted hard rock band with the crunch of a stone age queen, the cross-over appeal of a parkful of linkins and the melodicism of the hardest fighter of foos.'

The promising description proved too much for industry moguls and he soon earned his first live gig at the Eurosonic festival in the Netherlands on January 14th 2010, aimed at showcasing new talent to the music industry.

Over 2650 music professionals would attend to watch more than 250 European groups in 41 separate venues. The organisation boasted 'It's the ultimate platform for the European music industry.'

His fanbase were yet to hear so much as a note of his music, but that was about to change – here was the place that Steve would kick-start his new career. The song So Sad was posted on the Internet with a request to listeners to forward it to their friends.

Heartbreakingly for Brian, the lyrics seemed to be talking right at him. One verse asks 'Another one today has just quit you, you don't even think that it's cruel, what's it going to take just to get through? Don't you see that you're now the fool?'

When Brian learned of Steve's plans, he had just performed his largest show yet – selling out the enormous o2 Arena in Greenwich, London – just a stone's throw from the home of his university days. Despite the elation of the show, which took place on December 9th 2009, it couldn't hope to heal Brian's heart.

Months later, on May 11th 2010, Steve performed his first ever London solo show at the Barfly pub in Camden. Brian was somewhere between Columbia and Israel, taking a short break from his fast-paced world tour, but the last place he wanted to be was at his former drummer's solo debut. That night, the pub – one of Brian's old haunts – was notably absent of Placebo and their crew.

While relations couldn't have been more strained between Brian and his ex-drummer, it was a totally different vibe between new percussionist Steve Forrest and his ex-band Evaline – they were the support group chosen on tour the very next time Placebo played London – at Brixton Academy on September 27th 2010.

The show had to go on – and it did. Fifteen years, six albums and numerous accomplishments down the line, Brian led a group that stood strong.

He was a man of a million faces. The fallen angel. The lonely, heartbroken romantic. The vulnerable, abused young boy. The talented musician. The charity-donating socialist. The notorious cross-dresser. The selfish tart with a heart. The drug-crazed sex dwarf. The party animal. The angry politician. The yoga fanatic and Buddhist meditator. The man with the skin of a rhinoceros who was falling apart underneath it all – 'to the hell you take me for.'

Standing in unquestioning defiance of his detractors, Brian was finally learning not to shoulder the burdens of his public perception. As the career train pulls out of the station yet again, leaving the memories of Battle for the Sun far behind, he hopes to reach the enviable point he craves the most – the one where the music speaks for itself.

EPILOGUE – THE DEATH OF NANCY BOY.

So as the curtains close on yet another world tour – the sixth to date – has Brian Molko indeed grown older and wiser?

His life has certainly changed – from that of a fast-lane singer whose gifts from fans have included a threesome with a mother and a daughter, crates loaded full of champagne, and the offer of a young woman's virginity to that of a man whose 'life has been reduced to going to children's birthday parties.'

But all the better for it, Brian believed. With distaste and plaintive exasperation, he insisted 'I don't wanna be the drug-crazed sex dwarf anymore,' and announced Nancy Boy officially dead.

However, it was not before he hit headlines worldwide for his cross-dressing. His fashion sense has always been eccentric – over the years, he has gleefully offended countless punters and endured the cat calls of thousands of macho men. From a criminally short pelvis-skimming little black dress (John Richmond of course) to an all in one glittery number resembling not so much a fetish suit as an infant's romper suit, he has never been afraid to experiment.

'We were making quite a political statement in the context of that macho Britpop world during the mid-1990s by appearing on TOTP wearing dresses,' Brian chuckled. 'We wanted to stand out like a sore thumb, but what it did was create a caricature of the band – I'd see cartoons of me wearing a dress and having hairy legs. When you see that, you know you're a caricature.'

The mass humiliation was all for a greater good though – it inspired fans for over a decade to take on their own total aesthetic freedom. 'We played with the Gossip at a festival recently and you can see that Beth Ditto is an icon,' Brian said of the size-32 star who gave a whole new meaning to the word 'voluptuous.' Big girl, big voice, followed the logic, and Gossip albums flew off the shelves worldwide accordingly. With visible satisfaction, Brian recalled 'the music world is a lot more accepting now, and I think we played our own little part in that.'

There was another type of freedom worth fighting for too – freedom to love either gender. This is something that has been characteristic of Placebo from the very beginning. It was for this all important cause that Stefan fearlessly took to the stage in Lebanon with 'Homo' painted on his chest, and that Brian tirelessly marched the streets of Madrid in the hope of inspiring social change.

In the early years, one deluded journalist introduced Brian to his readers as a 'feisty young heterosexual.' However the penny finally dropped and a couple of years later, both Brian and Stefan were out and proud. Meanwhile the less visually impaired already understood that a man happy to parade in lacy dresses – and onstage of all places – might have more than a tenuous connection to batting for the other team.

Yet straight, bi, gay or even curious, it was the freedom he represented that was really important. Brian's other conquests to defend same-sex love included inciting the crowd to join him in a chant of 'Everyone is gay' at a festival in retaliation to its homophobic organiser. Before appearing, the bands had been asked to promise that they would promote nothing to do with homosexuality that day.

He also dared to perform live just miles from a border that separated the punishment for homosexual sex between death by public stoning and 'mere' imprisonment. Finally, he was more than happy to lock lips with Stefan in a public demonstration in Lithuania.

Disappointingly, Brian later claimed 'I regret being so frank about mine and Stefan's sexuality because it freaked people out so much.' Yet he conceded 'It was important for us to stand up and be counted. It was all about freedom and tolerance – and acceptance in a prejudiced world.' Thanks to the Placebo effect, conflicted homosexuals could hold their heads up that little bit higher.

Despite all the advantages of the Nancy Boy era, Brian does have obvious regrets. Ask him what he regrets the most about those early years, and he will admonish himself with an answer that leaves no room for misinterpretation. 'Keep talking like that and you're going to alienate a lot of people, you pretentious bastard.'

However his brazen honesty is part of what propelled him to the top over the years. Today, despite claiming a desire to be less brash, very little has changed. 'The fucking economic crisis makes me so bored,' he recently groaned to one bemused interviewer. 'What do you expect me to tell you?'

He's never been afraid to speak out, especially when it really matters. When a game of free association would more readily link Brian to 'cocaine' than 'musician' though, he knew things had to change. He felt there was far more to him than the confines of his media persona could ever give expression to.

He's had an eventful career, with fan requests including marriage proposals, insalubrious threesomes and invitations to deflower virgins, but with 10 million albums sold, to his credit what he'd most like to be remembered for is his music. It's for that reason above all that Nancy Boy is dead.

His ultimate goal? Never to be misunderstood. Older, wiser but eternally a child, this is something Brian would struggle with all his life. 'The first time I heard the Animals' 'Please don't let me be misunderstood', it just seemed to describe me completely,' he confirmed. 'The lyrics "I'm just a soul whose intentions are good, oh lord please don't let me be misunderstood" – it implies someone fucking up all of the time, which I do, but I have good intentions.'

As well as claiming it would be the title of his auto-biography, he also wished to put the line on his tombstone. 'It encapsulates how I see my own soul,' he mused.

While hopefully there will be no need for a tombstone for many years yet, it is a fitting epitaph for the corpse of Nancy Boy. Hopefully Brian Molko will win the battle never again to be misunderstood.

Extras

FILM INFLUENCES.

As a theatre school graduate Brian made a dramatic departure into singing, but just how much influence does he still derive from film?

BITTER MOON

This enthralling psychological thriller, directed by the lovably twisted Roman Polanski, has many links with the work of Placebo.

The film begins with an ill fated love affair between a young couple, Oscar and Mimi. When fickle Oscar tires of the relationship, which has been an addictive one, besotted Mimi vows to win him back at all costs. Seeing an opportunity to capitalise on her dependence, he uses her to entertain his most sadistic fantasies. The relationship has never been a conventional one, and at first this only enhances their trysts. However, things soon take on a more sinister theme.

When it seems as if Mimi can get no lower, he forces her to cut off her hair, and she surrenders the one source of power she has left – her beauty. To his amused surprise however, no amount of cruelty is sufficient to quell her love. Ultimately he does leave her, jilting her moments before a romantic reconciliation holiday. Mimi is left abandoned, hurt and confused on the plane as he makes his mad dash for liberation.

Free at last, Oscar embarks on a debauched journey of hedonism and casual sex. He is having a whirlwind of a time until a tragic accident leaves him a wheel-chair bound paraplegic. Now the roles are to reverse – he is the desperately needy one, who fears he will never be loved again.

To his surprise, Mimi agrees to be his carer, yet all is not what it seems – she has a vengeful agenda. She taunts him for the misdemeanours of his past, openly flaunting her colourful sex life in front of him while he lies helpless and unable to move, let alone participate. She abuses him with mental cruelty, leaving him lying in a scorching hot bath while she idly chats with friends on the phone.

She infuriates him by playing the role of a tender wife and ardent carer in public, but switching her sweet image of innocence the moment the pair are alone. Frustrations build until he cannot stand the jealousy, resentment and tension. Against the backdrop of a calm and seemingly idyllic summer cruise, tragedy strikes and no-one's lives will ever be the same again.

This is a tragic tale of revenge, emphasising the strong attachment that – to their misfortune – the two ultimately cannot sever. Whilst Mimi's payback at first seems liberating, her unrelenting and unhealthy desire for revenge proves that she is still desperately emotionally bound to him.

This theme of domination and submission and indeed of addictive relationships is one that Brian has addressed many times on the Sleeping With Ghosts album. The helpless wheelchair bound victim plays a part in Brian's lyrics as well.

Special Needs is 'the tale of a has-been told from a wheelchair. Someone reminisces about how the shoe is on the other foot and they worry about being written out of their ex's biography.'

Lyrically, the song depicts a liaison with a beautiful and glamorous woman who ultimately gets the upper hand. Everything that the singer once held dear in this fantasy tale is now decayed, whilst his ex-partner burns more brightly than ever before. Incidentally, Brian may have played out this scenario in real life with French partner Benedicte who has her own band, Melatonin. Rumour has it that her desire for musical success was part of the reason their liaison was torn apart.

'Remember me when your clinch your movie deal... and think of me stuck in my chair that has four wheels,' Brian laments. The song tells of fears that fame is transient and adoration unreal and superficial – and the character imagines that soon he too will suffer the fate he fears the most – that of a nobody. Brian encountered this helplessness as a lonely teenager in Luxembourg, and his memories serve only to heighten his fears. However in the words of the singer himself 'The past is just that – you can make your own future.'

Similarly Centrefolds captures the same desolation, addressing the abject fear of a 'washed up celebrity' who, remembering past conquests, balks at the prospect of settling for second best. 'It's hard to reconcile what I've become with the wounded child who lies deep inside,' he later sang, providing a window into his image of adoration – so at odds with his childhood past and earlier collapse of self-esteem.

Brian has described Centrefolds as a tale of degradation, its character fearing loss and taunts in the same way that the incapacitation of Oscar subjects him to ridicule and typecasts him as perpetually useless, someone whose life no longer has the luxury of a purpose. 'All the centrefolds that you can't afford have long since waved their last goodbyes,' Brian sings to himself, perhaps method acting as an adviser to himself. 'All the centrefolds… you've long since faded from their eyes.'

It deals also with Brian's fear of becoming old. This fear is partly explained by the well-meaning but somewhat disturbing words of his mother, who had told him as a child 'The moment you pop out of the womb, you start to decay.'

Meanwhile, 'six months off for bad behaviour' is a lyrical portrayal of Oscar's tragic accident, the one that spells the end of his life as a capable man. Stumbling drunkenly from a nightclub, a beauty on each arm, this sets the scene for a major collision with a vehicle, the same one that ultimately leaves him paralysed.

The story line of Bitter Moon seems to have inspired Brian more than once and the characters he provides could easily have been inspired by the tumultuous, ill-fated relationship of Oscar and Mimi.

THE SEVENTH SEAL.

This Ingmar Bergman film is a philosophical offering that provokes thought into one of Brian's hottest topics – the dark side of religion.

A knight, embittered by his life of war and brutality slowly loses all his faith in God, Desperate to see his wife and children, but bound by circumstance and seemingly sentenced to a life of misery, he challenges death to a game of chess. The prize for the winner? His own life.

This twisted Russian roulette and determination for battle, played out to the tune of sinister music, symbolises Brian's battle between following religion and reclaiming his own life and identity. He experienced immense frustration that he could not reconcile his bisexual feelings, his lust for life and keenness to try new experiences – no matter how unwholesome – with the rigidity and strict rule book that Christianity provided.

He appreciated the metaphorical imagery that Bible study had blessed him with, but ultimately disliked the repression of organised religion. He attended Sunday school until he reached 14 and flirted with becoming a born again Christian in his early 30s but for the most part of his life Brian had rejected God.

Early songs released fury by 'shedding the sceptre of Jesus' while

Passive Aggressive is one of Placebo's more famous auditory triumphs over the reign of religion, claiming that 'God's in crisis... fuck him, he's over.'

However it is Special K that this film most closely resembles. A song about addiction – whether it be to drugs, love, sex or religion – it features the words 'Can the saviour be for real, or are you just my seventh seal?' The song corresponds with the film, where the one man the knight confides in about his loss of faith turns out to be death himself – ironically disguised as the religious figure of a priest.

Metaphorical and deeply meaningful, both Special K and the film echo the questions of Alfred Adler, a psychologist who described religion as no more than 'child like dependency.' Those opinions match Brian's view of religion as an unhealthy addiction, a means of escaping guilt and fear. Bible quotes further increase the story's dramatic impact.

Brian subsequently purchased a jacket bearing the telling slogan 'he who fears death does not enjoy life' – the perfect testament to his attitude. Not only does it sum up the film but it reinforces the message that for him, freedom did win out after all.

FANTASTIC VOYAGE.

This light-hearted sci-fi thriller was an undeniable influence to Placebo, providing an inspiration for the video Special K. This was one where the band let their creative juices run wild. In a plot that mimics the film's story line, Brian is miniaturised and dropped through Steve's eye. The sight of Brian in a tiny spaceship and glittery spacesuit entertained fans across the globe. As Steve wryly commented in an interview, startling the group's detractors, 'That's the only way Brian'll ever get inside me!'

TWIN PEAKS

This film encapsulates Brian's vision of Luxembourg. The city that shaped his lonely childhood existence, he saw it as peaceful and idyllic on the outside but devastatingly traumatic within – just like Twin Peaks.

The film relives the singer's anguish. A brutal murder is set in an astonishingly tranquil small town of America. Residents of the beautiful region could barely have suspected the tragedies at its inner heart.

Reading much like the story of Burger Queen, where a gay goth struggles to survive in the cloistered, homophobic environment of tiny Luxembourg, and – pioneered by Brian's favourite director of all time, David Lynch – the series is uncharacteristically macabre.

Best described in the words of one of its characters, it is 'a beautiful dream and a terrible nightmare all at once.' Indeed, Luxembourg might have been his father's key to financial success and prowess, but to a young Brian who cared not for bulging bank balances, it marked only his downfall.

IRREVERSIBLE.

Brian enjoyed the films of Gaspar Noe so much that he was all too happy to hand over directing privileges for sexy video Protege Moi to him.

One of Noe's most memorable works, Irreversible has been cited as dark as it is disturbing. Noe has been noted for his portrayal of abject, brutal and senseless violence, seeing one of his characters pulped to death by a fire extinguisher when the film has scarcely begun.

Death, desire and danger prevail against a subtext devoid of morals – unsurprisingly, since Noe confesses to thriving on shock value. However the underwhelming rape scene allegedly provided more erotic pleasure to its audiences than the shock value he intended, and Belluci's acting failed to demonstrate the sort of hysteria a film buff might expect. Whilst Brian enjoyed the film, he claimed to prefer the more subtle love scenes in films such as Eyes Wide Shut. However it held a dark delight for him, which led to him christening it a 'very moral film.'

A two and a half hour journey into terror and malfeasance, it is an artistic and surprisingly sensual film. Some felt that the potential to hold up a mirror to the human condition was marred by over-sensationalism. It is a film that viewers will either love or hate and this is of course exactly how Noe intended it. Like him or not, he was responsible for creating Protege Moi as we know it today.

AMERICAN BEAUTY

This film provided inspiration for Slave to the Wage. Both the cinematic and the musical version have themes of entrapment in a low-paying rat race. Brian holds the subject of individuality and escapism from the daily grind very dear to his heart, rejecting the notion of becoming a cog in a wheel that benefits only those at the top.

An anthem of rebellion, its anti-establishment message was very clear.

Brian's distaste for 9-5 office jobs has been a part of his nature since the day he scornfully broke a shredding machine – the first and indeed last week of 'respectable employment' for the star.

He relished Kevin Spacey's portrayal of the rat race and all of its trappings, securing the film as a possible inspiration. Incidentally another Spacey film, the Usual Suspects, is a term of endearment coined by Brian to teasingly describe his long-standing fans.

CHRISTIANE F.

This is the troubling true story of a teenage heroin addict who, at the tender age of 12, turns to prostitution to fund her all-consuming habit. Alone and abandoned on the streets of Berlin, music is her only form of solace. A fervent Bowie fan, Christiane first smoked heroin after one of his concerts and the soundtrack to the movie features Bowie in memory of that.

Of course it wasn't just Bowie who featured. Brian was left heartbroken by the tragic tale and agreed to provide a soundtrack, Blackeyed, for the film adaptation, known as Engel und Joe.

Placebo might have been chosen for the Bowie connection but they fit the theme like a glove. The song is played out amid scenes of domestic violence, tears and triumph.

Brian has chased the dragon himself, claiming that he was 'an old romantic at heart and it was bound to happen', but he ultimately resisted its temptations, adding 'When you have to make a choice between talent, friends, life or heroin, you make that choice pretty quickly.' Brian had developed a strong survival instinct, just like the star of the film.

Today, the real-life Christiane F is in her 40s, and while she might be battling with methadone supplements, she is alive and healthy.

ONCE UPON A TIME IN THE WEST.

This popular spaghetti western might bear no similarity to Placebo's world in its plot, but musically the two have a lot in common. The eery, haunting and suspenseful tune of the Harmonica Man sounds very much like 'Protect Me From What I Want.' This illuminates the band's potential for writing film scores – which Placebo fans eagerly anticipate for the future.

IT'S IN THE WATER.

An unassuming lyric in the lively and impassioned Post Blue, it shares its title with a 1998 film about homosexuality. In small town America, an area of Texas as bigoted and repressed as Brian believed the terrains of Luxembourg to be, a sinister secret has emerged.

Chemicals that induce homosexuality have been let loose in the water supply, threatening to subvert the small town serenity the area has come to rely upon. Themes of both gay and lesbian love appear side by side and the moral values of these Texans begin to fall apart at the seams.

A message about the oppression faced by minorities, this is a matter close to Brian's heart and surely not far from his mind when he penned the refrain 'It's in the water, baby, it's between you and me.'

LIQUID SKY.

Yet another Placebo lyric, the film seems to appeal to Brian's penchant for sci-fi and fantasy. Aliens discover a chemical in human brains, released during orgasm, that leaks a potent life force energy. The aliens set about stealing the chemical, killing innocent humans in the process. In a curious twist, the story contains an androgynous female figure who takes on roles of both genders in the same film.

OTHER FILM FAVOURITES IN BRIEF.

Brian's all time favourite is the peculiar and seemingly plotless French movie La Haine.

His favourite Asian film is Lost in Translation. The tale of linguistic and cultural isolation without the luxuries of being able to speak in your mother tongue faced by strangers in a foreign city echoes Brian's isolation at constantly being on the road. Spending most of his year perpetually confined to a moving tour bus, Brian learned to love his nomadic lifestyle but appreciated the message nonetheless.

Brian claims to have worshipped Todd Haynes as a lowly drama student, little imagining he would one day be landing a part in one of his movies. Among the most enjoyable for him were Poison, based partly on Jean Genet's prison experiences and sister movie Dottie Gets Spanked. This was a ground-breakingly intense exploration into childhood sexuality and the ambiguity and novelty of early lust. It taps into Brian's enjoyment of innocence and lolita like ladies, such as the one pictured on the cover of Special Needs sampling her mother's bright red lipstick.

Etre et Avoir, set in a school in rural France, captured Brian's heart with its depiction of teaching young children. The sensitive soul admitted that it had brought him to tears on more than one occasion.

Jim Jarmusch and David Lynch are among Brian's favourite directors, and he can't resist yet another screening of Blue Velvet.

Finally, a film used by Brian to break up the monotony of tedious telephone interviews. If in the same situation one day, fans may want to take a leaf out of his book and seek light relief in the form of the Exotic Dances of Bettie Page...

BOOK INFLUENCES.

Here's a selection of some of the essential reading that inspired or entertained Brian over the years, and the novels he couldn't put down during long journeys on the tour bus.

PLEASE KILL ME – THE UNCENSORED ORAL HISTORY OF PUNK

Legs McNeil and Gillian McCain.
£12.99 – Abacus

Brian was photographed holding this book during a shoot with the NME in the autumn of 2000. Clad in a provocative T-shirt bearing the phrase 'Don't hate me cuz I'm beautiful', he posed with the tome before citing it as an all-time favourite.

The NME were unimpressed with his choice, reporting 'He'd like this collection of rock and roll classics to be photographed, convinced as he is that "it'll shock them."'

In fact, many Placebo fans were barely shocked at all, knowing already of his longstanding love affair with punk-rock. It was to be an interview that saw Brian christened the most hated rock-star in Britain – although some would say he was simply misunderstood.

The book traces the movement via classic acts such as the Stooges, the Ramones and the Pixies. Brian would claim that despite his unique sound, without punk-rock Placebo may never have existed. Aficionados will derive as much pleasure as Brian from this carefully crafted labour of love, providing a concise history of a much-loved genre.

UNCLE TOM'S CABIN

Harriet Beecher Stowe
£1.99 Wordsworth Editions Ltd

This provocative novel might seem innocent but in fact thinly disguises an underlying political meaning, discussing America's role in issues of racism and slavery. The book controversially suggests that misuse of Bible passages is responsible for the onset of black slavery. Commonly held beliefs also blame misinterpretation of Bible verses for homophobia and violence against women.

Brian makes reference to this book and its political undertones in the song Blue American, lamenting 'Read a book about Uncle Tom, where whitey bastard made a bomb, but now Ebonics rule our song, those motherfuckers got it wrong.'

The listless, resigned way in which the lyrics are delivered convey Brian's apathy and resignation at the evils of the world. It was written during a period of immense despair and dark depression – a time when he had all but given up, and the book matches this darkness.

It is a moral cautionary tale, criticizing not just racism and hypocrisy, but the prejudice tainted role of women in that era. Brian's attitude towards racism and sexism are summed up with three little words – 'God? She's black.

AFFLUENZA

Oliver James
£5.89 Vermillion

Yet another psychological-cum-political text, this book features the sickness that is affluenza. James looks at the obsessional need to earn more, and the desire not only to keep up with but to surpass the Joneses – a tendency to risk anything and everything in a bid to be the richest man. The author visits some of the most poverty-stricken countries of the world alongside the most wealthy, including Nigeria, Shanghai, New York and London.

From shattered economies to non-existent ones, he hints at the possibility that poor communities which are less striving may have a more profound happiness than their Western counterparts – one that does not rely on the fragility of materialism.

Brian has discussed the perils of the rat race and the money-hungry in

Slave to the Wage and has experienced desperately poor communities, ones that raise a smile despite just flocks of sheep and cows for company, on his visits to countries such as India. Finally, he had also experienced affluenza directly through his own loveless family.

Like the author, Brian has come under fire for being a Champagne socialist in his charitable endeavours – the fortunes of his family have never quite been forgiven or forgotten – and it seems that the two share a common interest.

OUR LADY OF THE FLOWERS

Jean Genet
£6.19 Olympia Press

This is a novel penned by an French author with a penchant for strong absinthe and unconventional sadomasochistic pleasure. If Brian's lyrics would advise you, this is a winning combination.

Identifying as neither gay nor straight, but unabashedly enjoying homosexual pleasures in prison, the author is the subject of extreme ambiguity. The majority of his works, translated for the benefit of both French and English audiences, were written behind bars, where his misadventures had led him. His unbridled fantasies, fuelled by an excess of testosterone and a pleasingly over-active imagination, flow freely through the pages for all those who dare to join him.

The honest and astonishingly candid stories hold back nothing, rather like Brian's own early work – raw, shamelessly unsophisticated and without the need for finesse. The singer relished this approach, name checking the author as one he enjoyed during college. As perhaps the greatest accolade of all, the title of the book was adapted for Placebo song Lady of the Flowers – believed to capture the same frustration and longing.

PERFUME – THE STORY OF A MURDERER

Patrick Suskind
£8.99 Penguin Classics

One of Brian's favourite on-tour companions, he found a particular affinity with this ghostly thriller. The book features an orphaned child with an extraordinary sense of smell. He becomes a perfumist but in his quest for perfection, seeks to recreate the most sought after scent of all on Paris's perverted back streets – that of a virgin. To exact the fragrance, he embarks on a bloodthirsty killing spree across the streets of the capital. Professional expertise is his alibi although, hungry for young blood, one suspects he would need little excuse. Here is someone clearly impassioned by his work, much to the chagrin of his innocent female victims. It is a piece of work that Brian has described as both 'sensual' and 'violent'. Here as in Leni and This Picture, it is a winning creative combination.

INVISIBLE MONSTERS

Chuck Palahniuk
£7.99 Vintage

This novel satisfies Brian's clear appetite for film adaptations and it is not his only treasured book by the same writer. Penned by the author of the world famous film and novel Fight Club, the central character in this novel is a prestigious fashion model.

At first sight, she seems to have it all, but tragedy strikes and a car accident renders her not only speechless but grossly disfigured. She undergoes total transformation from the gorgeous and much coveted object of desire that she was as her former self, to an invisible monster – hideously unattractive and more shunned than smiled at. She faces a fate she has never known – that of an ugly woman who by the mere nature of her compromised physicality, is now invisible to the world.

The story bears a remarkable similarity to Centrefolds, where Brian expresses his fear at losing the status of a celebrity. It recounts the character's despair at losing all that she holds dear in her current, cruelly transient identity. Brian has expressed a consistent belief – cynically or sensibly – that fame is superficial and ultimately a machine that will chew you up and spit you out. For someone who appears to have it all, perhaps this cautionary tale kept his ego in check during his party-fuelled tour days.

EXQUISITE CORPSE

Poppy Z Brite
£7.99 Gollancz

Brian has barely concealed his delight in the media at the prospect of a good gothic horror novel. He has an appetite for the unusual and frequently reads the works of Brite. The author, whose achievements include a whole host of horror stories and a biography of Courtney Love, penned a particular favourite of his known as Exquisite Corpse.

The book features a depressive serial killer recently released from the confines of his prison cell. He hits New Orleans, embarking on a journey of decadence, rediscovery and homosexual love. His partner shares his 'dangerous desires' and as the synopsis reports, 'leaves a trail of blood from London to the USA.' Brian's trail of blood – and spunk – however is perhaps the most legendary of all. The jury is out on whether he believes he can beat the record on this gory gothic novel.

ABSINTHE: HISTORY IN A BOTTLE

Barnaby Conrad
£14.99 Chronicle Books

A gift from myself to Brian at an inebriated DJ night at the Barfly, this details the history and various uses of the dangerously appealing 'green fairy.' Brian received several miniatures the same year to accompany the novel from various gift-bearers and found the book an intriguing accompaniment. He is pictured posing alongside the book on numerous radio press sites.

UNDER THE SKIN

Michael Faber
£7.99 Canongate Books Ltd

This is another sample of Brian's on tour reading, mirroring his self-confessed sci-fi obsession. The book features, in his words, 'a civilisation of mutant dogs, who kidnap humans and vivisect them.' Ludicrously untrue, yet pure escapism for the stresses of a rock-star on tour, it is yet another novel that deserves pride of place among the Placebo favourites.

MUSICAL INFLUENCES.

Brian has certainly made his feelings clear when it comes to the musical shit list. He has denounced 50 Cent as 'hideously unmusical', blasted Ian Brown as 'someone I can't respect', and described Pete Doherty as 'someone whose voice sounds like a cat being strangled.' Even Kanye West has not escaped his attentions – whilst it 'might be neat pop… it's totally meaningless.' So how about the tick list?

The following quotes document Brian's love affair with music – and in particular the greats that inspired him, shaping the unprecedented sound that is Placebo today.

'Jacques Brel tears the heart out of my chest – it fucks with my head. It makes me want to go and rewrite every song I've ever written.'

'Scott Walker gives me the biggest hard-on – the tenderness and humanity in his music blows me away.'

'Linkin Park is kind of unmissable. You'd have to live in Lebanon. Or not even Lebanon, but live under a rock to have missed Linkin Park.'

'Peaches – I appreciate a woman who can scare me knowing that I like it.'

'Mindless Self Indulgence – their show is an absolutely unique experience. I don't say that lightly and I can't say that about many bands, but I really recommend catching them live.'

'Flaming Lips shows are like children's birthday parties on acid – totally glorious.'

'We went to see Sonic Youth recently and we turned around – they were doing a greatest hits set – and went 'My God, I'm really surprised they haven't sued us yet.'

'At the Drive In is an incredible experience – it gives you complete faith in rock and roll. The passion and lack of cynicism is so refreshing… awe-inspiring.'

'Sonic Youth changed my life. They gave me a love of dissonance, which can be quite beautiful. I tried to copy them and I did it so badly that I ended up sounding like myself.'

'I'd like to have shared a bed with Billie Holliday. I'd like to think she'd have sounded the same in the sack as onstage. She had a beautiful voice.'

'The strangest and most gloriously beautiful thing I've ever seen is the Polyphonic Spree. They're quite a strong band – 27 people in robes playing horns, singing music that basically sounds like Christian music – but it's the most uplifting experience of my life. When I saw them at Chelmsford, they had a town cryer introduce them. It was completely freaky, but it made me cry, it was so gorgeous.

Here are a few that didn't meet with Brian's approval:

'Fuck Britney – she's so homogenised.'

'50 Cent? I don't wanna be shot, but I can't remember ever having heard anything this unmusical.'

Finally, a word from Simon Breed on why he believes he is among Placebo's greatest influences himself:

'I can see in Pure Morning bits of the Breed song Perfect Hangover – about waking up and you've got no skin and it's a blazing dawn. On the cover of English Summer Rain, there was a verse 'I can't sleep without your breathing' – that's [Breed song] Faithless Broken Powerless, which goes 'To sleep without your breathing is more than I can take.' Brian's similar lyrically, which is great of him – but Placebo's much more pop, much shinier – and Breed was darker.'

Authors Note - My Placebo.

From Brazil to Brussels, Istanbul to Iceland, I've seen Placebo's live show over 50 times in 20 unique countries. In my 12 year love affair with the group, I've visited four continents, united by one common theme - a desire to see the band I adore.

In my pursuit of Placebo, I've stayed in both luxury hotel suites and ill advised unheated cabins, shivering inches from the December snow. I've seen shows both on Brian's birthday and my own. I've encountered the singer in some unusual places too. A favourite was in an Atlanta bar at the illegal age of 18, where he was drunkenly smearing MAC Cosmetics over a female fan and bringing a whole new meaning to the phrase 'badly applied makeup.'

Meanwhile a little closer to home, much to my surprise, he's also sidled past my local North London bus stop. Of course what really counts is the music, and I've seen the band tour 5 of their 6 albums, from tiny acoustic shows to packed out stadiums, gigs as obscure as the official Italian fan club show and as mainstream as the Wembley Arena and o2 Arena in London.

Since then I've watched their distinctive brand of mischief and melancholy in Slovenia, Iceland, Brazil, Turkey, Japan, Switzerland, Bulgaria, Greece, the USA, Malaysia, France, Canada and Singapore to name but a few.

My journey began one morning in 1998, as a teenager. I instantly connected with Placebo on hearing Pure Morning. Smarting from a particularly bad breakup, I became vaguely irritated to see a hung-over man wandering down the side of a building collide with my TV screen. 'Who does he think he is? It's not possible to walk down a building,' I sneered.

My friend had very different matters on her mind. 'Is that a man?' she asked. 'Obviously a man,' I retorted with heavy sarcasm. Besides the prominent Adam's apple, his gender was obvious to me. Yet his androgynous appearance was to stir up the excitement of international media for many years to come.

We turned the sound up and begrudgingly I had to admit that the song was brilliant. Fuelled by extreme curiosity, I bought the album Without You I'm Nothing the next day and was addicted from that moment forwards. It delivered an impact beyond anything I'd ever experienced. I felt I recognised Brian in his songs and it was like hearing the voice of a long lost friend I'd forgotten I knew.

I'd battled bereavement, a tragic love affair, and countless frustrations and in the years to come, Placebo became the sound track to my pain. They mirrored my feelings and kept me buoyant - their emotional candour was my sanctuary. I lived out loss, regret, sorrow and of course elation and joy through their colourful palette of songs.

One of my most memorable moments was seeing the group in Byblos, Lebanon. Astonishingly beautiful even in the wake of a perilous civil war, this was a place Brian gushingly described as not only his childhood home but as the 'Paris of the Middle East'. He wasn't mistaken.

I wasn't sure what to expect from the live show in a place where mere homosexuality alone is tantamount to a prison sentence. From the moment Stefan walked onstage however, I was delighted to see the dangerously controversial slogan 'Homo' painted across his chest. I waited for an uprising but all I could hear were screams of approval. Placebo received a generous, voluptuously warm welcome and Blackeyed sent a largely male audience into indisputable elation. In a war torn and tragically repressed country, this crowd must have felt metaphorically blackeyed all of the time.

Despite the baking heat and the invisible yet ever present threats of discrimination, these proud 'homo goblins' played a blinding performance - and one that I would not have missed for the world.

My first foray into seeing the group was equally as memorable. It involved a trip to Germany in 2001 to visit two random strangers who had promised to accompany me to the band's Bremen concert, a few months past my 16th birthday. I'd allayed my mother's fears by claiming that we'd met several times before. Little did she know! I went off into the unknown armed with little more than a packet of cigarettes and an overnight bag. That was my first glimpse of Placebo in a foreign land and it wasn't to be the last. From that moment forwards, I captured both in memory and in print the changing faces of a group who, no matter what they do, will always have a powerful impact on me like no other and a special place in my heart.

Steve Forrest says 'I like music because it allows you to be everything you're not supposed to be.' Stefan says 'I like music because it makes my life worth living.' Brian's reasons for adoring music are abundantly clear in the pages of this book. And as for me? I like music because not only does it match your every emotion - passion, fear, longing, bitterness. sadness and of course joy, but because, unlike people, music is the one thing that will never let you down.

CPSIA information can be obtained at www.ICGtesting.com
Printed in the USA
BVOW081141170612

292825BV00004B/6/P